The History of
the United States
1876–1976

edited by
Frank Freidel
Harvard University

A Garland Series

Realities and Illusions
1886–1931
The Autobiography of
Raymond Moley

edited
with foreword and epilogue
by Frank Freidel

Garland Publishing, Inc.
New York and London
1980

Library of Congress Cataloging in Publication Data

Moley, Raymond, 1886–
  Realities and illusions, 1886–1931.

  (The History of the United States, 1876–1976)
  Includes bibliographical references and index.
  1. Moley, Raymond, 1886–   2. Political scien-
tists—United States—Biography. I. Freidel, Frank
Burt. II. Title. III. Series.
JC251.M56A37   320′.092′4 [B]   78-13887
ISBN 0-8240-9692-4

Printed on acid-free, 250-year-life paper
Manufactured in the United States of America

Contents

Foreword

Raymond Moley was the first spectacular example at the presidential level of a new kind of expert who has become essential in American politics and government. He was the thoroughly trained professional academic, equally proficient in the classroom and in government service. As the head of Franklin D. Roosevelt's "Brains Trust," he was responsible during the campaign of 1932 for the formulation of policies and their presentation in speeches that would win votes. During the interregnum following the election and the first "Hundred Days" of the new administration, he was Roosevelt's chief adviser, helping transform the proposals into the realities of the first New Deal. Moley wrote two fine accounts of these experiences, **After Seven Years** (1939) and (with the assistance of Elliot A. Rosen) **The First New Deal** (1966).

There remained to be told another important story, how Moley had developed into the kind of a person who could be so valuable to Roosevelt — into the prototype of the academic in Washington. There had always, of course, been some interchange between the groves of academe and the halls of politics. President John Quincy Adams had been briefly a Harvard professor, and Justice Joseph Story continued to teach at Harvard Law School while serving on the Supreme Court. Woodrow Wilson had been President of Princeton until little more than two years before he became President of the United States. Academic experts, chiefly scientists (but including one predecessor of Moley's in political science from Columbia University) had lent their skills to the government as early as the Civil War years. But it was during the Progressive years and World War I that first state governments like Wisconsin, then city governments like Chicago, and finally the federal government began to make extensive use of talent from the universities. Those who staffed "The Inquiry" to prepare President Wilson for the Versailles conference were direct forerunners of the Brains Trust.

There were two major questions. Where had Moley obtained the professional skills that he demonstrated in running the Brains Trust? Even more important, where had he obtained the ideas that became a component of the first New Deal? Several people urged Moley to write a professional and intellectual autobiography to cover up to the New Deal, and also the decades since, during which he had moved away from it to the right. But first Moley wrote a biography of one of his boyhood heroes, the Irish patriot Daniel O'Connell. It was not until he was in his mid-eighties that in response to the urging of his editor, William B. Goodman, then at Harcourt, Brace, he began his autobiography.

As an account of the intellectual influences upon the chief Brain-truster, it is illuminating. There was the populism of Bryan, an almost romantic strain, in Moley's Ohio boyhood. He was caught up in the excitement of the movement, even as was the poet Vachel Lindsay in Illinois. Moley's respect for Bryan persisted, and Bryan's anti-imperialism and distaste for foreign ventures became a permanent component of his viewpoint. Then there was Henry George's call for tax reform as a means of reforming the American economy, the single tax on land, which in more sophisticated forms had a lifelong attraction for Moley. **Progress and Poverty** led Moley to one of George's most ardent disciples, the renowned reformer, Tom L. Johnson. The leader and trainer of an outstanding array of Ohio reformers, Johnson was more realist than doctrinaire, and so, always, was Moley. From Johnson and others around him like Newton D. Baker, under whom Moley briefly studied law, he learned much about practical politics and effective administration. He became convinced, for example, that public regulation was superior to public ownership of utilities. Johnson was so emphatically Moley's ideal that in **After Seven Years** he has suggested that early in the Great Depression he felt that what the country needed was someone to do on a national scale what Johnson had done in Cleveland. "There was no Tom Johnson. But out of the field, by January, 1932, it seemed to me that the buoyant, likable man in Albany was the only hope" (p.4).

In his academic training, Moley came under the influence of Charles A. Beard of Columbia University, the progressive historian and political scientist. Moley admired Johnson from afar, cheering his political speeches at rallies. He came to know Beard closely and warmly as a teacher, adviser of his doctoral thesis, and sponsor in helping him up the academic ladder. It was a lasting relationship, in which was some parallel between Beard's evolving views from the 1920s into the 1940s, and those of Moley. He writes in an unusually informed way of Beard's dramatic resignation from Columbia University during World War I. The chapters on Beard are a contribution to knowledge of the historian.

It is Moley's own early career that did most to prepare him for his later important duties, and this Moley traces well, as he went from high school teacher to Columbia professor, and from mayor of his hometown, Olmsted Falls, Ohio, up through a wide array of service enterprises. He directed Americanization in Ohio during World War I, became director of the Cleveland Foundation, an influential social service agency, and conducted surveys and wrote reports on the administration of criminal justice in a number of states. In the process he acquired administrative skills and became especially effective in gathering, clarifying, and presenting complex data in readable form. He was indefatigable as a speaker and writer. His talents and his energy were of exactly the sort Governor Roosevelt needed at the beginning of 1932 as he prepared for his national campaign for President. Moley's ideas, with their roots in American reform movements of the late nineteenth and early twentieth centuries, were broadly compatible with those of a presidential candidate ready to embark upon bold experimentation to combat the Great Depression. All Moley's experience had prepared him admirably for this moment.

This is Moley's account of his intellectual and political education. It is rather general on figures he viewed from afar from Bryan through Johnson. Thereafter, in its account of his career in Ohio and New York it is rich with personal recollections and observations. It adds significantly to an understanding of the continuity from the populists and progressives to the New Dealers, and is especially vital in showing how Moley, one of the new political scientists, came to be a prominent contributor to national politics and government.

There was more Moley wished to explain in his autobiography. He wished to cover the decades after his departure and alienation from Roosevelt, years not covered in his two previous accounts of the New Deal. This part of the memoir did not progress well. He wrote sketches of a number of prominent Republicans with whom he was associated, beginning with Wendell Willkie. Few of these added much to the deft accounts in **27 Masters of Politics** (1949). Above all, he wanted to write about his relationship with Richard Nixon, whom he greatly admired. But Moley had several serious bouts of illness, and became increasingly depressed as the Watergate crisis intensified. After Nixon's resignation, Moley continued at his task with a heavy heart, not condoning Nixon but confessing in private that he still loved him. An uncompleted page on Nixon was in his typewriter when he died early in 1975.

Had Moley lived and been his earlier, vital, incisive self, his autobiography would have gone through another draft or more. He was a perfectionist. Nonetheless, there is so much of interest and use in these pages that it is better for them to appear in what he would have considered less than final form than not at all. In consequence there are here reproduced almost all of the chapters of the autobiography up to the point of the Brains Trust. There has been substantial deletion of repetitions, occasional commonplace passages, and lengthy quotations from both the writings of Moley and others. The pages on Johnson have been rearranged. Suspension points, thus . . ., indicate deletions; square brackets [ ] enclose the editor's interpolations.

Only the last two chapters go beyond the point where Moley became Roosevelt's campaign adviser. An editor's note introduces them. The remaining chapters from the 1930s into the 1970s have not been reproduced, but the Epilogue draws upon them briefly.

A full copy of the unedited manuscript is to be found in the Raymond Moley papers, Hoover Institution on War, Revolution and Peace, Stanford, California.

James E. Sargent assisted Moley in his work on the autobiography.

I am grateful to Sarah Stewart for typing and assistance. Frances Sleeper Moley has helped with advice and encouragement; it is to her that Raymond Moley would have wanted his last book dedicated.

Harvard University   **Frank Freidel**
February, 1979

1
A Wonderful Place
for Growing Up

The panic of 1893, which scattered distress over so many of the American people, by a singular chance contributed for me a source of great happiness in many years of my early life. For Felix James Moley, my father, after several years in which he barely made ends meet in his "gent's furnishings" store in Berea, Ohio, found the going so hard in 1893 that he gave up the struggle and moved his family and business three miles west and settled in some property in Olmsted Falls which my grandfather's thrift and energy had left to my grandmother.

The story of what had happened in the family's fortunes was not very clear in my seven-year-old brain. But the advantages of our new location in Olmsted Falls soon dawned upon me. I entered school that fall and settled down to the infinitely complex business of a boy's life shortly before my seventh birthday.

Olmsted Falls was bisected from north to south by the Rocky River, and from east to west by the main line of the Lake Shore and Michigan Southern Railroad. Both the river and the railroad were to be matters of vivid interest in the many years that followed our removal. And the big house which Grandmother gave us to occupy, which stood at the junction of the river and the railroad, offered fabulous opportunities for a boy's exploitation. My grandfather built it to provide him with a store and residence under the same roof. The store occupied the front of the main building; the dining room, kitchen and "parlor" and small porch had been added to the main building later. Above the store was a large room originally designed as a ballroom, but during most of my earlier years it was rented as a lodge hall to the Odd Fellows. The ten living rooms were behind, beside and on the second floor. The real source of fun and entertainment was the basement. It had been rented, in the years before we moved in, for a saloon. The main room had the old bar in one corner with a cool storage cellar behind. The main room had a pool table (with pockets) and a billiard table (without pockets), and a "pigeon hole table" for the

1

unskilled. One of the conditions imposed by my mother before consenting
to move was the ouster of the saloon. And so all this space was ours —
which included living rooms formerly occupied by the family of the saloon-
keeper. There was a barber chair down there, for my grandfather's
establishment had also included space for a tonsorial artist. This chair
played a large part in my early life, for located in the basement it was a cool
and comfortable seat for my hours of reading in the hot summers.

The land on which this commodious building was located stood next to
the railroad and sloped down to the river at its rear. To the south the Moley
property included three stores built as a unit. These were occupied by the
town barber and his family, a considerable grocery store and meat market,
and another store only casually occupied. Beyond this structure was the
property of the miller who, at the level of the river, had his sizable grist mill
with a dam which raised the level of the river for three quarters of a mile
upstream.

But that basement was to be the center of my life for years of growing
up. It was mine by virtue of the fact that the older members of the family
had other interests. I entertained a very few of the boys of my own age for
pool playing, wrestling (we had a mat in the basement) and boxing. I
acquired a very considerable skill at the pool table, which skill remained
with me for many years.

The pathway leading from the house to the river was well worn in all
seasons. For in the winter it led to the lake above the dam which provided
skating. The utility of this considerable head of water played a part in the
economy of the town. It provided energy for the mill which was the center
to which the farmers for miles around brought their grain for processing.
At the dead of winter the ice on the river was cut and gathered into
icehouses for the grocer, the butcher and the saloon-keeper.

If anyone thought about ice and water pollution in those years, he kept
it a secret, for the users of the ice were quite indifferent about keeping it
from contacts with food and drink. And the boys with whom I enjoyed
skating used to slake their thirst with long draughts of the river water
under the ice. It was cold and fairly clear and this seemed to us complete
freedom from dangerous germs. The only cases of typhoid I heard about
were in the summer and fall and were attributed to the dust on the fruit
which was eaten raw.

Below the dam the river found its way among rocks in a gorge. This
continued for a few miles on the way downstream. At one spot the river
widened and provided a swimming hole which found great favor with the

younger generation of boys. It was for boys only for swimming garments were dispensed with. Wandering among the rocks was a diversion of mine. It was a route for quiet contemplation which I confess consisted of formulating arguments with which I might overwhelm my brother and sister who were nine and seven years my seniors. At certain places along the path there were level spots among the rocks and in my imaginings I named these as cities in the country. Later, when I reached fifteen or sixteen, as my passion for politics and campaigning directed my behavior and my reading widened, I imagined that I was campaigning and that I had speaking engagements in those imagined cities. As material for speeches, I used some of the more purple passages from Henry George's **Progress and Poverty**, or selections from a cheap four-volume set of orations edited by the immortal Bryan. There were in that collection wonderful examples of rhetoric from speeches of my hero Daniel O'Connell. As to Bob Ingersoll, which Bryan religiously kept from his collection, I secured [his orations] from other sources. [I memorized] the great Ingersoll's great lecture on Napoleon, and among many other odds and ends my memory retains the words today.

This early preoccupation with classical oratory, together with the reading of English essays by Burke and Macaulay, and the quotations in Park's **Grammar** served me well. They gave me a feeling for words and a practice in oral composition. . . .

The circumstances which brought our family to Olmsted Falls in 1893 were in part related to the personalities and lives of my antecedents. Neither I nor any other member of my immediate family seemed to have been much interested in the genealogical pursuit of information beyond what he learned from our two grandmothers, one of which, on my mother's side, was known to us as a hard bitten yankee named Jane Chourchward. Her husband in her first marriage and my grandfather was John Fairchild. He lived on a large farm on the edge of neighboring Berea and his business interests consisted of two or three wooden bowl factories in various parts of Northern Ohio.

He was a native of Connecticut, and the girl that he married had the maiden name of Fletcher. Her parents came from Massachusetts and migrated to a small town near Medina, Ohio. In my pursuit of information of where the Fairchilds and Fletchers came from, I met with the following answer from my grandmother, "I don't know as they came from anywhere."

On the other hand, I was much more successful in obtaining information from my father's mother who was Irish and quite productive of information. Grandmother Moley, whose name was Mary Anne, was the daughter of Joseph Kane of Dublin, who was a civil engineer. He was entered in Trinity College in that city in 1821 and the records say that his father, Nicholas, was a "gentleman." This meant that he could afford to pay his son's tuition. He graduated four years later and apparently was somewhat successful as a civil engineer.

My grandfather, Hipolyte Molé, was born in France and as a boy joined the circus. He suffered a fall from a horse and while mending his broken leg, he learned the tailoring trade after which he migrated to Dublin and set himself up as a "French tailor." My grandfather Kane employed him to teach his daughter French and the outcome was a marriage.

The couple lived in Dublin for some years and my father, who was the second son, was born there in 1846. This was in the middle of the great potato famine, and in 1847 or 1848 my grandfather's family migrated to the United States and after a short stay in New York ended up in Olmsted Falls, Ohio. According to the stories that my grandmother told me, my grandfather had as a customer in his shop in Dublin the great Irish Liberator, Daniel O'Connell, and it was because of the stories that she told me about O'Connell that I entertained a boundless admiration for the Irish leader and resolved in the course of the last few years to write a biography of him.

2

A Village Populist

There was a good deal of excitement in the main street and particularly before my father's store on that July day in 1896 when the Cleveland **Plain Dealer** arrived at the post office. For high and centered on the first page was the handsome face of a man named William Jennings Bryan, and the headline said that he had been nominated for President by the Democratic Convention meeting in Chicago. I was there with my father who was excitedly talking with some men who had gathered around the chairs in front of the store. It seemed that everyone was asking the same question, "Who is this man Bryan?"

I had that question in my mind too. For while I was two months short of my tenth birthday, I was a steady reader of the Cleveland **Press** which we had in the evening from the paperboy who distributed the two newspapers which reached most of the people in the village. And the **Press**, an important factor among the growing Scripps chain, was hotly Democratic and had been full of accounts of the struggle over the money question at the Convention in Chicago.

I had long since been taught by my father to believe that it was right and just to belong to the Democratic Party. For the Republicans represented the conspiracy which was responsible for the debts whose shadow darkened his life as a businessman. Two weeks before we had not been so surprised when the newspapers displayed a picture of William McKinley who had been nominated by the Republicans at St. Louis, for McKinley was a name well known in Ohio. He had served as Governor of the state since 1892. And his sponsor, Mark Hanna, a resident of Cleveland, had been abundantly portrayed in the press as a bloated friend of the rich and an exploiter of the poor working man. For it seemed automatic that all working men were poor.

For many years after that Democratic Convention, there lingered in published accounts the romantic idea that Bryan, a relatively unknown country lawyer who dabbled in politics, had secured a newspaper

5

assignment to cover the Republican Convention in St. Louis, and that later as a delegate from Nebraska at the Democratic Convention had borrowed fifty dollars for his expenses and to everybody's surprise had, during the debate on the platform, swept the Convention with an improvised oration. In short, that Bryan had really been a "dark horse" nominee.

There is little truth in that legend. Bryan was very much a candidate for the nomination and had very considerable support beyond his state. . . .

Even the immortal "Cross of Gold" speech, which was delivered in the debate over the platform, had been meticulously, lovingly constructed bit by bit on scores of platforms, including the floor of the House of Representatives. The figure of speech which concluded the speech had been phrased and rephrased until it rolled up to a conclusion of supreme emotional power. Even the striking bodily gesture which accompanied the end, arms outstretched, made witnesses feel that they were witnessing another crucifixion. [1]

It was my great good fortune to learn my first lessons in national politics during a campaign of such commanding public interest. There had been nothing like it since 1860. The art of oratory had been Bryan's passion since his early college days in Illinois. Public speaking had been his profession since he moved to Nebraska in 1887. And since the Democratic Party in 1896 was badly split over the policies pursued by President Cleveland, and, because of the ideology involved, denied the support of the money people who supported Cleveland, its candidate had little newspaper and financial resources to build a national campaign organization. So the burden of the campaign fell upon the broad shoulders of the candidate himself. . . .

Bryan had the skill of a true teacher in phrasing his argument in such simple terms that acceptance of his conclusion was almost automatic. Years later I witnessed an example of this talent for simplifying things. He was in Cleveland and spoke at one of the famous City Club luncheons. He was in Ohio supporting the interests of prohibition. Ohio had two propositions for amendments to the state constitution, one of them by the drys, another by the wets. The wet amendment had only a few words. The drys proposal was much longer.

Bryan had samples of the two versions. Holding them up as if he were addressing a gathering of illiterates, he told them to vote the short word "no" on the short amendment, and the long word "yes" on the longer dry amendment.

It happened that the City Club had long had a reputation for sophistication and intelligence. One might have thought that the people there, most of whom were not in sympathy with Bryan's views, would have felt insulted by this bit of simple instruction. But the obvious sincerity of the speaker, his complete lack of awareness that his audience was any higher in education than a lot of children, won the admiration of the crowd. For it seemed to explain to them the secret of Bryan's vast influence over a generation of Americans.

Despite the opposition of most of the nation's newspaper owners, the reporters who accompanied Bryan, like his audiences, came to be captured by their admiration for the man whom their bosses were determined to destroy. These veteran and proverbially cynical observers of the political scene were softened by a man whom they came to believe was passionately in earnest. They were by the nature of their assignment compelled to suffer the same traveling discomforts and wearing routine as the candidate. They came to admire the sheer physical endurance of the man, his unfailing courtesy, and indeed the joy he had from his performance of his mission. . . .

As the weeks passed after Bryan's nomination, and the press carried more and more news of the campaign, the political talk out in Olmsted Falls grew more heated. A good proportion of the farmers who came to the village for shopping and to bring their produce to the stores or the mill were stalwart Republicans. But in the village there was quite a proportion of Democrats. The arguments in and on the sidewalk before my father's store made up in heat for their lack of facts and logic. One of the more popular arguments was that if "Free Silver" won, the dollar would be worth only fifty-three cents. The "fact" upon which this was based was that in American currency the Mexican peso's exchange value was only fifty-three cents.

I cannot claim that I knew much about the money question. But I came to know a lot about Bryan and he took complete possession of my loyalty and affection. I secured a fairly good picture of his handsome profile and that became a pin-up in my room for several years. I vigorously butted in on the conversations that were almost continuous in and around our store. That September when I returned to school, this time to the fourth grade in the "intermediate" room, I became a bit of a nuisance among the boys. In politics they were a mixed lot, with the indifferent in the majority. But I became known as a sort of fanatic with my partisanship, and when Bryan lost I persuaded my mother to keep me at home the rest of the week, for I could not bear the taunts of my friends after the confident claims I had made about Bryan's chances in the election.

I was thrifty enough, however, to turn a few honest pennies by selling buttons. I was able to purchase a lot of them with the faces of Bryan and Sewall on the Democratic ones, and McKinley and Hobart on the others. They were sold for five cents and produced a two-cent profit. Even with the money Hanna was spending for McKinley, buttons in those years were not given away.

I believe that the most significant fact that became fixed in my mind in that campaign was that "hard times" was not something inevitable in nature like dry weather or a fire or a flood. It was something that someone was responsible for in Washington or a sinister place called Wall Street or in the banks in Cleveland.

The fact of "hard times" and debt and shortage of money we had known ever since we had removed to Olmsted Falls. In fact, I had even noted even before we left Berea that my father was always having trouble about debts. I well remember that when he returned from the bank after renewing a loan by signing a new note, that when the old note came back he carefully tore out the signature.

I noted the worried look on his face and overheard the many arguments he had with my not too sympathetic mother. She was a pure yankee. Before her marriage she had served her father in his business affairs and those affairs were, despite his bad health, quite prosperous. Apparently she could not understand or find much sympathy for the troubles of her husband.

He was a man with an infinite capacity for making friends. He was a super salesman. But as a manager he seemed to lack foresight and judgment. I heard a "drummer" once tell him that he overpriced his goods. He was also fighting the growing competition with the stores in Cleveland where people from the suburbs were to an increasing extent doing their shopping. His father had set him up in business in Berea and during his lifetime had provided the managing genius to keep him going. But since grandfather died in 1886, the son Felix had been on his own.

In those years of the depression, which incidentally were the same years in which Mr. Rockefeller was building the University of Chicago, the **Press** had plenty to say about its fellow Clevelander. Some of this must have reached my mother who remarked more than once that every time old Rockefeller gave another million to the University of Chicago, the price of coal oil went up a penny.

Despite the patronage of many prosperous farmers in the countryside around Olmsted Falls, there were not a few townsmen who were living close to the poverty line. But this I took to be the normal state of affairs in which some people like the druggist had more than the road worker.

Somehow everybody seemed to make ends meet and the really poor and shiftless were the recipients of help from the neighbors.

During the year 1894 the town had a glimpse of the reaction to the depression that prevailed over the land, for a contingent of the "army" of the unemployed which had been mobilized by Jacob Coxey stopped in Olmsted Falls on its way to Washington. The townspeople made the visitors feel at home, gave them food and drink, and wished them well. Coxey himself, who lived in Massillon, Ohio, had been in the news a great deal that year. His "army" suffered a considerable erosion as it marched toward Washington, but enough reached there for a parade on May Day up Pennsylvania Avenue.

In my personal life the shortage of money was perennially acute. Whenever I asked my father for a nickel or a penny, I was reminded of "debts to pay" and hard times. But prior to 1896 and the coming of Bryan I was led to believe that our troubles were due to some unnamed bad people, never that the roots were in Washington and that there were things that Congress could do about it.

Out in Olmsted Falls we knew little of the great effort Mark Hanna was making to defeat Bryan, although he lived at the western edge of Cleveland only a dozen miles away. We knew something from the Cleveland **Press** which always from those early days pictured the paunchy National Chairman, suited in garments with dollar signs imprinted upon them. But the bales of his literature reached us and precious little did we have on the Democratic side. My father had acquired a large campaign print which he displayed in his store window. It showed the map of the United States contrived to show the outline of a dog. The dog's body was in silver, the tail — New England, New York and New Jersey — was in gold. And the words said, "Will the dog wag the tail or the tail wag the dog?"

What I could not know in those autumn days of 1896 was that incredible as it might seem, that tail was destined to wag the dog in both parties and in the nation for years to come. The master who had charge of the wagging that year and for eight years to come was Mark Hanna. In managing the promotion of his friend McKinley, he raised more money and applied better management in that campaign than had ever before been seen in American politics. . . .

Years later, at Columbia, my friend and adviser, the liberal Professor Charles A. Beard, told me a story about 1896. His father, who was a bank director in a town in Indiana, came home from his office one day that summer and said with great satisfaction that [the bank had given a large sum] to the Hanna fund. Son Charles, who had already learned something of politics and business practices, questioned the ethics of his father's action. The response was that since he was the custodian of that money, he was entitled to use as much of it as was necessary to protect it from bank robbers, embezzlers, and people like Bryan who were intent upon destroying its value.

The language was probably no more bitter than it had been in the Jackson era, but in 1896 there were more and bigger means of projecting it. The campaign of Bryan was referred to by the New York **Tribune** as a "conspiracy against the Ten Commandments." I wonder now, as we all look back over the many years since that hectic autumn, and in the light of all the political and economic changes that have come and, I hope, of moral enlightenment and of improved taste and decorum, what those defenders of the Ten Commandments might be thinking as they look down from whatever Heavenly station they occupy, about the methods they used to discredit Bryan.

Perhaps the most damaging blow to Bryan's chances was a rise in the price of wheat in the final weeks of the campaign. In August the price was about forty-seven cents a bushel. It rose steadily from that figure until, at the time of the election, it was near eighty-five cents. Some Bryan supporters hinted of a dark plot, manipulating the price to help McKinley. But a more probable cause was the failure of crops abroad which lessened the farmers' interest in Bryan's cause.

At the tender age I had reached in 1896, attachments are largely emotional. The Bryan personality captured me as it must have affected thousands of other boys. He seemed the perfect gentle knight out of the romantic West, unbelievably handsome, young, courtly, brave, indomitable. . . .

3

Public School with Diversions

The anguish I suffered with the Bryan defeat was softened by the eternal consolation of youth, "next time." But since another election was four years in the future there were tasks and problems enough to occupy me in the interim. The main one was my schooling.

The center of my life so far as education went was a brick structure built by the village at some time in the past, perhaps when the local revenues were more adequate because of flourishing private enterprise. It rose two stories on a large square of village-owned land which served a double purpose as a park with a bandstand, a reminder of days when there was actually a local "silver cornet" band of townspeople who had long since died or scattered when prosperity deserted the area and the country.

The structure consisted of two stories. The first floor with a hallway included two schoolrooms, one for the three primary grades and the other for the three "intermediate" classes. Up the stairway was a larger room which was sometimes called "high school" but more accurately was mostly referred to as "upstairs." Here there sat and studied the pupils of the remaining four grades which would roughly be described as seven through ten. The two rooms downstairs were in charge of maiden ladies who were changed from year to year at the caprice of the elected Board of Education.

In charge of the upper grades in my earlier days was a man who proudly carried the title of superintendent. He had always been a leading figure in village affairs. . . .

I had passed without much effort through the grades up to the fifth when I conceived a belief that I could easily assume the tasks of the people in the seventh grade. But my teacher, a maiden lady of the village, hesitated to yield to my plea. She said that because my father was a member of the Board of Education, promoting me would be interpreted as an act of favoritism. This seems to have been my first intimation of the workings of politics in local affairs, also evidence of the ways of bureaucracy.

I will not say that I bitterly complained to my father about my teacher's failure to recognize superior qualities of scholarship but demurred because of political consequences. But for some reason my father joined with other members of the Board, fired the teacher and employed for the intermediate room a hard-faced disciplinarian, Mary McKean. She immediately yielded to my arguments and I was promoted to the seventh grade and moved upstairs. Miss McKean was to figure in my life in Olmsted Falls for some years.

One morning early in the new school year I went with my books up a long series of stairs and was duly enrolled in the seventh grade. This opened new vistas for now I could watch the older students recite and enjoy the stimulation of Will Locke's instruction. He was a most attractive man of about thirty years who had completed a course in law at the University of Michigan. Why he drifted into teaching I never knew for he had all the attributes of a successful lawyer. He was handsome, articulate and brilliantly intelligent. I learned a great deal from him that was outside the curriculum, for after a year or so we became fast friends. With his example before me and my political instincts, a decision to become a lawyer became almost automatic.

Another event which provided me with some spending money of my own earning was the purchase of the town newspaper route from an older boy who was leaving town. The purchase price of the monopoly of ten dollars I borrowed from Grandmother Moley. (She never minded that I considered the money as a gift.) The townspeople preferred an evening paper. Only the grocer-butcher took the morning **Plain Dealer** by mail. The evening papers were the Cleveland **Press** which was, as I have noted, liberal and in national affairs Democratic, and the **News and Herald**, solidly Republican. I sold about twenty-five of each and they were distributed throughout the village. I picked them up at four in the afternoon at the railroad station and used my bicycle for distribution. This business gave me something like a dollar a week in profits and the dealings with the customers made me fairly well known in the village. The latter was an advantage later in my teaching and political ambitions. I retained the newspaper route for the next five years.

The outbreak of the war with Spain in the spring of 1898 gave the gossipers before my father's store a lively subject to talk about. The geographical names involved some difficulties in pronunciation and considerable manhandling of the Spanish language. But generally everyone agreed that considering the blowing up of the **Maine** (which the yellow press assumed prematurely was the work of Spain) and the alleged cruelties against the poor Cubans, the Spanish deserved a whipping, and patriotism waxed high with the news of American victories. Politics for the moment was forgotten but a few perceptive observers in Washington realized that with the assumption of external responsibilities, the issues would be changed for years to come, especially in 1900. Bits of news about my hero told me that Bryan had volunteered in a letter to the President who delayed his answer and that the orator had assumed the initiative and with the cooperation of the Nebraska Governor had helped form a regiment of the National Guard and had been commissioned Colonel. The history of Bryan's military career makes rather dismal reading, for the regiment was encamped in a swampy place near Jacksonville and while it was mustered into the Federal service in July, hostilities ceased before it could be moved anywhere near the fighting. . . . Altogether it was a wretched incident which did not embellish Bryan's reputation.

But he emerged with an issue which in the next two years he exploited in speeches and in writings. It was a crusade against imperialism, a call to the American people to remain secure within their own borders and, following Washington's dictum, to avoid entangling alliances. In this stand against expansion and the exaltation of military power, Bryan had good reason to protest, for in certain circles in Washington and in the yellow press, there was plenty of nonsensical chauvinism. And Theodore Roosevelt, elected Governor of New York in 1898, largely through the popularity he exploited by his rather dubious military record, took the leadership in the flag waving and saber rattling. Beveridge, Lodge and other expansionists in the Senate were most articulate.

In reply, Bryan demonstrated innocence bordering on naivete. This is well illustrated by a choice bit of rhetoric which in various forms and arrangement of words and phrases was to ring forth from scores of Chautauqua platforms in the years to come:

> Behold a republic rising securely upon the foundation stones quarried by revolutionary patriots from the mountains of eternal truth. . . . Behold a republic increasing in population, in wealth, in strength and in influence, solving the problems of civilization and hastening the coming of a common brotherhood — a republic which shakes thrones and dissolves aristocracies by its peerless example and gives light and inspiration to those who sit in darkness. . . . Behold a republic standing erect while all nations around are bowed beneath the weight of their armaments. Behold a republic whose flag is loved while theirs are only feared.

The excesses of this war of words between isolationism and imperialism were enough to raise doubts even in my teenage mind. I never lost my admiration for Bryan but I could not enjoy his complacency. I was swept a long way by his beautiful prose but I was unwilling to place my faith in a policy of non-resistance.

Moreover, things were happening on the domestic scene which were also portrayed in the papers I sold. A surge of business activity came with the termination of the Spanish War which commanded attention. A wave of big incorporations and mergers was sweeping the business world which was to extend into the new century. As I have noted, the new supplies of gold and the accelerated use of checkbook money had almost eliminated bimetalism as a political and economic issue. Inflation in a much greater volume was coming with positive effects upon the prices of farm products. As the two parties squared off in the summer of 1900, the Presidential candidates were automatically nominated.

I was far less emotionally stirred by the campaign of 1900 than I had been four years earlier. My sympathy for Bryan was unshaken, for the rhetoric about the cause of peace won my support. But my support was less vocal.

What happened was that the country, no longer subdued by hard times, was not in the mood to find agreement with Bryan's pacifism. It seemed that the victory of our arms over the weak and incompetent Spanish forces, and the sudden acquisition of dependencies overseas had been a sort of taste of blood for the American people. . . .

Bryan's vote was, however, only slightly less than in 1896. . . . The consistency of [the] vote in the three elections in which he was a candidate . . . must have been due to the hold which he had on the affections of such an immense proportion of the American people. For he was the first candidate of a major party to sound the alarm against the ruthless predatory character which national growth and the march of invention and technology had permitted in the world of business. The extent to which the crusade which Bryan carried on in the years from 1892 when he first appeared on the national scene until well into the new century has, I believe, quite properly been regarded as the prelude and inspiration of the great age of progressivism which swept the country for the greater part of two decades. It is true that his indictment lacked clear specifics and that his proposed remedies were nostrums rather than remedies. But he was everlastingly right in attributing injustice, wastefulness and social anarchy to the business community of his time.

Looking back three-quarters of a century, it is clear to me that Bryan's major contribution to my political education was to impart the fact that there were ascertainable causes for the inequities that were so apparent, even in the little world that I knew in my childhood and youth. That there was something called a system which was at fault and that a sovereign government had the power to impose corrective measures upon that system. Indeed Bryan's great shortcoming was that he believed an omnipotent government had intelligence which matched its power. . . .

It is true that Bryan's appeal ignited my latent prejudices and fell far short of feeding my mind. And it is difficult to determine the point in my progress toward maturity when my prejudices became viable convictions. That part of my early education came only when the influences of other leaders attacked the issues raised by Bryan with more specific and practical answers. But for all the years of Bryan's life, despite my disagreement with the views he held, at the end my respect and affection for the man remained. He did not awaken my interest in politics; my father and an innate instinct did that. But he gave me a glimpse of the issues and some hints upon which other influences might build.

Those who either remember or otherwise know of Bryan only as he appeared in the twilight of his life miss the immense significance of the man in shaping the moral sense of his generation in matters political. It was the supreme tragedy of his life that the curtain had to fall so soon after the sordid scene in the Scopes trial in Tennessee.

In early September, 1901, shortly before my fifteenth birthday, I went with my mother and my sister Nell on a visit to the Pan American Exposition in Buffalo. On the first day after our arrival we visited the attractions at the Exposition, but the second day we spent at Niagara Falls to escape the crowds that were expected because of the presence of President McKinley. The following day we returned to the Exposition while McKinley visited Niagara Falls. He returned in the afternoon and held a reception at the Temple of Music on the Fairgrounds.

We were in a building next to the Temple when there fluttered through the crowd the tragic news, "The President is shot."

I immediately left my companions and ran over toward the Temple of Music. I noticed that a crowd was gathering at the rear door of the building and I joined it. I soon saw the interest of the crowd when the rear door opened and two policemen emerged half dragging the assassin, Czolgosz. Someone near me shouted, "That's him. Let's hang 'im."

There was a carriage drawn by two horses waiting, one of the closed sort with the driver on top and which can "turn on a dime." The police officers moved toward the carriage and the crowd followed. The driver escaped the crowd by starting the horses and making a sharp turn. So there was avoided what might have been a lynching.

After I rejoined my mother and sister, we decided to take the evening train to Cleveland. The city was seething with excited rumors about the President's condition.

McKinley lived eight days and died, more a victim of bungling surgical attention than the assassin's bullet.

I could not know at the time that what happened at Buffalo was more than a tragedy. For it was not long before the man who succeeded as President would usher in a new political and economic era.

The McKinley-Hanna regime had made good the promises it made in 1896. In the phrases used in that campaign, McKinley really proved to be the "advance agent for prosperity." Under his presidency the smoke again came from factory chimneys and the worker's dinner pail was filled.

But the cause of social and economic justice for which Bryan had argued with such eloquence outlived Bryan's two defeats. And in a turn of supreme irony, this provided with somewhat different language the major theme of McKinley's successor.

It was quite clear that Theodore Roosevelt, whether sincere or not, believed that the wave of the future was toward the reform of business and industrial practices, toward a recognition of the rights of labor, of investors and of the consuming public generally.

In the great industrial expansion that followed the election of McKinley there had been at the turn of the century a series of great mergers such as the creation of the United States Steel Corporation. And what was called the "trust" problem was concerned with legal means to prevent these industrial giants from an inevitable monopoly. The McKinley administration had been most hospitable to this trend toward concentration.

Roosevelt, despite disclaimers at the time he entered the White House that he intended in no way to change the policies of his predecessor, was regarded by observers as cut from an entirely different pattern and was motivated by an entirely different attitude toward the business community. Most of the early Roosevelt activities, however, were limited to preachments against irresponsible business.

4

Tom L. Johnson,
Disciple of Henry George

It hardly needs saying that the characters in the early chapters of this book, whom I consider as having contributed to my political education, were remote figures I knew then only through reading what I could about them. For the most part this was in the newspapers I carried, the Cleveland **Press** and the **News and Herald**. I absorbed what they printed during my afternoon jaunts on my newspaper route. This was supplemented by more reading in the evenings at home or during the day after I entered college in the small college library where several of the current magazines were kept and such books as were pertinent. I did not have much chance to talk with anyone about national affairs and politics, for [my teacher] Will Locke could only reflect what I had read in the newspapers.

When Tom Johnson became a factor in my education, there were the writings of Henry George himself. And my much used copy of **Progress and Poverty** purchased in 1901 when I was fifteen has markings to show the fact that I read it with considerable care but not much understanding except to note the main thrust of his extraordinary argument. I accepted it much as I had Bryan's discourses on fiscal policy but with a difference.

The reason I discovered Johnson was because he preached the doctrines of George and my attachment to Johnson soon converted me from the populism of Bryan to the more sophisticated doctrines of the progressives, except that Johnson brought his liberal ideas into the government of a big city.

Young as I was, I came to realize in 1901 that something more than [the] populist solutions proposed by Bryan were necessary to meet the problems that I felt were confronting the nation, and my interests were shifting to the activities and proposals of more sophisticated reformers.

McKinley's policies had indeed succeeded so well that writers in the press were beginning to complain about what was to be an issue for years to come. It was called Big Business, and its manifestation in the years around the turn of the century was a series of mergers. It seemed that the old Trust had been succeeded by the incorporation of many giant corporations, which some writers predicted were on the way to the domination of the country.

It is true that Bryan had sounded the warning about the danger in what he called the Trusts, but he had never supplied the specifics of the new capitalism which by 1901 was appearing in the form of the great corporations like United States Steel and the Standard Oil Company. The voice of organized labor was beginning to be heard through the columns of the press and some magazines that I began to read. Attracted by the large profits of the large corporations, leaders of some of the unions began to demand a larger share for the worker. And it began to dawn upon the Democrats in an industrial town like Cleveland that Bryan's inflationary remedy might help the farmers but it would also raise prices at the grocery store.

In April, 1901, the news reached Olmsted Falls that Tom L. Johnson had been elected Mayor of Cleveland. The newspapers had carried the news of his campaign for two months, so that I knew something of his life and ideas from what I had read. His name was rather well known because he had represented the Twenty-First District in Congress for two terms from 1890 to 1894. This District included the village of Olmsted Falls. He had first entered politics at the suggestion of Henry George.

Tom (not Thomas) Johnson had crowded two brilliantly successful careers into his relatively short life of fifty-six years when he died in 1911. But he always said that he wanted to be remembered as a disciple of Henry George. It was the reading of a book by Henry George that started his thinking about social problems. He formed a warm friendship with George in the 1880s. He was managing George's campaign for Mayor of New York when the master died in 1897, and he directed that he be buried near George's grave in Greenwood Cemetery, Brooklyn.

When in 1901 the election of Johnson as Cleveland's Mayor brought his name prominently to the attention of all of Northern Ohio, he found a public fairly well prepared to accept his leadership and his ideas. For, in part because of his many speeches and his activity in Congress, he had given considerable currency to George's ideas. In fact, Johnson apparently had brought George himself to Cleveland for a lecture in the early 1890s. Also there had been a good deal of material in the Cleveland **Press** which closely followed the doings of social reformers.

I had thus heard a considerable amount about George and something called "Single Tax." My copy of **Progress and Poverty** was acquired about the time of Johnson's election. The leading liberals in Cleveland, and they were numerous, were [called] Georgists. A Single Tax Club was formed which was still flourishing when I moved to Cleveland ten years later. It met regularly on Sunday to hear one of its members give his special speech on Georgism. There was a weekly journal called **The Ground Hog** which was largely written and published by a printer whom I knew in later years.

I had learned that George was a native of Philadelphia, who at the age of fifteen went to sea. In his worldwide travels he saw and was oppressed by what he saw of poverty in such cities as Calcutta. Finally he ended his voyages in San Francisco. He had learned the printer's trade at sea and found employment in some of the shops in the Bay Region, and soon moved up to journalism. He apparently did not derive his ideas about what he called "land monopoly" from the economics textbooks, but from observing what was happening in San Francisco and Northern California. He noted with moral indignation that a few individuals, through speculation in land, had accumulated large fortunes while the generality of the people remained poor. The question which was always in what he wrote or spoke was whether these accumulations of wealth were due to real labor or management or merely the possession of land which a crowding population made valuable.

Realizing that he needed intensive study of economic science, he went East and immersed himself in a study of the classical economists. To his surprise he found that not only had the French Physiocrats a century before perceived what he had learned in California, but had invented a remedy which was essentially a single tax on land.

(Pierre Samuel Dupont was a prominent Physiocrat before his move to the United States, where he founded the business which bears his name. Indeed, one of the members of that family became one of the advisers in the Johnson Administration in Cleveland.)

He also found a great deal of inspiration in the writings of Ricardo. His famous **Canons of Taxation** are almost exactly the same as certain principles in Adam Smith's **Wealth of Nations**. His great book **Progress and Poverty**, which emerged from his studies, soon attained worldwide attention.

In 1881, two years after **Progress and Poverty** was published, he was in Ireland lending his advice to the Parnell Party. Curiously, there is a link between George and the reforms of Sun Yat Sen in China, for during Sun's exile in the United States and England he grew to know of George's work, perhaps through John Stuart Mill with whom George had a considerable correspondence. (The present land reforms in Taiwan were based upon ideas carried over from the mainland by Chiang Kai-shek and his people.)

George's ideas were largely responsible for the system of land taxation adopted about 1890 in Australia.

At the age of sixteen I was quite unable to grasp the economic argument presented by **Progress and Poverty**. But the beauty of George's language and the simplicity with which he expressed his major contentions struck my admiration. The major concept, which I considered to be the real contribution of George, is marked in my old book, not only for its literary excellence, but its message:

> Take now ... some hard-headed businessman, who has no theories, but knows how to make money. Say to him: "There is a little village; in ten years it will be a great city — in ten years the railroad will have taken the place of the stage-coach, the electric light of the candle; it will abound with all the machinery and improvements that so enormously multiply the effective power of labor. Will, in ten years, interests be any higher?"
>
> He will tell you, "No!"
>
> "Will the wages of common labor be higher, will it be easier for a man who has nothing but his labor to make an independent living?"
>
> He will tell you "No!"
>
> "What then will be higher?"
>
> "Rent; the value of land. Go, get yourself a piece of ground and hold possession."
>
> And if, under such circumstances, you take his advice, you need do nothing more. You may sit down and smoke your pipe; you may lie around like the Lazzaroni of Naples or the Leperos of Mexico; you may go up in a balloon, or down in a hole in the ground; and without doing one stroke of work, without adding one iota to the wealth of the community, in ten years you will be rich! In the new city you may have a luxurious mansion; but among its public buildings will be an almshouse.

The way to correct this injustice was, according to George, to make land common property, not by actual confiscation of the land but, in his words, to confiscate the rent. This would, he said, preserve the principle of free enterprise while taking back in the form of taxes the "unearned increment" previously taken by the owner of the land.

The modern Georgist offers a prescription which it is believed carries out the purpose of George, but makes the change more palatable to the land owner. He would, through a change in assessing practice, shift some of the burden of the property tax from the improvements (buildings, etc.) to the land. This might be done in whatever proportion the public would determine. This is called "Land (or Site) Value Taxation." It is now considered wholly impractical to speak of a Single Tax. I am not sufficiently informed to be certain, but I believe that George himself never used the expression Single Tax. It is also important to note that George was strongly opposed to socialism. One of the chapters in **Progress and Poverty** is devoted to an argument against the Marxian thesis.

I hesitate to draw conclusions from quite inadequate data, but I suggest that the fact that Johnson had a good deal of mechanical genius caused him to hope for much more social amelioration from the adoption of the George idea than most people now would expect. The basis of his fortune was the money he made at twenty-two by the invention of a street railway fare box. This gadget accomplished many things. It assured honesty in the conductor and the passenger alike, as well as greatly facilitating the collection of fares. I have wondered about the Georgists' belief that many wonderful results will come from the adoption of the George idea, including the immensely complicated problems of abolishing poverty. The mechanical mind considers a special problem to be similar to a mechanical failure. A more-or-less simple device will cure the difficulty. And there is no question but George and his disciples believed that a change in the incidence of taxation would lead to certain Utopian results, including the abolition of poverty and peace among nations. Indeed this is not only suggested but substantially promised in some of the rhetoric in the concluding chapter of **Progress and Poverty**.

A great many years later I came to know another mechanical genius, John C. Lincoln. His chief achievement in the world of industry was the founding of the Lincoln Electric Company of Cleveland. His inventions, which numbered more than fifty over his lifetime, included the immensely important arc welder. He became interested in George after hearing him speak in Cleveland in the early 1890s. He then read a great deal of George's writings and lavishly supported Georgist activities. In 1947 he founded the Lincoln Foundation and dedicated it to the promotion of George's ideas as stated in **Progress and Poverty**. [2] To him the taking of rent by the "owner" of land was legalized "stealing," and the remedy could come through a radical revision of the tax laws.

It is true that both Johnson and Lincoln were aware of many ways to ameliorate social distress and both supported them. But they were convinced that at the heart of social problems was a great injustice underlying all others. It was like a cancerous infection in the very marrow of the bones of the social organism.

Johnson entered the business world at a time when the potential of electricity was in the full tide of exploitation. The beginnings of what were to be vast industries were appearing, and one of these which drew Johnson to its service was the electric street railway. As I have said, he was employed in this business in Louisville when he invented his fare box. With the money he earned from this invention, he actually bought a street railway system in Indianapolis. Success followed success in various cities, and finally he found himself in Cleveland competing . . . with the interests of the mighty Mark Hanna. The need for steel for the rails and other equipment carried him into steel manufacturing, and he built plants in Johnstown, Pennsylvania, and Lorain, Ohio.

He was no doubt headed for great leadership in the business world when a curious thing happened. On a train from Indianapolis to Cleveland, a news butcher dropped a book at his side. He picked it up and at the end of the line he paid the price of a half dollar. The book was called **Social Problems** by a man named Henry George. This was in 1883. The young man, not yet thirty years of age, became absorbed in what he read. It is a common characteristic with men of action that they learn more rapidly through their ears than with their eyes. Governor Smith of New York had a habit of saying, when a book was recommended, that he would rather see the author. Johnson first gave the book to his lawyer and asked his opinion. Then he sought out George himself. The two became fast friends. Thoroughly "sold" on George's ideas, he asked what he could do to further the cause. When he was advised to enter politics, he answered that while he could make money, he could neither speak nor behave in the way a politician was supposed to. George assured him that he could learn.

Following that, there were several years during which Johnson, while pursuing his business activities, gave a considerable part of his time to how he could implement the George theories and promote a wide public understanding of them. He also saw a great deal of George, especially in 1886 when George was one of the unsuccessful candidates (along with the young Theodore Roosevelt) for Mayor of New York. In 1888 he ran as a Democrat against Theodore Burton for Congress in Ohio's Twenty-First District and lost. But in 1890 he challenged Burton to a debate, proposing, as he told the story later in a memoir, that the speeches be limited to ten minutes. He knew that Burton, who was ponderous and wordy, could not win such a test. Johnson, who spoke with a great economy of words, won the debate and the election then and in 1892. In 1894 the great panic of 1893 was on and Burton regained his seat.

Johnson's service in Congress was hardly noteworthy, although he was able, with the cooperation of five other members, to spread the whole text of George's book **Protection of Free Trade** in the Congressional Record. He and his colleagues then put the pieces of the book together, had it printed at Johnson's expense, and because it had appeared in the Record had the Government frank it [for mailing]. The demand for this free book was so great that more than a million copies were distributed.

In 1896 Johnson, as a Democrat and former Congressman, was confronted with a fundamental decision. He had no faith in Bryan's proposals for reform, but supported him as a matter of party unity. He never believed bimetallism to be anything but a palliative. By the turn of the century, Johnson had divested himself of substantially all of his business interests in preparation for his campaign for Mayor of Cleveland.

His steel interests in plants in Johnstown and Lorain ultimately became a part of the immense United States Steel Corporation. Various interests acquired his street railway properties. [3]

The social and political philosophy developed by Johnson essentially followed the ideas of George, but his application of the term monopoly went far beyond land.

5
College
and a Year of Teaching

Hard and fast economic limitations barred me from the enjoyment of four years at a first-rate high school and another four years at a good college. Instead, I absorbed what was taught at the school in Olmsted Falls up to and including the tenth grade, and three years at a quite impoverished Methodist college with the high-sounding name of Baldwin University.

While the school in Olmsted Falls offered instruction in two of the normal high school years and the people in the village spoke of a "high school," we had no such certification until I secured it several years after my graduation in 1902. My diploma simply said that I had completed my studies in the "public school."

While Will Locke did a great deal to train my thinking, especially in mathematics and in the rules of grammar, there was no training in written composition and no requirement in reading classical literature. Indeed, the school had no library at all. Nothing beyond a two-volume set of a deadly dull history of Ohio which was a gift from Columbus. My graduation "oration" on the subject "The Height of Human Ambition" (well sprinkled with quotes and quite noble in its hortatory passages) was my sole contribution to the writing art in my public school years.

At home I read everything in sight, borrowed many volumes of Scott and Cooper from my aunt in Berea, and as a literary effort tried to make a play of the novel **Ivanhoe**, a task which I abandoned after writing a few pages of what was to be the first act.

After my graduation, my rather over-average size and strength suggested that I ought to get out and make a living. And so, in the summer that followed, I first had a job in a Cleveland manufacturing plant, and later employment in a Michigan stone quarry of which my brother-in-law was superintendent. My sister Nell, when I returned from Michigan in September, insisted that I should be enrolled in Baldwin University three miles away from home in Berea. (This institution ultimately merged with Ger-

24

man-Wallace College, and now is Baldwin-Wallace College.)

My lack of anything like the credits for entering a properly accredited college was of no consideration. With only about 100 students, the paramount need of Baldwin was for more enrollees. The tuition, which was only about $30 a quarter, was in some way raised at home. Transportation was by rail on the Lake Shore.

While I was officially registered as a "prep" student, the limitations of the curriculum and the small student body compelled the administration of the college to throw open to all students, regardless of their preparation, all courses. There was no offering in American history or government and so I turned to English. The professor in that subject was a kindly but not very exciting product of Harvard where he had finished with a master's degree. But my passion for literature and the resources of the little college library sufficed. Also his course in rhetoric began my training in English composition. I also took advantage of an arrangement that Baldwin had with German-Wallace College to elect a course in French. All modern languages were offered at German-Wallace, a short walk from Baldwin.

German-Wallace was a college supported by the German Methodist Conference. Its student body was considerably larger than that of Baldwin and its academic standards were considerably higher. Some of the professors were natives of Germany and, therefore, its offering in that language was rather rich. I regretted later that I neglected the opportunity to elect courses in that language. My teacher in French was of German extraction and possessed the strictness and efficiency which were the tradition of the fatherland.

The first and the second years at Baldwin passed without incident. I realized quite well the limitations of the institution, its rather thin curriculum, and the lack of talent in the faculty. It should be said, however, that considering the meager salaries which the college could afford, the dedication of the professors made up for what they lacked in talent. In my second year I resolved to carve out from the curriculum as many courses as the administration permitted. There was more English, more French, Spanish, economics, and more mathematics. As in the first year, the library offered much that the courses lacked.

At the end of the second year at Baldwin I felt that my education so far had imposed a burden on the family's exchequer, to which I felt unwilling to add. The meager profits from my father's store had never been enough to meet expenses. Nell and, for certain periods, my brother Jim lived at home. My mother and my sister Nell added something to the budget by taking in school teachers for board and bed. And for gangs of special workers on the railroad they often provided lunches. Also my grandmother contributed something to the till. But the balance was fairly thin and I decided to do the only thing which my preparation seemed to provide, which was school teaching.

A vacancy appeared in a rural school four miles from Olmstcd Falls. This school, named Kennedy Ridge, where it was located, was the typical red school house with all eight grades and pupils ranging from six to sixteen. The president of the School Board I knew slightly as a customer at my father's store. I took the county examination and secured my first teacher's certificate. The School Board hired me. The pay was $35 a month for nine months. I secured board and bed at a farmer's house and I set forth in a career which was to extend far into my life.

I was two weeks short of eighteen when I called my brood of about forty to order. As I look back at that year on Kennedy Ridge, certain substantial gains stand out. Most important I was self-supporting for the first time in my life. The $35 seems small today but it went quite a long way in 1904. It paid my keep at the farmer's house, bought my clothes, and supplied my recreational needs which consisted of dances and an occasional theater outing in Cleveland.

I was also able to carry some courses with private lessons by professors at Baldwin. These courses I took at professors' homes on Saturdays and on one evening every week. The midweek engagement I was able to meet by walking two miles to one of the interurbans which branched out from Cleveland. Then I was compelled to change to another interurban which carried me to Berea. I don't wish to add a heroic touch to this extracurricular undertaking but in the winter months it was quite a task to plough through the snow to the first interurban and wait in a shed without a door for the connection, and then back to my lodgings on Kennedy Ridge after the return trip. But it gave me credits which stood me well in completing my final year at Baldwin.

An incidental gain was the development of a sense of responsibility. It was not easy to maintain discipline in a school with such a range of ages. Some of the older boys, who were able to come only late in the fall after the final harvest, were of my own age. As I remember, my troubles, however, were not with these elders. It was the ten or twelve year olds who needed an occasional tanning with sticks I cut from the trees nearby. And the small fry of six to nine were quite beyond my teaching skills.

When spring came I found that there had been a change in the School Board. My friend, the president when I was hired, had been supplanted by another farmer who, because he had been a teacher himself in his earlier years, was particularly difficult to deal with.

In this case, my new boss, despite his fussiness, made a wise decision. He said that after visiting several of the parents of my younger pupils he had decided that I should be supplanted by a woman teacher. In short, I was fired. Now, as I look back, this was the only job I ever held which ended in a dismissal. I accepted his decision without protest, for despite the unbounded confidence I had in my capacity, I had to admit to myself that teaching very young children was beyond me.

After some cogitation and a great deal of study of the Baldwin catalogue, I conceived the bold plan of returning to college for another year and, by an incredible accumulation of credits, actually qualified for graduation by the end of the next school year. The loose regulations imposed by the college administration and the generally low standards of scholarship of the faculty encouraged me to believe that I could, after the two earlier years of college study beyond the tenth grade, complete the requirement for a degree. What was involved was clearing up several subjects in summer school and, during the coming year, electing and passing what generally required two years of residence. It was my luck to have impressed the new president of the college, a former businessman named George B. Rogers, that I was equal to the program I outlined. He offered to cooperate by tutoring me in Latin, for this was a minimum requirement for the degree of Bachelor of Philosophy which was given when the student was offered no Greek.

President Rogers and my old friend and teacher George Collier had some heated words about admitting me to the senior class which ended when Rogers flexed his presidential muscles. Collier satisfied his pride and the honor of the institution by telling me that if I succeeded in getting a degree after only three years of residence beyond the tenth grade, the institution would suffer irreparable damage. My response to this was that the reputation of the college would never suffer from numbering me among its alumni. And my mental note was that if they had considered the low standards some years earlier, the plan I proposed would have been impossible. It should be noted that my exploit in ploughing through the curriculum stirred things up so that in the next year measures were taken to stiffen the requirements. My boast about never disgracing my alma mater was made good years later when I shared the joint honor of most distinguished graduate with a young man who, after playing with the Los Angeles Rams, was, for a year or so, coach of the Atlanta Falcons.

And so the summer passed and the following winter and I graduated in a class that numbered only five. The point was that in some courses I studied the professor rather than the required reading. In others I worked hard. And in two courses in philosophy and religion my comments in class earned a private warning from the professor that I was in danger of losing my faith. Perhaps he was prejudiced because I flaunted my Catholic church membership, giving as my senior oration a paper on Daniel O'Connell.

I offer this account of my college education certainly with no intent to claim brilliance or for burning the midnight oil. For in the only test which is worthy of note, by examinations over the next few years for teacher's certificates, I was not a straight A student, except in literature. Night study was never productive in my life. I had plenty of time for sports and my studying in those years was mostly done before breakfast. What I had done within the four corners of the printed requirements was quite unusual but not irregular.

Whether I might have been better educated at the end of my twentieth year had I attended a college with stricter requirements ... is pure speculation and hardly relevant. I simply lacked the financial resources to do anything other than what I did. I had acquired enough money from my grandmother for tuition and incidental expenses such as railway fare. I had lived at home where the labor of my family provided food. And I had enough time aside from my busy college schedule to maintain contact with political happenings.

6
Johnson:
What a City Learned from a Man

One of the many correspondents from abroad who visited Cleveland during the Johnson years asked the Mayor to tell him about the street railway controversy. [4] Johnson took him to the window of his office and pointed to the people in the street. "Ask the first person you meet down there," was the answer. This was hardly an exaggeration, for Johnson conceived his first responsibility to be public education. But not only the people of Cleveland learned the meaning of Johnson's liberalism. The word went out through the reaches of the nation. In those years when what came to be called progressivism was growing, the city of Cleveland was at the center of national attention. It was . . . "The city on a hill."

In his autobiography written during the last months of his life, Johnson stated the principle which guided him in all his efforts for reform. This definition is phrased in the idiom of his time. But what he did in applying his principle in his administration as Mayor indicated a sophisticated understanding of realities perhaps greater than any of his contemporaries in the great dissent of those years. He sought to remove or at any rate to lessen the influence of what he called "Privilege."

The most important lessons that came through to me from my reading about Johnson, and which remained as foundation stones in my political philosophy, were these. And I believe these were also learned by the perceptive people of Cleveland at that time.

1. That a liberal government is not necessarily inefficient.

Too often the public is prone to excuse bungling, incompetent management of government in an administration which is supposed to be more concerned with helping the needy and providing justice than it is about what the same government is doing with the taxpayer's money. The warm-hearted, God bless them, are not always the clear-headed, God keep them. In many of the states and cities over the land, governments elected because of their promises to the needy and underprivileged find the tasks of government beyond their assortment of skills.

Johnson, [during his] brilliant business career in the years before he

entered politics, had successfully contended with the tycoons who owned
what we now would call mass transportation and which in those days was
the street railway system, and later when his need for steel rails led him
into the steel manufacturing business, [with] the colossal companies
which dominated the steel business.

As mayor he applied the same clear and energetic efficiency to the
city's business affairs he had used in winning his fortune.

2. The second lesson, to which most of this chapter and all of the next
is devoted, was that while what he called privilege in the entire body politic
should be effectively restrained and, if possible, abolished, there was a
way short of socialism to attain the desired end. This, I believe, he taught
the city while he was teaching himself. For while there always flickered
behind the bright face of progressivism the flare of socialism, he found a
way to establish a just settlement of the street railway controversy without
government ownership. We shall see in another chapter how this was
accomplished in settling the transit controversy. But at this point I shall
concentrate a bit upon the process which led me to escape the lure of
socialism.

I must carry my reader back to those early years of the new century to
emphasize [how attractive] socialism was to the young, idealistic, educated
American.

As [we viewed] the state as it existed with plutocracy on every side,
monopolizing the means of production, dominating the agencies of
government with all the power that money could bring, dictating the prices
Americans had to pay for living, we all sought for some saving formula.
And many found this in socialism.

Socialism had swept over the so-called intellectual classes in England,
sweeping Shaw and other luminaries with its intoxicating influence. We
felt the influence here. The flood of socialist literature was almost overwhelming. It seemed so easy. Simply take the means of production
together with almost all property interests into the beneficent arms of a
thing called Government. How could anything owned by the government,
which meant, in the simplistic thinking of the day, the "people," be
anything but just for the "people"? It seemed to so many just as simple as
that.

In those years local applications of socialism were [popular].
Municipal ownership of public utilities was [sometimes] adopted ... ,
especially in the production and distribution of electric power. This
fashion, which reached its peak of popularity in 1910, continued well into
the next two decades. Harold Ickes and George Norris were great in-

fluences upon [Franklin D.] Roosevelt, and federal law was revised to provide that preferences in the sale of electric power from federal production plants should go to states and communities with local owner-ship.

In the agreement, described in the next chapter, Johnson in his negotiations with the street car companies decided that private ownership could be successfully harnessed with government control. This com-monsense solution of Johnson forever after kept me away from socialist solutions. . . .

During those years when the vogue of socialism was taking hold in England and in some parts of the United States, I happened to be exposed to strong pressure to embrace Marxism in a somewhat extreme form.

There were two brothers in Olmsted Falls, sons of a German radical immigrant who had, somewhat before I entered Baldwin, gone away to college. They were Will and Frank Bohn. Will, the elder, had been sent to the University of Michigan where, after completing his graduate work, he taught English for a while. I had spent many hours with him when I at-tended summer school there in 1907 and 1909. Later he became a worker in the Socialist Party and for a time held some sort of paid office. When I was on the Columbia faculty, he was director of the Socialist Rand School in Union Square. Two or three times I gave speeches at the School because of invitations from Bohn. Still later in the 1950s and 1960s he was on the masthead of the liberal magazine **New Leader.** I had, however, lost track of him after the Rand School experience. [5]

During my teaching years in Olmsted Falls, Frank Bohn spent con-siderable time there where his family still owned property. His visits were usually in the summers. He had taken his doctorate at Ohio State in history and drifted into the Socialist Party. He was a virile, strapping fellow who told highly exciting tales about his activities in the labor troubles of the Northwest. I realized that these tales lost nothing for truth's sake in the telling. But it was true that he had co-authored a small book with Bill Haywood and had traveled with him among the I.W.W.s in Idaho and Montana. In those years and for a long time thereafter, he made a living lecturing before middle-class groups across the country. Otherwise, he was a gay, fancy-free, lazy type. The people in Olmsted Falls found him most attractive and never minded the brazen way he sponged his keep on his visits. We saw a great deal of each other and he most vigorously tried to make me a convert. There was no doubt about his radicalism (according to what he said). Once he said that he would be willing to see half the population of the United States die in the revolution for the sake of socialism.

I realized that such talk was really the outpouring of his romantic disposition. But in some of our more serious talks, he was quite persuasive. I was induced to read two books on socialism by Edmund Kelley which I found quite persuasive. I am sure that I might have become a convert except for three negative factors.

First, I was a Catholic and I had studied enough to know that socialism was quite godless. Certainly Frank Bohn was godless enough.

Another deterrent was my appraisal of the two Bohns, Frank especially, who gloried in his Bohemian ways which seemed to me slovenly, irresponsible and even, in what he occasionally worked at, incompetent. I pondered on what would happen to the work of the world which needs doing with the likes of this educated vagabond in a position of power. This distrust of the radical type has grown as I have known so many in my journey through life. In rejecting the basic principles of a capitalistic society, they also turn against the standards of workmanship that go with it. In the days of the New Deal this incompetence was everywhere apparent. The Democratic Roosevelt ran a very disorderly ship. One Under Secretary told me that his boss was such a mystic that he had to see that the work of the Department got done. Since the Under Secretary was himself a notorious dreamer, I said to myself, "God help the Department." For every generality, exceptions must be taken. In our time Milwaukee and Bridgeport have had Socialist mayors who were kept in office for repeated terms because they were competent administrators. And I also had before me the example of Johnson, the reformer who was the incomparable administrator.

I have discussed in some detail Johnson's concepts of justice which he labored so long to realize. Also his efforts to educate the public and his care of the political organization through which he retained power. There remains a comment on his great capacity as a civil administrator.

He carried into his administration of the city government the genius for administration which had marked his successful business career. The innovations he conceived and put into operation spread their influence far and wide. Municipal control of utilities, smart police administration, new departures in welfare organization, street construction, repairing and lighting, and all of the other household duties which make urban life tolerable, were done with such efficiency that the inhabitants came to take them as matters of routine.

Foremost in the art of good administration is the capacity to select competent subordinates. One of his better and more famous selections was a minister named Harris R. Cooley, who was chosen as Welfare Director. Under his leadership the various charitable and correctional activities were moved out from rookeries in the city to an immense farm purchased by the city. There he established decent humane establishments — one for minor offenders, another for the indigent, another for the dependent old people, and another for the tubercular patients. Modern welfare administration owes Cooley a great debt.

His police chief, Fred Kohler, whom Johnson promoted from the ranks, was a far-sighted humanitarian in handling offenders but a firm believer in discipline. Theodore Roosevelt on one occasion hailed him as the "best Police Chief in the United States."

The Mayor of Toledo, Brand Whitlock, who as a former newspaper-man was having trouble with managing the city's affairs, once asked Johnson what was required in a good executive. Johnson answered that he must make decisions quickly and count on being right two-thirds of the time.

But Johnson, in his autobiography, impatiently brushes aside the truly remarkable administrative achievements during his service as Mayor. "To give good government," he wrote, "wasn't the thing I was in public life for. While we need to give the people clean and well lighted streets, pure water, free access to the parks, public baths and comfort stations, a good police department, careful market inspection, a rigid system of weights and measures, and to make charitable and correctional institutions aid the unfortunate and correct the wrong doers, and do the hundred and one things that a municipality ought to do for its inhabitants — while we tried to do all these things and even to outstrip other cities in doing them, we never lost sight of the fact that they were not fundamental."

What he said "we tried to do" he did. And while he quite correctly rated justice above efficiency, he would probably agree with the proposition that it is best to have both.

7

Johnson:
Private Ownership — Public Control

It was a cold night in November, 1907. I stood in an immense crowd at Sixth and Superior in Cleveland. We were watching the moving statistics of the election returns displayed on a large screen high and across the Plain Dealer Building. The arc lights threw the scene into harsh brightness and cut the blackness of the streets and buildings in the background with slashes, pools and swaths of whiteness. Tom L. Johnson had been elected for the fourth time since 1901 and as his majority grew on the screen, the joyous tumult of the crowd increased. It seemed that the people who had reelected this man were trying to match in their enthusiasm such celebrations as New Year's Eve or a presidential election. I joined in the emotions of that night although I was not a Cleveland voter and I never knew nor was to know Johnson, except through the press and as an attendant at his meetings.

The campaign that had terminated in the election that day was the culmination of a long battle against the interests that held property rights in the street railway system of the city. In preparing for this test, those interests had mobilized money and influence of every available sort. The old Hanna machine was still a potent force, its tentacles reaching as far as the State House in Columbus and the White House in Washington. President Roosevelt had taken a hand and gave his open influence to persuade Theodore Elijah Burton, long a Congressman in the Twenty-First District, to run against Johnson. Burton was the brightest Republican star that the GOP could offer. He had been Hanna's lieutenant, managing the home forces while the Senator was tending store in Washington. After Hanna's death in 1904, Burton had been left the virtual head of the Party in Ohio.

The campaign that year had exceeded anything Cleveland had known before in bitterness, excitement and general interest. Not only had President Roosevelt made it an issue of party loyalty, but William H. Taft, Ohio-born Secretary of War and President-to-be, and James R. Garfield,

Secretary of the Interior and son of a President, joined in. There was wrangling in the streets, the clubs, the schools and the homes. The major issue was the nature of the prospective franchises to be given to the street railway lines, the rate of fare, and the extent of city control. Deeper than all that, however, the campaign epitomized the division between the philosophy of individualism as exemplified in the McKinley-Hanna era, and the liberal philosophy of the first years of the century.

But Burton's classical style and stuffy platform image, together with his imperfect understanding of the issues involved, made him no match for the virile, informed and resourceful Johnson. And Johnson's fight for popular causes and his efficient administration of the city's affairs had long since won for him the enthusiastic support of the Cleveland electorate. It was everywhere regarded as the last desperate stand of the Bourbons and that when Johnson won, he would substantially have his way in determining the status of the street railway for years to come.

In the excitement of that night in Cleveland, I almost forgot that earlier in the evening I had been declared a winner in my candidacy for Clerk of Olmsted Falls village.

Johnson's struggle for the first six years of his Administration took the form of setting up competitive [streetcar] lines favored by him and the City Council, which was firmly pro-Johnson, and at other times striving to give the franchises governing the old lines when they expired to interests favored by Johnson. So fierce was the battle that at one time the rails of one of Johnson's lines were laid on top of the pavement paralleling the rails of the Company. Through the long contest, the courts controlled by the Establishment issued an avalanche of injunctions which Baker, as City Solicitor, resisted with great legal skill.

Realizing that the victory over Burton marked the moment for a settlement, Johnson, on the day after the election, wrote a letter to the Company suggesting that their representatives meet with the Mayor and the Council to consider the terms of a final settlement. He noted that many of the franchises of the Company's lines were up for renewal and that the City Council would hold the decisive hand in fixing the terms of the new grants. The logic of Johnson's position was quite clear. He and the City Council which he dominated were in a position to dictate terms.

Preliminary negotiations resulted in the selection by the Company of Frederick G. Goff to confer with Johnson and reach a final settlement of the long controversy. Goff, of whom we shall hear a great deal later in this narrative, was a lawyer of remarkably liberal opinions who, nevertheless, had the confidence of the entire business community. He was at the time of his appointment a partner in the law firm of Kline, Carr, Tolles and Goff, which was generally known as "Rockefeller's law firm." He had served for a while as Mayor of the suburban town of Glenville and, to the horror of the sporting element, had halted betting at the race track there. He was a sturdy, forceful individual who was to play a great part in the life of Cleveland. He was soon to leave the law to become President of the Cleveland Trust Company.

There was great mutual respect between Goff and Johnson and they soon whipped together a plan. Because of certain questions of valuation which were submitted to Judge Robert W. Tayler of the Federal Court, the final plan which the Council passed in the form of an ordinance was to be called the Tayler Plan.

While it is true that Johnson said in the beginning that his ultimate aim was ownership by the City of all the street railway lines, some radicals and socialists questioned why he agreed to a settlement leaving the properties in the hands of the private Company. His reply to this was that it really made no difference to the car riders whether the lines were publicly owned or not, so long as their rights and convenience were protected. No doubt, Johnson, as a pragmatist, conceived that there would always be the danger if the lines were publicly owned that there would, in the years ahead, be incompetent or corrupt people governing the city who would use the immensely valuable properties for political patronage. For Johnson, the fine product of private enterprise himself, was no visionary believer in public ownership. The agreement reached by Johnson and Goff was a most ingenious combination of private ownership and public control and supervision. . . .

I had not been able intelligently to understand the long struggle over the street railways. But the Johnson-Goff agreement and the Tayler plan were easy to comprehend. One feature of the plan which especially interested me was the manner in which Johnson had protected the public interest without resorting to what he had stated to be his ultimate objective years ago when the controversy began.

One of the cardinal dogmas of the Progressive era was that all types of monopoly should be government owned. This was especially stressed in the case of public utilities such as street railways, gas and electric utilities. As a result of the widespread feeling that only in public ownership could the public interest be protected, municipal ownership, especially plants producing electricity, spread like wildfire through the states. A reaction against this set in some years later when it was discovered that the production and transmission of electric power by large private or Federal plants made municipal plants, necessarily smaller in size, uneconomical. Even in Cleveland, where a municipal plant was built during the Baker Administration, it was found better after some years to sell the plant to the Cleveland Electrical Illumination Company, a company owned by private investors. The improvement in methods of regulation hastened the reaction, for it came to be recognized that if the rates to the public were fair, it was of lesser importance who owned the property.

So Johnson's willingness to leave ownership with the Company was an act of statesmanship and foresight in a year when public ownership was one of the cardinal objectives of the liberals. . . .

What won Johnson great popular support from the beginning was his effort to relieve small home owners of some of their tax burden. This he achieved by putting pressure on the assessors, most of whom were dominated by his Democratic political organization, to raise the valuations on land property, especially unused land, held for speculation. Soon a Johnson man was elected County Auditor, an individual who held office for many years beyond the life of Johnson. To bring out the necessity for heavier land taxes, he established tax schools out in the residential areas which were taught by some of his lieutenants, including Peter Witt.

As the crusade proceeded, it was found that prevailing standards of taxation were not only protected by state laws, but by state boards of equalization and the courts. Indeed, so firm was his belief that higher land taxation was the ultimate goal that his long struggle for cheaper street transportation was a secondary issue. He pointed out that whatever people saved by cheaper transportation to and from work, and which enabled them to move farther into the suburbs, would be wiped out by the higher prices for homes and higher rent exacted by land speculators. A Georgist newspaperman whom I knew coined a phrase which was framed and shown in many offices in my time, "THE LORD GIVETH AND THE LANDLORD TAKETH AWAY." . . .

In the course of his earlier political activity, Johnson had acquired considerable skill as a public speaker. I found my way to Cleveland many times in those years and remember well the fascination of those platform performances. He spoke in the clear crisp idiom to which he had become accustomed in his life as a businessman. His voice was moderately but pleasantly high pitched, and clear and penetrating. His speeches were always brief and unadorned. He was physically a big man, considerably overweight. His face, up to the end, had a remarkably youthful color and freshness.

In his incessant round of public appearances during his service as

Mayor, he was always hospitable to questions from the audience. Even the most lowly and inarticulate and the most hostile received courteous attention. When the question was not audible or its answer required a few moments of thought, Johnson gained time by inviting the questioner to the platform. The question then repeated and the well considered answer were part of the continuous process of education which he conceived to be his major mission as Mayor.

In all of his campaigns, except perhaps his first one, he used a tent for his meetings. This was an innovation which fascinated the people of the city. His purpose in using the tent was not only to add a bit of showmanship to his political meetings but, as he said, to make his audience feel comfortable and to accommodate larger gatherings. The tent was transported and erected from vacant lot to vacant lot, and when he campaigned for Governor of Ohio in 1903, he traveled with the tent through the counties of the state.

I remember well that in 1903 Hanna, in opposing the Johnson candidacy for Governor, himself used a tent for his appearance in Berea. In his remarks, Hanna spoke of Johnson and his tent as a circus. The next week Johnson and his tent appeared and in his reply to Hanna, he complimented the Senator on his imitation, but he added that he was at a loss to distinguish between his circus tent and Hanna's canvas auditorium.

In all of Johnson's political performances, he had a brilliant supporting cast. Foremost among his lieutenants was Newton D. Baker, who came to Cleveland at the invitation of a well known Cleveland lawyer who had known him in his home town of Martinsburg, West Virginia. He received his college education at Johns Hopkins where, in the course of his residence, he came to know Woodrow Wilson, a graduate student. They lived at the same boarding house for a time. Meeting Wilson was a great experience in Baker's life. He learned a great deal in their conversations and also from listening to some of the lectures which Wilson delivered while finishing his thesis which became well known under the name **Congressional Government**. It was often noted that Baker's style of public speaking closely resembled that of Wilson. After Johns Hopkins, Baker received his law schooling at Washington and Lee. He practiced for a short time in Martinsburg before moving to Cleveland.

After Johnson became Mayor he took Baker into his Administration as Law Director. In 1903 he was elected City Solicitor, an office which he held until he was elected Mayor in 1912. With his talent for exposition and his flawless diction, he had the role in Johnson's meetings of expounding the economic and legal case for his superior's policies, just as he served Wilson as a cabinet officer.

Peter Witt had been a labor official and at one time was a severe critic of Johnson. But the great capacity of Johnson to enlist capable assistants won him over and he served in the Johnson campaigns as the champion of the exploited and the scourge of the rich establishment. He had matchless talent for bitter invective and caustic humor. During the Johnson years he served as City Clerk and when Baker became Mayor, as Street Railway Commissioner. In 1916 he was a candidate for Mayor to succeed Baker but was defeated. This substantially ended the Johnson dynasty, but not the Johnson tradition.

When I became active in the life of Cleveland after 1916, I enjoyed [Witt's] friendship. He once agreed upon a plan to work together on a biography of Johnson but nothing ever came of the idea. Later, when Baker returned to Cleveland after his service as Secretary of War, I came to know him quite well. He served as the leading citizen of Cleveland until his death in 1936. In 1932 he was seriously projected as Democratic candidate for President but he did nothing to encourage the effort to draft him. In my contacts with him after I was serving as one of Roosevelt's advisers, I found that Baker had grave reservations about the character and capacity of FDR.

Beyond Baker and Witt, Johnson's regime was rich in talented men. One of the foremost of these was Frederick C. Howe, who, first as a member of the City Council and then as State Senator, was a speaker at Johnson's meetings. He was a scholarly man with burning compassion for the underprivileged. He wrote several books on urban problems. When, after Roosevelt's inauguration in 1933, I had some prominence in the new Administration, Howe came to my office, hoping for an opportunity to serve. He had lived through the long years since Johnson's time in relative obscurity, but he apparently believed that Roosevelt represented the revival of a national stage of the Johnson ideas. In his old age his dim spirit seemed to nourish some of the old fire. I persuaded George Peek, head of the Agricultural Adjustment Administration, to make him Consumer's Counsel and he stirred considerable consternation among businessmen with his radical comments in the press.

Johnson's attitude toward party politics was mostly orthodox. He believed that in making secure his own ascendancy and the realization of his ideas of reform, he needed the support of a strong, well nourished party. He assured this by giving the patronage to the party workers, but giving them lower ranks of the service. The department heads and the policy makers he needed at his side, he selected himself with an uncanny genius for the recognition of talent.

Since he realized that there could be no royal succession to carry on the reforms that he cherished and to a degree achieved, he realized that he must leave behind an educated citizenry capable of making the right decisions at the polls and in the currents of public opinion. This required public education through political leadership. The people, he insisted, must be taught to understand what should be done in their interests. They must demand excellence in government for years to come. Some years after Johnson's death, I heard Newton Baker say (when he was leaving Cleveland to become Secretary of War) that he conceived that the "preaching function" of a high official [was] of the greatest importance. This he had learned from Johnson.

During the Johnson years almost every person in Cleveland was able to discuss coherently such complicated issues as franchises, property rights, taxation, and the public interest of public utilities.

I came to recognize this sophistication among the people of Cleveland when in 1912 I went there as a resident. It was a heady and inspiring environment. Among my colleagues in school and later at the University, in my social contacts, in the City Club downtown, people were alert and articulate. It was a feeling I had about the atmosphere in my classrooms, for in those years the young ones sat at the feet of their elders, not over them in the judgment seat. Cleveland, despite its controversies and upsets, maintained its distinction more than two decades after Johnson's death.

8

Learning from the Muckrakers

My outlook during the Johnson decade went well beyond municipal affairs and the ideas of Henry George. The final years of the old century and the first ones of the new had seen a great consolidation of economic power in the incorporation of the industrial giants. The success of the McKinley Administration in bringing about economic recovery had firmly established the Republican Party in power in the nation and the state of Ohio. Only in corners like Cleveland, in most of the big cities, and in the South did the Democratic Party win elections. Since the prevailing interest of the Republican Party was business-oriented, government looked favorably upon these combinations. And a goodly number of their representatives sat in the seats of political power, including the United States Senate.

Thoughtful and sometimes politically minded people began to question this ascendancy of the rich, and their protests found plenty of exposure in the press which still had to appear as the people's friend, despite the wealth of those who owned the newspapers. In 1903 a dear friend and schoolmate was scheduled to graduate from the Olmsted Falls school as I had the year before. A short time before the end of the term he fell ill with typhoid fever and he asked me to prepare and deliver his graduation "oration." I undertook to comply and since the fulminations of Theodore Roosevelt about good and bad business seemed to be popular, I selected **The Trust Problem** as my subject. I found considerable information in the Baldwin Library, especially some of Roosevelt's speeches and various articles in the magazines. Thus I found it easy to arraign the big corporations for their sins and omissions. But when I came to the remedy, I found myself completely without ideas. It is true that TR suggested a remedy. He called it "pitiless publicity." But this made no sense to me then. How could telling about an evil cure that evil? So I ended my script by saying that we had met the challenge of George III in the American Revolution and the revolt of the South over slavery and so we could grapple with the aggregations of great wealth.

My own experience in magazine publishing and writing quickens my interest in describing what came to be known as "muckraking" in the first decade in this century. The rise and fall of these magazines within ten short years reminds me of what I have witnessed in the years since, when such stalwarts as the **Saturday Evening Post** and **Colliers** have followed the **Literary Digest** into the shade. And even such a gorgeous latecomer as **Look** lived a short life. Magazines, like the styles of women's headdresses, have their birth, their day of flowering, their fading glory, their struggle to live by introducing innovations, and their death. But in their short vogue, the "muckraking" magazines had great influence in stirring their readers' indignation. And I was one of their most devoted patrons.

Nothing that I learned in the college library or in serious books that I read at home or in my daily hour with the Cleveland press did so much to stimulate my interest in national affairs as these magazines. They had originated in certain printing innovations which permitted them to be sold at a low price, even within the tight limits of my purse. There were also the novels, cheaply printed, which dealt with the same subjects at greater length.

When the old century was nearing its end, the number of magazines with national circulation had been reduced to four fairly prosperous journals which were published monthly. They were **Harper's**, **Scribner's**, **Century** and **The Atlantic**. Their contents were mostly literary, their price sufficiently high to assure them a limited readership of mostly educated people. They eschewed sensationalism in deference to [the] general gentility of their readers, and they hesitated to [attack] the political and economic establishment for the obvious reason that their publishers were so close to the politico-economic people who ruled the Republican Party.

A new type of journal saw its beginning with S.S. McClure, Frank A. Munsey, and John Brisben Walker, who published respectively **McClure's Magazine**, **Munsey's**, and the **Cosmopolitan** at strikingly lower prices. It is unnecessary here to describe the mechanical innovations which made the lower prices possible. But it is worthwhile to note that the great increase in public literacy through the growth and improvement of the school system provided a vastly wider market for cheaper reading. In a short time larger sales produced the economies of mass production and distribution, and the price of most of these newcomers dropped to ten cents. And then there came great competition for material sufficiently sensational to assure a new type of reader.

The key to a fat circulation they found to be what was called "the literature of exposure." ... Since the low price brought them within my modest means, I was able to buy them at Beswick's store in Berea, where several years before I bought the **Tip Top Weekly** for the exciting Frank Merriwell stories.

Among the most exciting articles which I read were Ida M. Tarbell's about John D. Rockefeller and the Standard Oil Company, Lincoln Steffens' series on corruption in American cities (which made Cleveland a distinguished exception), Ray Stannard Baker's exposure of the conditions in the coal mines during the early years of the labor movement, and somewhat later David Graham Phillips' attacks upon the Senate, and Thomas W. Lawson's diatribes about high finance. Also high in the muckraking list was Upton Sinclair's novel about the Chicago stockyards, **The Jungle**. . . .

By 1908 and 1909 these attacks on politicians and businesses had become so extreme and irresponsible that apparently the public became bored and indifferent. They suffered the fate of Savonarola, who was left naked to his enemies when he pressed his attacks too far. The famous monk was hanged and burned. The sensational magazines, with few exceptions, simply sputtered and died of circulation troubles.

Also, in the three years beginning in 1910 the newspapers had many more subjects for news. At the beginning of 1910, in March, there was the revolt in Congress that overthrew Speaker Cannon. This was the work of authentic Progressives like George Norris. In 1910 the feud between the returned Theodore Roosevelt and President Taft erupted. Important legislation in Congress claimed considerable newspaper space, and the rivalry in the Democratic Party for the presidential nomination attained importance as a split in the Republican ranks threatened. There is a sort of Gresham's Law in news purveying. Real events which are newsworthy drive out the best products of fevered imaginations.

My own appetite for the sensational stuff had lessened after I reached voting age in 1907, but during that period several works of fiction had appeared in book form that I found interesting.

Upton Sinclair's **Jungle** made his reputation. He wrote many books after that in his long life but nothing ever rivaled his exposure of the stockyards. Indeed it was on the wave of indignation created by that book that one of TR's favorite pieces of legislation passed in Congress. In 1908 when I enjoyed a vacation in Chicago I was most concerned in visiting the stockyards where I found the place placarded by notices favoring the proprietors. They were not, the visitor was assured, making over two percent on their investment. All of this in response to the Sinclair book inspired indignation and the passage of the Food and Drug Act.

David Graham Phillips was, aside from his magazine writing, a prolific novelist. I found his political stories fascinating. The most outstanding political novel of those days was Winston Churchill's **Coniston**, a story of a political boss in New Hampshire.

There were also several novels touching on the race question and glorifying the South by a highly gifted but inflammatory preacher, Thomas Dixon. The best known of his novels was **The Leopard's Spots**. One of his books was made into a famous movie, **The Birth of a Nation**. Perhaps the sympathy for the post-bellum South which his biased novels awakened in me caused me, despite my Unionist heritage, to conceive a strong sympathy for the first President Johnson. I remember doing an essay in college defending him. It was highly laudatory of that much abused and persecuted President.

One of the notable products of the muckraking years was the vogue of the historical novel. I am not sufficiently informed to say whether the serious and well drafted historical novels of those years were inspired by the flood of political fiction and non-fiction that came from the muckraking writers. I only suggest that they came in the same period. I was most interested in some of these fine works of fiction, and their value to my education was that they led me to the reading of real history. It seems strange but history was an almost completely neglected department of study at Baldwin. The only course that I can remember is English history which was given by the professor of English literature.

I do not feel competent to explore the extent to which the muckrakers inspired the Progressive era in political life. It is hard to determine which preceded the other, the politician or the writer. Both politician and writer were dependent upon a receptive public opinion and both contributed to the slant of that opinion. Perhaps it is safe to say that the writers made the way easier for such figures as La Follette, Norris, Roosevelt, and others.

My own concern in looking back is to determine how much I profited from what I read of these sensational attacks upon business and organized politics. Certainly there was little in their outcries to suggest what might be done to curb the excesses and terminate the evils which flourished in a capitalist society.

It was some years later, after the full flowering of the Progressive movement, that the behavior of corporations was quite considerably tempered to resist and refute the critics. I saw evidence of this in my visit to the stockyards in the summer of 1908. ... In the long run the greatest contribution made by the Progressive movement was the reformation that it produced in business's relations with the public.

As my account of the years after 1907 shows, I was able to take little time from my personal affairs for the national political scene except to follow with intense interest the final acts in Johnson's crusade against the street railway interest. My energies were largely given to my school, to picking up a few courses in law evenings and Saturdays, and to the minute duties of my office as Village Clerk.

9

My New High School
and Village Politics

The summer after my graduation from college was a time of hard thinking, of faraway dreams and, in the end, the acceptance of certain realities. Nothing had shaken my ambition to be a lawyer, an idea which had been instilled in me by Will Locke, my teacher. Beyond that I saw politics and public office as my destiny. American habits and traditions pointed to the law as the gateway to public life, for one must make a living while pursuing the unremunerative trade of politics. The alternative was inherited money which had projected such luminaries as Theodore Roosevelt, who was at that time enjoying his elective term. But destiny doomed me to be poor.

In any event, I needed a job after such a lengthy educational experience. Village opinion, which my parents reflected, decided that it was up to me to earn a living. Since I had been a devoted newspaper reader, I had developed the idea that it might be a wonderful life writing about politics, and my proficiency in my English courses led me to believe that I might have a talent for writing. And so I haunted the editors' offices in Cleveland, seeking a job as a reporter. But it seemed that no editor on any of the newspapers in Cleveland was impressed either by my appearance or my scanty qualifications. Finally, since the summer was passing and I was not saved, I looked for employment nearer home.

The school at Olmsted Falls had enjoyed good years, for Will Locke had resigned at the time of my graduation and was spending his time attempting to practice law as a side issue to his growing habit of drinking. After one disastrous year with an incompetent superintendent, Mary McKean, the teacher who had engineered my promotion to the seventh grade, was made superintendent. She had lived at our home for several years during the school months and I grew to know her well. Indeed I flattered myself as one of her favorites. Another tie with my interests was the fact that her brother, Ed McKean, was the star shortstop with the Cleveland Indians, a team that in the 1890s vied with the Baltimore Orioles

46

for the honors in the old National League. However, Miss McKean never mentioned his name and I was afraid to bring up the subject. Presumably there had been a quarrel in the McKean family because Ed had carried on a partnership with Cleveland's star wrestler Tom Jenkins in the saloon business.

As superintendent, Miss McKean had imposed iron discipline and had won the respect of the community by her teaching skills. She had decided that the final two years should be the foundation of a new high school and had induced the Board of Education to employ a fourth teacher to have charge of the seventh and eighth grades, holding forth in a room "upstairs" which had originally been designed as a stage for school plays.

In the spring of 1906 she had resigned to accept an appointment in the Elyria High School and the Board had chosen as her successor a woman named Parmelee. Then the woman who had taught the seventh and eighth grades resigned and that created a vacancy late in the summer. And so after failing in my attempt to enter journalism, I drifted into what Samuel Johnson called "the universal refuge of educated indigents." I applied for the vacancy and was employed. The salary was $45 per month.

My relations with Miss Parmelee were cordial enough. She permitted me to make the courses in English in the ninth and tenth grade of real high school quality. And I helped with the discipline. But her personality and the fact that she could not quite measure up to Miss McKean's standards created some unhappiness in the village. So at the end of the year she was dismissed and through the solicitations of Will Locke I was employed as the new superintendent. The salary was $70 a month, a princely income in that environment and in those years. Indeed a rather loose-living friend, a classmate of mine in Baldwin, said when he heard the news that "with all that money you could keep a woman in Cleveland."

But the new responsibility which my appointment imposed upon me made such alluring suggestions seem quite irrelevant and, of course, highly improper. The person known in the village as "superintendent" was regarded as quite a figure. He ranked with the two preachers and the priest as one of the leading intellectuals. And the fact that I would only reach voting age after school opened in the fall, and that I was known to everybody as only yesterday a schoolboy, made the problem still more serious. Indeed it was quite a task after school started to stop the older boys from calling me by my first name.

Above all, I knew that I needed all the skills as a teacher and all the new ideas about education to master the position, which would be watched closely by almost everyone in the village.

So I decided that I would attend the summer session at the University of Michigan at Ann Arbor. There I enrolled in some courses in teaching methods and, because it seemed like a good opportunity, an advanced course in Shakespeare. The fine Shakespeare collection in the University library was available for collateral reading.

When school opened in September I was confronted with a rather disturbing decision, for a man in the village who was interested in politics was getting together a slate of independent candidates to run in the coming election. He asked me to let him enter my name as a candidate for clerk of the village. At that moment I had not reached my twenty-first birthday but he said that since I would be qualified when I took office, I could become a candidate. As I look back at that decision, I am still amazed at my presumption. In the first place the people in the village would expect the head of their school to be completely neutral in political matters. Moreover, and most important, the incumbent in that office, Art Atkinson, was a good friend and a member of the School Board that had elected me. He would be my opponent at the election.

The solicitation was not marred by any hint of bad feelings. My campaigning consisted only of visits around the village in which I said nothing of a pejorative nature about my opponent. And he didn't seem to care much about winning. I won and after the election I called at his house. He gathered the books together and after giving them to me, he instructed me in the duties of the office. I hardly realized at the time what a decent thing he was doing. It seems as if he were teaching me a lesson in good behavior. Whether he actually was doing that, I learned from that man my first and best lesson in politics, a lesson which Burke expressed in the word magnanimity.

Atkinson was a farmer with considerable acreage outside the village but to provide educational opportunity for his numerous children he lived in a house near the school. His children were well dressed and well behaved. I am sure that without any intention to heap coals of fire on my head, he never opposed me in matters that came before the School Board of which he became president the next year. Whenever I proposed an expenditure which would improve the school, I could count upon his support. He would occasionally remind some penny pinching colleague that since he was a considerable taxpayer, he was always giving priority to the education of his children.

I have long since learned that wealth or high office or stature does not necessarily go with greatness. This man ranks with anyone I ever knew in all my days in public life.

The passing of my first year as superintendent was a good indication that it was successful. The townspeople who took pride and considerable interest in their school have little to judge the quality of a teacher except the presence or absence of trouble. I have often heard School Board members render a favorable judgment for a teacher by calling attention to the absence of "kicking" in the community. I attempted no serious innovations and the habit of good order which Miss McKean's discipline had created greatly helped. At the meeting of the School Board in the spring, the verdict was that since there had been "no kicking," I deserved another year.

During that year, however, I moved seriously to upgrade the upper grades and moved toward recognition as a second-grade three-year high school. That recognition required certification by the State Superintendent of Schools. Firmly believing in direct action, I found my opportunity when the State Superintendent, a man named Jones, was scheduled to give an address at a county teacher's meeting in Cleveland. I attended and when the speaker returned to his dressing room backstage, he found an eager young school administrator waiting for him. Perhaps my obvious concern about improving my school was what captured his professional interest for he gave me on that occasion and in subsequent correspondence very friendly attention. I described the school, its facilities, its courses and the teaching talent. He then told me that in order to win certification, I must build a library and add several new courses, including physics. And the latter would require considerable laboratory equipment.

I then returned to the Board and with strong support from Atkinson the missing facilities were authorized. I helped with the expense of buying books for the library by organizing a concert and set the students upon the community selling tickets. And then finally when I had met all requirements, I reported to the State Superintendent. The day the certificate arrived with the great seal of Ohio emblazoned upon it was marked by great rejoicing at the school, an occasion when the lower grades from "downstairs" were allowed to come up to the "big room." At the end of that year we graduated the first class under the new status of the school. That was in the spring of 1909, a year which was to prove momentous in my life as well as in the history of the school.

Despite my feeling that I had earned a certain security of tenure by my success, there were certain factors which disturbed me. At the election of Board members that spring, Art Atkinson for some reason did not run again. The previous year two new members had been elected to the School Board, one of whom was a man named Charles Harding, whose career some years earlier as superintendent had been so successful that it had become village folklore. He was an opinionated man who no doubt viewed my innovations with some suspicion. But I well realized that I must deal with him with some care, and I called at his farm before the Board meeting and boldly asked him for a two-year contract as an expression of confidence. He did not agree and I withdrew the suggestion. He then said some words of praise for my teaching which he said was reflected in the attitude of the students. But he said my writing was dreadful as compared with the Spencerian standards which he admired. I was compelled to agree and said I would attend some classes that summer in a business school in Cleveland. At the Board meeting I recommended a change in the arithmetic texts which had been used for many years. They were publications of the American Book Company which corporation had traditionally exercised great influence in local affairs. The new texts I had recommended were also publications of the American Book Company and, as a matter of routine, the Company had sent samples to all Board members. This infuriated Mr. Harding who charged that it was an attempted bribe. He also said that the old texts were good enough since they dated back to his administration. When he finished his defense of the status quo, he quoted the line from Pope, ''Be not the first by whom the new is tried.'' Someone has said that repartee is what you think of on the way home. I have since wondered why I did not reply with Pope's next line, ''nor to be the last to lay the old aside.'' But even if I had thought of the reply, it would have been unwise to use it. So I said that since the American Book Company had been up to its old tricks, I would change my recommendation to a publication of Ginn and Company. This seemed to satisfy everybody. The new, I hoped, pure texts were adopted and I was duly hired for the year beginning in the autumn of 1909.

While the matters raised by Harding were thus resolved, his disposition to peer over my shoulder in school affairs was not pleasant. I felt quite certain that he intended to dominate the school by a sort of remote control, and coming just at the moment when my spirits were rather high because of my successful completion of two good years, the prospect of more trouble with him disturbed me. In October, however, destiny intervened. Charles Harding died of typhoid fever. My experience with him, however, established in my mind a proposition which in later years was confirmed by many instances which did not concern me personally. This, which is now pretty well established in education, is that former professional teachers make very bad members of school governing boards from rural school systems to big universities. The professional member is likely to pick at details rather than to judge overall results.

That summer I returned to the University of Michigan, after an unsuccessful effort to improve my handwriting. This time I enrolled in two courses in the law school to help when, after a year, I attempted to enter the second year in law school. I also took a course in the English drama, for I entertained at that time an idea that I wanted to be a drama critic rather than a lawyer. At the end of the term I had a serious talk with the professor, telling him of my dilemma. After he heard my story, he said that I should stick to the law. I took the hint and forever dropped the dream of writing about the theater for pay and free admissions.

10

Two Disasters and a Decision

In terms of remunerative labor, the thirty-two months of my life between the Christmas holidays in 1909 and September, 1912 were a complete loss. The reason for this interruption in the course of my teaching career was a catastrophic illness which knocked at the gate of my complacency. I saved some of that period from complete loss by rounding out the formal college education which Baldwin had failed to provide. I read a good deal, wrote a small unpublished book about Shakespeare, and did a lot of thinking.

My school year at Olmsted Falls ended in May, 1909, quite successfully. I secured reelection for another year, and presumably because of my proven competence in the village school, was given supervision of the six district schools of Olmsted Township. This responsibility was to be assumed in the fall of that year and since it would take another day in my week and entail visiting these schools on Saturdays, I was to receive an additional ten dollars a month from the Township Board.

My plans for the coming year were made quite without calculation of the burden which I was bestowing upon my physical capabilities. Nor did I take note of certain warnings which my body sounded that summer when I spent two months at the University of Michigan. I had never worried about the demands I made on my constitution. Indeed as a schoolboy, I was quite a physical culturist, reading and practicing the lessons taught by Bernarr MacFadden in his magazine and books.

Nothing bothered me that summer except certain fits of depression when I began doubting whether I was ever likely to succeed. This was strange, considering my habitual confidence in myself. Perhaps these fits were due to some hidden physical malaise. But I am quite sure that no medical examination would have found cause for alarm.

When school was resumed in September, I confronted a full schedule. I spent the normal five days teaching and supervising things at Olmsted Falls. Then, according to my agreement with the Township Board of

Education, I spent Saturdays visiting the district schools. They were scattered out on an average of two miles from my home in the village. The roads were especially muddy that year. Pavements were for the future when motor transport took over. My means of transportation was the old family horse and a light buggy, such as doctors used in the country. So six days were taken.

Two evenings were mortgaged for a course in real property which was given by Newton Baker at the Cleveland Law School, a private commercial school owned by a prominent lawyer in Cleveland. This was really a foolish addition to my week, for it involved driving three miles to Berea and then taking the interurban to Cleveland. After the class, it meant a return trip which ended shortly before midnight. The duties of village clerk were minimal but I ran and was elected without opposition.

I developed a cough in October which I assumed would pass as many others had in a week or so. But this continued and got worse. So one evening when I reached Berea on the first leg of my trip to the law class, I decided to call on a doctor I knew. He found my temperature to be 100 and said that no doubt it had been running at that level for some time. His examination of my sputum confirmed his guess that I was suffering from tuberculosis. The news which I received was confirmed the following week by a Cleveland specialist, and I was told to seek treatment in the West.

The Cleveland specialist, Dr. John Lowman, whose memory is honored now in the name of a building in the Western Reserve Medical School, was rather severe in his instructions. He said that my case was moderately advanced, that I should go to a sanatarium he knew in Silver City, New Mexico, and stay there a year. When I asked if I would recover, he said bluntly that he was a physician, not a prophet, but that if I followed orders, I would improve. And so I resigned my school jobs, my village clerk's office, and on the day after Christmas I set forth on the trip to Silver City.

Everything had happened so suddenly that I hardly had time to consider the full meaning of this disaster. But weeks and months of reflection in Silver City brought it all home. My teaching career, which had begun so happily more than three years before, was ended, perhaps forever. The money I had saved for law school was soon gone. And even after a year, if I recovered, I had no prospect of getting the money to take a law course which, because of this interruption, might be for the full three years. The termination of my service at the village school cost me many hours of regret, for I loved to teach and the association with the students meant a great deal.

But I found an antidote to regrets, not only in what reading I had taken with me, but in the reports of my improvement. The books I was able to carry with me included a set of Emerson's **Essays**, Carlyle's **Essay on Burns**, two books of Shakespeare criticism, and the fourth volume of Ward's **English Poets**. These books are here with me as I write. In the Carlyle I heavily underscored a passage which gave me no end of satisfaction in the depressing days after my arrival:

> Manhood begins when we have in any way made truce with Necessity; begins when we have surrendered to Necessity, as the most part only do; but begins joyfully and hopefully when we have reconciled ourselves to Necessity; and thus in reality conquered over it, and find that in Necessity we are free.

The sanitarium to which Dr. Lowman sent me was about three miles north of Silver City, higher up in the mountains of southwestern New Mexico. There are large copper deposits up there and a considerable refinery at nearby Santa Rita. The altitude at the sanatarium was said to be about 6000 feet. There are cold freezing nights in the winter months, but bright sun almost every day, a suitable variation for clearing diseased lungs. The routine does not vary. A good night's sleep, rest before and after meals, and sit in the sun most of the day.

The morning after my arrival Dr. LeRoy Peters came to see me. He was then about thirty-five. He had migrated from Chicago a few years before with tuberculosis of the larynx and had spent two years recovering. His disposition was bouncy and optimistic. His professional skill was of a high order, spreading his name throughout the Southwest. Later, after my time under his care, he moved to Albuquerque where he was medical director of St. Joseph's Sanatorium. He carefully examined me. In those days X-rays were not used for diagnosis. The stethoscope sufficed. His examination showed infection in both lungs from the sixth rib upward. He confirmed Dr. Lowman's diagnosis of a moderately advanced case. My blood pressure was alarmingly high, higher than it has ever been since. This he attributed to the altitude. He said that if I responded to treatment, I would have the infection arrested in "six to nine" months, and he cheered me by declaring that I would probably live twenty-five years. My temperature, which was 100 degrees the night of arrival, dropped to normal in two days and never during my whole stay in New Mexico went higher.

My recovery, which was quite remarkable, was shown in the monthly examination, and in April my case was declared arrested.

At about that time my good friend, John Bonsey, for whom, as I noted earlier, I wrote and delivered a commencement paper in 1903, was a telegraph operator on the New York Central in Olmsted Falls when I left there. He decided shortly after my arrival in New Mexico to quit his job and follow me. In New Mexico he secured a job as an operator with the Santa Fe by carefully denying his union membership. He was stationed in a small village called Buchanan, located on a branch line in North Central New Mexico. So, with the doctor's permission, I went up there to live with John in April. We greatly enjoyed those days and nights. He was busy during the days with his railway duties. I spent my time reading some books which the land agent had gathered. We kept house in a one-room affair out on the mesa. At night we dragged our beds out under the stars. That was the year of Haley's Comet, and it kept vigil with us nightly. In June, when the days were getting hot, I returned to Olmsted Falls.

Before leaving Silver City I secured an appointment for the coming school year as principal of the three-room school at Santa Rita, for Dr. Peters vouched for my health. I had every intention of returning in the fall to take up the business of school teaching again.

It was most pleasant to find myself back in the home town. I greatly enjoyed resuming life among my old friends and former students. A month after my return, John Bonsey resigned his job with the Santa Fe and returned to the New York Central in Olmsted Falls.

I had every reason to believe that I could live the normal life that had characterized other summers at home. I slept out in the open and regularly took my temperature every morning and afternoon. But a sense of euphoria induced by my quick recovery led me to make a series of mistakes which ended in another disaster. The first was a game of tennis which I played on a hot afternoon in early August. The next morning before rising I was horrified to note that I had a temperature of ninety-eight degrees which meant over ninety-nine degrees in the afternoon. I knew then that the exercise had torn open the sleeping infection and that I was in trouble.

Dr. Lowman was on a vacation when I visited Cleveland the next day but another doctor examined me and declared that "the bugs are active again."

Back home I decided to alter my plans completely. It would never do to return to Santa Rita and endeavor to teach school with active tuberculosis. So I wrote resigning the appointment. I then decided to follow the example of a former classmate at Baldwin University, a Berea boy named John Morrissey. He apparently had been troubled by weak lungs and left Berea and took a law degree at the Law School of the University of Colorado at

Boulder. The news in Berea told that he was practicing law in Denver in 1910 and doing well.

I solved the money problem, at least for a year, by borrowing $350 from Grandmother Moley. I made the necessary preparations and arrived in Denver on the afternoon of September 3, 1910.

Had I been able to see Dr. Lowman, he would have dissuaded me from an attempt to undertake the arduous task of a law student with a temperature rising above ninety-nine every afternoon and a persistent cough. I foolishly believed that a high dry climate would soon restore the arrested case that I had thrown away on the tennis court. But ambition is the great creator of illusion.

On my arrival in Denver I registered at the old Oxford Hotel near the railway station. Then I called my old friend John Morrissey at his office where fortunately — or unfortunately as it proved — I found him on a Saturday afternoon. I met him at dinner and told him of my plans to go to Boulder. After dinner he suggested that we take a "tram" out to an amusement park. We spent an hour or so watching the dancing, and on our return to town the crowd on the "tram" was so great that we were compelled to crawl in a window. I left him at the hotel and went up to the room to which I had been assigned. The clerk was very sorry but due to congestion he had been compelled to put two other guests in my room. They were asleep when I arrived.

After unlocking the door and entering the room, I coughed softly to make sure that I would not awaken my sleeping companions. And I immediately tasted what I knew to be blood. In the lighted bathroom my fear was confirmed. It was a considerable hemorrhage. This had never happened before but my experience told me what to do. I got into bed and rested quietly on my back. After a few moments I called the desk and asked for a doctor. The doctor was a woman and she did all that anyone could do. Put an ice pack on my chest and administered a strong sleeping pill.

I slept profoundly and when I awakened my two sleeping companions were gone. Since I was always hungry in the morning, I ordered a heavy breakfast and ate it. This was another of what had already been a tragic series of mistakes. Then followed a most distressing day. I tried repeatedly to reach Morrissey but since it was Sunday I had no success. [6]

Twice that morning and once in the early afternoon, there were more effusions of blood. The woman doctor of the night before had vanished. Finally in the middle of the afternoon I spoke with the man at the desk and explained my serious condition and implored him to get me a doctor. Shortly after, a doctor phoned. I explained and his very intelligent and helpful reply was that he was not a lung specialist but would have someone call me who was better equipped to help.

I have always believed that this good turn by a doctor I never saw and whose name I never knew was the turning point in a series of incidents which might have taken my life. For in those years Denver, as well as many cities in the Southwest, was ridden with quacks who preyed upon the thousands of "lungers" who were sent by Eastern doctors, who told their patients that all they needed was the dry air and — God help us — exercise. In other words, the "roughing it" advice they gave claimed more lives in the West than all the Indian wars. What happened that afternoon was providential, for the doctor who came to see me in response to the promise I had received over the telephone was without doubt the most renowned specialist in Denver. Dr. Henry Sewall was vastly more than a physician. He was called a physiological chemist, one of the pioneers in what came to be known as bio-chemistry.

That afternoon, however, he was only the physician taking the steps appropriate to my critical condition. He gave me a brief examination, asked me a few questions, specifically my home address and the name of my mother, arranged to have a nurse come and remain overnight, and to have me moved to St. Luke's Hospital the next morning.

The next morning as the nurse was taking my temperature, I stole a glance at the thermometer. It was 105. I was moved to the hospital where Dr. Sewall made sure to say that my illness was not TB, for in those days, due to the immense number of "lungers," the hospitals had to deny them admittance.

During the first week my temperature fell below 100 and I believed that I was on the way to recovery. This was good news when my mother arrived. But in the second week the temperature took a turn for the worse. It reached 102 degrees or more every afternoon. My experience the winter before told me what that meant. If these very high temperatures continue for a month or so, the disease, which in a young person is so acute, is likely to have spread so widely that recovery is probably impossible.

The supreme proof of my good fortune in having as a physician a man who had already achieved high distinction as a scientist came after I had been in the hospital about three weeks.

Dr. Sewall recognized as I did that unless the infection could be checked, the outlook was bad. He therefore decided upon what he told me months later was an experiment which came of his long studies in biological chemistry. He injected what he told me was a serum taken from the neck of an infected horse. As I remember, the stuff was called "streptolytic" serum. The mischief which was bent on destroying me was what was called a mixed infection, in which the TB bacilli are supplemented by streptococcus and pneumococcus microbes. These intruders are what cause the fever, for the TB "bugs" are not virulent enough to cause high temperatures.

The effect of the injection was amazing, for the temperature dropped the next day from the routine 102 to 99 degrees, and it never went above 100 in all the months I remained in Denver. After another two weeks, my mother found an apartment near the hospital with a sleeping porch and I began the long and familiar business of "chasing the cure." Dr. Sewall called frequently, when on his visits to the hospital, and kept us cheered with encouraging predictions of ultimate recovery.

When the temperature fell to normal I started a regimen of daily walks and in November the question arose about my getting on with my law studies. I had learned from John Morrissey that the University of Denver had a law school in downtown Denver where the classes were held afternoons and evenings. I asked Dr. Sewall about this and he strongly advised against it. He said that downtown there was too much dust and my old enemies the "streps" might get me again. But he said that he would not object to my taking graduate courses in the liberal arts division of the University of Denver which was two or three miles out on the "tram." This advice placed before me a profoundly important decision. I said that I wanted a few days to think.

I had always considered the profession of law merely as an avenue to public life and politics. With this barred, what was the alternative? It was rare good fortune for me that in the election two weeks before, Woodrow Wilson had been elected Governor of New Jersey. I had admired Wilson for many years, for when I gathered college catalogues at the turn of the century, I noted in the Princeton catalogue that there was a man named Woodrow Wilson whose title was McCormick Professor of Jurisprudence. ... I had been amazed at the time that somebody could get paid for teaching politics which to me at that time meant something quite different than the classical stuff which went by that name at Princeton.

From this time I had followed the career of this man. I read whatever I could find about him or by him. I noted that he had been elected president of Princeton in 1902, and since he was pretty much in the public eye after that, he was not hard to follow. In 1908 he delivered some lectures at Columbia University and my favorite magazine columnist, Samuel Blythe, ran a piece in the **Saturday Evening Post** on his page "Who's Who and Why" about something Wilson had said in those lectures. In discussing the presidency, he said that the President "is the national voice." Therefore, said Blythe, Dr. Wilson naturally wants to be President. This was one of the earliest notices of Wilson's presidential availability.

A bit later, there was considerable news about Wilson's controversy at Princeton about the location of the proposed Graduate School. His resignation as president of Princeton followed, and very recently his nomination as the Democratic candidate for Governor. I summed all this up as applying to my own career. If a professor could get into politics at the high level of the office of governor, why should I go on grubbing at the law? Why not be a professor? It is probable that Dr. Sewall encouraged my choice of a career, since his whole life until he came to Denver was in the academic world.

And so the decision was made and I registered for courses in political science and economics, traveling to the University three times a week. In January my mother left for home and I moved to a sanatarium for convalescents.

Since my studies were not at all difficult, I spent a great deal of time that winter at the Denver Public Library, reading Shakespearean criticism and making notes for a small book which I completed the following year. It rests securely among the unpublished manuscripts in my files. I concluded after finishing it that I was not equipped to venture into the crowded field of Shakespearean scholars.

The busy schedule which I had for the winter months of 1911 seemed to prosper my convalescence. So as the summer was drawing to a close, I proposed to Dr. Sewall that I return to Ohio, especially because for two winters I had been a heavy burden which my family was ill equipped to bear.

The loan from my Grandmother Moley had long since been exhausted and I well understood the managing that went on at home to meet the costs of my long stay in Denver. The death of my mother's mother, however, brought to her some securities which paid good dividends, although I suspect that she hocked some of them to secure a considerable loan. But I was greatly helped by the monthly loan from my friend John Bonsey, who had remained in Ohio with a good job with the New York Central. In 1916 he fell ill of tuberculosis and I was able to repay all that he had loaned.

Dr. Sewall agreed to my return to Ohio but he warned me that I must return to a dry climate by March, "the pneumonia month on the shores of the Great Lakes." [7]

When I returned to Olmsted Falls, I was determined that this time I must make sure that my recovery should be permanent. I was resolved to make no more mistakes. I suppose that I should have sought some remunerative work but so far as teaching was concerned, Dr. Sewall's orders that I return to the West to avoid the bad spring months stood in the way. I was ill equipped for any other sort of employment except common labor. So I decided, quite selfishly, I admit, that I could do more for myself and my long-suffering family in a year or two by further preparation for teaching. I decided to continue my graduate work by taking some courses at Oberlin.

The high standards at Oberlin would not admit me as a candidate for the M.A. on the basis of my graduation from Baldwin. So I had to throw in several other odds and ends of eduation which I had gathered on the way. These included some courses I had finished at the summer terms at Ann Arbor, two legal courses I had taken privately at the Cleveland Law School, and what I had taken at the University of Denver the preceding winter. I then arranged to go to Oberlin on the train three days a week for the first semester only since I assumed that I must return to Denver in March.

Meanwhile the political pot was boiling in Olmsted Falls. An old friend, Bob Fletcher, was a retired contractor who had moved out to Olmsted Falls. He was then in his hale and hearty seventies. Unlike most of the former Cleveland residents, whom the natives contemptuously called the "Four Hundred," Fletcher's associations and sympathies were with the "natives." I could rate very well as a "native" since my father and grandfather had lived there since before the Civil War.

Shortly after my arrival he told me that I should run for Mayor. He promised to manage my campaign and run for the Council himself. He said that the Four Hundred were determined to take over the town government and institute a lot of what they called "improvements" which were probably not necessary and would be incompetently managed. He said further that if I ran and was elected, we could, working together with a majority of the Council, institute some real improvements with more efficiency than they could show.

I agreed to run with the proviso that I would have to return West in the spring. We planned to meet that possibility by having Fletcher as president of the Council take over for me.

It was a lively campaign, for the Four Hundred had a slate of candidates, including a blue-nosed yankee for Mayor. This man was a Unitarian and Fletcher had a curious way of defining my opponent's faith:

"You know what he is? He's a second handed Jew." I asked what he meant by that expression. "A Jew," he answered, "thinks that Christ ain't come yet. But a Unitarian says that He came but wasn't no good.''

That is a definition which I have never heard since.

In the election I was successful and our slate won a good majority of the Council. In that majority my father was numbered.

Fletcher and I decided that the first and most important of our improvements would be to bring electric lights to the village. Our plan was to purchase the electric power from some outside source, measure it at the village limits and then, after providing lighting for the streets, sell the power to the residents at a price which would pay the cost of the public installations. To raise the money for these installations, which included the lines through the village, we proposed a bond issue to be submitted to the voters. We easily won that vote since some of the commuters who were friendly to me came over to our side, and the rest of the Four Hundred could not very well oppose a greatly needed addition to the life of the village. Now with the money we realized from the bond issue, Fletcher managed the installation of the lines.

The problem remained to make contracts for the power. At first there were two possible sources. One was the offer of the interurban railway that passed through Berea. The terms were satisfactory but the objection was that electric lighting from the lines of an electric railway was unsatisfactory because the lights were lowered whenever a car of the line started. The other possibility was to buy power from the municipally owned plant in Berea. The town of Berea offered to sell us what we needed and build the transmission line to us.

I then remembered Tom Johnson's final view of public ownership. His opinion was that it is not necessary to have government ownership if service can be had from privately owned utilities with adequate protection for the rate payers, and that the danger in public ownership, which means politically oriented ownership, is inefficiency or corruption, or both. I could not be sure that the Berea plant would give reliable service, and I doubted whether the municipal plant could long compete with the big Cleveland Electric Illuminating Company. So I rejected the offer. My judgment was vindicated a few years later when the municipality sold their plant to the private company.

We were at this pass when a man came to see me. He represented the Milligan Company, a subsidiary of the great Doherty power empire. He said they were building a big plant in Lorain and since they were extending a transmission line in the direction of Cleveland, they would like to have Olmsted Falls as a customer. I was immediately interested for it was evident that since their line would pass close to our village, we might get a very good bargain.

After some negotiating about a guarantee of continuous and reliable service, they agreed to a figure which would give us a substantial profit which we could use to pay for the street lighting. The figure they fixed in making a ten-year contract was so low that a few years later they appealed to the village to grant an increase. At that time the village clerk could not find the old contract. He appealed to me for a copy. My habit of saving all important papers served well. I had a copy and the company was held to the old rate for the life of the contract.

The lessons I learned from this experience conditioned my views on the subject of public utilities for all the years after. Our experience in bringing in electric power to the people in Olmsted Falls involved microscopic amounts. But the principle of private versus public ownership was the same as that which was involved in later years in the Tennessee Valley, Grand Coulee and Hells Canyon. When the public interest is concerned, it is best to leave ownership and management in private hands with strict public regulation of rates to the public and access to the courts for enforcement.

When construction is of such massive proportions, as was true of the Hoover Dam, it may be necessary in a few cases to bring in the government to raise the huge costs of construction. But the provision that Mr. Hoover made to have contracts for the sale of power which will cover the outlays of the government until the whole project is paid for is a wise protection of all concerned.

It is true that old fashioned progressives may rant about the "power trust" and claim that only with public ownership can the public be protected, but this belongs to another age. Control is what is needed, not ownership.

11
Cleveland's Finest Years

In calling the roll of distinguished cities, Cleveland, in the twenty years following the election of Tom L. Johnson, will never rank near the top with those which left great art and architecture to grace the centuries. Nor will it rank high in such planning marvels as Haussman created for Napoleon the Lesser.

But it had a singular virtue all its own. It can be claimed that in those years it had a record of social and political innovation and general public enlightenment that give it shining distinction among the most shabby urban centers of the early twentieth century. Life was, to perceptive citizens, an exciting experience and to me, coming after twenty years in a village broken by a period of illness, an exciting adventure of the mind.

I was carried along during the nine Johnson years as a witness and then from 1912 to 1923 as a resident and later, in a small way, a participant in the life of Cleveland.

With the coming of spring, 1912 I was reminded of my promise to Dr. Sewall to return for a spell to the high and dry climate of the West. I consulted Dr. Lowman who had originally sent me to New Mexico. After an examination he declared me well enough to face the bitter spring winds off Lake Erie, and advised me to stay. When I asked him for a definition of how to stay well, he gave me this advice:

"Respect fatigue. Never eat a heavy meal or exercise when you are tired. And once a week go to bed at eight o'clock."

It was a very busy spring. There were my courses at Oberlin to finish. Also my duties as Mayor, for Bob Fletcher and I were supervising the construction of the lines which would carry electricity through the village. The newspapers were full of political news, for there was a bitter feud between Theodore Roosevelt and Taft over the Republican nomination. Since this break gave the Democrats hope for the first time in fifteen years, the Democratic nomination was a tempting prize. Finally there was among my concerns the getting of a teaching job for the coming year.

Ohio, traditionally a mother of Presidents, was pregnant that year with a quite promising hopeful, Judson Harmon, the Democratic Governor. The Governor was a serious candidate. He was a Cincinnati lawyer and judge who had served in the final years of the Cleveland Administration as Attorney General. In 1912 he was in his second term as Governor.

Baker, Mayor of Cleveland, was opposed to the nomination of Harmon, not only because he believed Harmon to be too conservative, but because of the traditional rivalry between Northern and Southern Ohio. More important, Baker was passionately supporting Woodrow Wilson whom he knew when they were both at Johns Hopkins. I watched the Wilson-Harmon contest with great interest because of my admiration for Wilson.

I saw an opening to help when Harmon's manager accused Wilson of bigotry. It seemed that Harmon's manager, Ed Moore of Youngstown, an ardent Catholic, had found some references in Wilson's writings to Catholics as Papists. Since this expression was anathema to Catholics of that generation, Moore claimed that this use of the term indicated prejudice on the part of Wilson who had Protestant clergymen on both sides of his family.

In the course of the winter I had looked up and read everything about Wilson in the Oberlin library. I had found a reprint of a speech Wilson had made to a convention of Protestant clergymen, and in his remarks he had drawn an invidious comparison between Protestant ministers and Catholic priests in their concern for the people in their communities. His remarks indicated that since priests carried with them certain attributes of divinity their status and their services far outweighed the worldly and secular image created by the Protestant ministers. This, it seemed to me, was ample proof of Wilson's complete freedom from bias. And so I prepared a letter to the **Plain Dealer** which was bristling with quotations. I sought and obtained an interview with Baker. I showed him the letter and told him of my discovery of the Wilson speech. He thought I had made a real point and used his influence with the editor to publish it. He said, incidentally, that he had never seen this particular speech of Wilson's.

This was my first important meeting with Baker.

At the Baltimore Convention later that summer Baker's great speech against the unit rule did a great deal to win the nomination for Wilson and enabled Baker's delegates pledged to Wilson to break the solid Harmon delegation from Ohio. In the balloting, however, Harmon received 148 votes on the first ballot.

Baker was essentially a liberal in the true and classic sense of that word. His support of the principle of freedom of speech and the press was shown in his administration of the War Department during the First World War, and his defense of the press in his later law practice. Despite the charge of socialism during the Johnson years and during his terms as Mayor, he was a firm believer in the institution of private enterprise. This was shown in some of his notable speeches in the TVA litigation, in which he represented the companies affected by the Government's adventure in state socialism.

When he left office at the end of the Wilson Administration, he was determined never to serve in public office again. And in 1932, when some of his protégés sought to get him the nomination, he gave them absolutely no encouragement. [8]

When he returned to Cleveland in 1921 and formed a law firm, he entered into the civic life of the city. In those years, when I served as Director of the Cleveland Foundation, I came to know Baker quite well. We both served on several committees. Altogether, I am sure that if he had been nominated and elected and had his health permitted, he would have been one of our great Presidents.

Baker's style in public speaking invites comparison with his friend, Woodrow Wilson. Emerging from the age of flamboyant oratory of the Bryan-Bob Ingersoll type, Baker, like Wilson, favored the conversational mode of a good college lecturer. There were few gestures other than the lifted finger for emphasis. His discourse was a marvel of sentence structure, for the words came in obedience to the discipline of a well ordered mind.

First on the list in 1912, however, was to get a job, a good one, if possible, but anything for the next year to make me self-supporting. It was not easy that year for the teaching market was tight.

I knew something of West High School, at that time the only city high school west of the Cuyahoga River. I learned that a loyal graduate of Oberlin was Principal and that he was at the moment in Oberlin. So I went to see him. In the course of our talk he said that there was no opening at the moment. I felt, however, that I had registered an impression.

With the aid of a teacher's agency to provide me with clues, I traveled far and wide in Northern Ohio with no success. Finally, I conceived the idea that I might have better luck with the Catholic high school. A prominent Catholic priest on Cleveland's West Side was supervisor of the high schools in the entire Diocese. I went to see him and told my story and offered my credentials. When he asked why I wanted to teach in a Catholic high school, I made one of the most unfortunate blunders of my life.

"Because," I said, "I think I am being discriminated against because I am a Catholic."

This was a double mistake. First, because I was indicating that having exhausted my first choices, I had turned to Catholic schools as a last resort, an affront to the very schools that this man was directing. The other mistake is shown in what the reverend father said:

"You Catholic boys are always whining about discrimination when all that stands against you is your own incompetence. Go on and make good and you will find that Protestants will take you without a thought about your religion. I would not think of hiring you after that remark."

So I left his rectory without a job, with my ego smarting after his lashing, a reminder forever of the lessons I learned that day.

One morning about that time I was on the train bound for Oberlin when I noted in the newspaper that J.M.H. Frederick had been elected Superintendent of the Cleveland schools. This rang all sorts of bells in my mind. In response to these, I fashioned a plan which took me off the train at Elyria, halfway to Oberlin, and to a car on the interurban bound back to Cleveland. For I had a slight acquaintance with Frederick.

He had been Superintendent of Schools in Lakewood, a big suburb of Cleveland, for some years and a member of the examining board which passed on teacher's certificates. In the course of my career, I had taken the examination three times. Frederick had marked the papers in English literature and my grades had been inordinately high, on the last occasion being 100 per cent. Apparently this had been sufficiently unusual to bring me some attention from Frederick, who congratulated me and at two or three county teacher's meetings had mentioned my interest in English, his own favorite subject. I knew from the papers that he had resigned his position in Lakewood after some controversy and, since he still held his membership on the Examining Board, occupied an office in the old county courthouse. I went directly there and since it was still fairly early in the morning, he was not too busy to see me before the rush of people who would besiege the new Cleveland Superintendent.

Frederick was a giant of a man, outstanding in any crowd. He was also an educator of the old school, a strict disciplinarian, and inflexible in his very high standards. He was also a school politician of considerable talent which accounted for his rise in the profession. Now after his vindication had come with his election by the Cleveland Board, he was at the moment enjoying the triumph. He was destined to serve his full five-year term. He greeted me pleasantly and listened with apparent interest as I told him of my adventures since my teaching at Olmsted Falls, and especially of my continued studies and my present need of a job. He said he would certainly keep me in mind. So I had touched two bases, Simpson, the Principal at West High School, and the man at headquarters who would have the final say.

My good luck continued, for in June while I was on a train bound for a national meeting of school administrators in Chicago, I met Frederick again. This time our conversation was about politics and I distinctly remember that he said that he was for Taft, if it meant that his vote would be one of the few that the distracted President would have. I did not reveal my own choice.

In Chicago the man at the teacher's agency told me to see the Superintendent from South Omaha who was looking for a high school teacher who could, in addition to a schedule of classes, coach the football team. My desperate need for a job prompted me to accept.

When school days returned, I presented myself in South Omaha and started my teaching assignments. When I met the football squad, I made a few pleasant remarks and laid down a few rules about discipline. From what I could learn in these first days, it appeared that in football South Omaha's high school team was high in its class. This was a surpirse, for in my conferences with the Superintendent, he had regarded the coaching part of my assignment as secondary and, knowing little of the site of the city and the high school, I had not taken the task seriously. But I was reassured when I had a conference with some of the "veterans" on the team, especially the captain and star quarterback, for I realized that the team could do a lot about managing itself with me to encourage the boys and maintain discipline.

On my way to the boarding house that evening, I had only slight concern about the job. Indeed it seemed like a pleasant prospect.

But when I reached the place where I had engaged a room, there was a telegram for me. When I opened the message, the contents overwhelmed me with joy. It was from David Simpson of West High and he asked me to fill a vacancy in his faculty that had appeared at the last minute. The news was so good that I wondered if someone was playing a trick. Hence when I responded in a telegram directly to Simpson, I asked for a confirmation. The confirmation came and I retired to a sleepless night of decision.

On the side of returning to Ohio and to Cleveland of all possible places, the advantages were overwhelming. This offer carried with it limitless possibilities. But there was the moral question of leaving South Omaha after a week's service.

Those were the days when teachers were hired and fired and paid like common laborers. Boards of Education considered it routine to dismiss a teacher overnight for the most capricious reasons. There were no rules, adopted after years of pressure from teachers, regarding tenure. Teachers' unions were unthought of and so were union contracts. In a situation like the one I faced, it was the individual teacher against the big school establishment, the Superintendent with the Board behind him.

I weighed the values one against the other. It would be a matter of temporary inconvenience for the school to get another teacher. But to me it was a turning point in my life. I was sure that I would be unlikely to get another chance like the one at West High. I decided to leave.

The next day I told the Superintendent all the reasons for accepting the Cleveland offer. He was sympathetic enough and accepted my resignation. The high school Principal was a bit unpleasant but this merely strengthened my determination to leave.

I found as I was preparing for the train that I was short of money, a quite normal circumstance with me. So I borrowed the necessary train fare from a kindly Catholic priest. Once again the Church of Rome was the Good Samaritan. I borrowed again when I arrived in Cleveland to repay the priest.

Whatever moralists may say about how I resolved that crisis, I found that at West High David Simpson reassured me.

I faced something like this decision years later when despite my acceptance of a position on the faculty of the University of Minnesota, I accepted the Directorship of the Cleveland Foundation. In that case the University, in a wholly friendly way, acquiesced in my decision to accept the offer in Cleveland, and instead of requiring a resignation gave me a leave of absence. This, I have always regarded as most generous.

David Simpson had spent many years at West High as a teacher and Principal. In Cleveland in those years the high school Principal was a well known institution. He was a dominant factor in the cultural and civic life of his jurisdiction. Simpson was a man of superior academic equipment and general culture. He was an impressive figure with a full and greying beard. He looked older than his fifty years. Once, when Mayor Baker came to speak in the high school auditorium, Simpson, in introducing him, said that to prove that he was younger than he looked, he revealed that he had been a student at the feet of the boyish-looking Mayor. He referred to his study at the Cleveland Law School in Baker's course in Real Property, the course I had taken briefly before my illness.

Simpson followed a tradition established by his predecessor who did not believe in assigning the subjects to teachers who had specialized in them. The idea was that with their superior knowledge, they would aim above the heads of their students. So Simpson, ignoring my interest in civil government and history, assigned two sections of ancient history and two in geometry. Two years later, when he gave me two sections in freshman English, which meant reading endless compositions, I protested, saying, "I can't do justice to these children." He answered, "They don't want justice, they want mercy."

Most of the faculty were in their late middle years and seemed settled there for life. Three were refugees from the miserable salaries paid them as professors in Baldwin University, my alma mater.

I found teaching ancient history quite enjoyable. To liven the subject, I made an arrangement with a young woman whose subject was arts and crafts to supervise my students in making drawings of important buildings in ancient Greece and Rome. Also I introduced map books to be filled in and assigned considerable reading in the little school library. I worked my students to the limit but kept them interested.

My major outside interest that winter was the writing of the essay required for the master's degree. In casting about for a subject which carried with it some flavor of the law, I selected the Cleveland Municipal Court. This court modeled after the Chicago Municipal Court was an innovation in the administration of justice. It supplanted the old justices of the peace and had civil and criminal jurisdiction, since the judges acted as examining magistrates. It was a compact court with a chief justice whose duties were mostly administrative. It had eight or nine judges elected in the municipal election. The plans for the new court had been made by a committee of the Cleveland Bar Association. In consulting one of the members of that committee, I learned that the most constructive member had been a lawyer named Manuel Levine, who was elected a judge when the court was launched. I sought him out and established not only an invaluable contact with the civic life of the city, but won a warm and generous friend. In all my eleven years in Cleveland, Levine taught me most and helped me most. He was like so many of Johnson's former protégés, a humanitarian and a bit of a philosopher. He had been given a small job by Johnson in the City Solicitor's office.

As our friendship developed, he took me to lunch on many Saturdays. From what he told me in these meetings I was able to describe in my essay not only the nature and purpose served by the Municipal Court but a great deal of the social life of the city which the Court served. For Levine, without leaning too far toward that permissiveness which has characterized later developments in jurisprudence, was quite familiar at first hand with the

complex life of Cleveland. He called my attention to the writings of Roscoe
Pound on the problems of administering justice in a great city, a departure
from formal judicial administration which came to be called "sociological
jurisprudence."

Levine, the innovator, was already looking beyond his contribution to
the creation of the Court, to the development within it of a division which
he called the Conciliation Panel. This was a court without lawyers in which
small civil disputes were disposed of by agreement of the parties under the
encouragement and supervision of the assigned judge. In his reading and
his contacts with natives of the Scandinavian countries, he found that
something similar to this had been introduced into the practice of the
courts in the Dakotas by natives of the Scandinavian countries. There, it
had suited the problems of a rural population. Levine's contribution was its
introduction into the teeming and contentious life of a city. Following the
example established in Cleveland, many other such tribunals were later
established in other cities. Mostly these are called "small claims courts."

The following summer I submitted the completed essay and was
granted the M.A. degree. I have always since been listed in the Oberlin
class of 1913.

I made further use of this essay. In a shortened form I sent it to the
National Municipal Review, and saw the first of my writings in print.

The second year at West High passed without serious incident except
an attack of rheumatism which hospitalized me for the first six weeks of the
fall term. A pleasant diversion during the winter was coaching the debating
team. We had only fair results, losing one of the two debates with the other
city high schools. This may have been the result of poor coaching or poor
material. When spring came, I decided to further my preparation for
college teaching by taking a leave of absence for graduate study. In
planning for this, I consulted Professor Karl F. Geiser with whom I had
studied political science at Oberlin. One of his passionate interests in
teaching had been to prepare a few students for graduate study. He was a
thorough scholar and strict disciplinarian. This may have been due to his
German ancestry and also his graduate study in Berlin. His preference for
his students who elected graduate work was Columbia and during the year
I spent there, there were ten other Oberlin students.

When I seriously began to consider another year of graduate study,
Geiser strongly urged me to select Columbia, largely because I would have
the advantage there of the advice and inspiration of Charles A. Beard.
Probably through the influence of Geiser, Oberlin that spring had selected
Beard as Commencement speaker.

This gave me the opportunity to see and hear him and if possible to have a conference with him. This was easily accomplished for after the program I saw Beard in his dressing room. . . . He advised me to come to his office at Columbia when I arrived in New York in September. Meanwhile he suggested a list of readings during the summer. Also he suggested that I brush up on my French and German, a reading familiarity with these languages being a requirement for the doctorate.

During the summer months, which I spent at home in Olmsted Falls, I seriously followed Beard's suggestions. I was fairly sure of my reading knowledge of French, although languages have never been easy for me. But I bitterly regretted then that ten years before I had not availed myself, while a student at Baldwin, of the German courses taught by the excellent native Germans at German-Wallace. However, I started at the bottom with a German primer. I was engaged in this when in August the great war exploded in Europe. I continued my German and Professor Geiser got me a copy of Woodrow Wilson's book, **The State**, translated into German. This sufficed as a pony. The outbreak of the war brought troubled years to Geiser on the Oberlin campus.

I visited Geiser in Oberlin that August and found him greatly agitated. He had in class and in discussions around the campus been highly critical of British policy. Impressed by his views I found myself to be far from an enthusiastic supporter of the Allies, but I kept my views to myself until the danger of involvement of the United States became serious. Then I vigorously opposed our participation.

In Geiser's case, his German origins, his name, his graduate studies in Berlin and his outspoken criticism of the British made him a mark for the wave of intolerance that swept American life, especially on the college campuses. Indeed the sentiment became so heated in Oberlin that Geiser suffered intense mental anguish. This prompted some of his more extreme critics to speak of his dismissal. But while no official action was taken, since the president of Oberlin was a great and respected liberal, Henry Churchill King, Geiser's classroom performance suffered.

Those whose memory goes back only to World War II cannot realize the intensity of pro-English and anti-German opinion in World War I. The intolerance extended to everything German. Professors of German deserted by students often transferred to other subjects or left the profession. School boards across the country eliminated German from the curricula. German music was dropped from concerts. In my own home I simply did not play Beethoven on the Victrola. I was at Western Reserve University after 1916 and witnessed the changes there which were attributable to anti-German sentiment. Professor Springstein changed his name to Mountcastle. At Barnard I learned later the good and kindly Professor Wilhelm Broun became Will Brown. Perhaps it is a sign of social progress that there was no revulsion against German culture in the 1940s.

In September, with what money I had saved in the preceding years, but with the assurance of credit if I chose later to borrow, I found myself in New York and at Columbia. It was my first view of a city in which I was destined to spend so much of my later life.

12
Columbia and Beard
before the War

I shall have a great deal to say in this narrative of the contrast between the Columbia University I knew as a student in the autumn of 1914 and the Columbia I lived with as a member of the faculty after 1923. Under the leadership of John W. Burgess, who founded the Faculty of Political Science, and Nicholas Murray Butler, who assumed the presidency in 1902, there had been gathered, at least in the humanities, an array of brilliant scholars which, without doubt, exceeded in original exploration of their chosen fields not only any other individual university in America, but in sheer aggregate of talent, all of the major universities combined. All over the nation Columbia was the graduate school where most college undergraduate teachers sent their students for post-graduate study in the social sciences. I had intended to go there ever since I knew Geiser of Oberlin.

In the summer after my decision to ask for a leave of absence at West High, and my interview with Beard at Oberlin, I had remained at home in Olmsted Falls reading and somewhat indifferently studying a German grammar. The war in Europe which broke out in August was somewhat disturbing but its great impact, which was felt along the Atlantic seaboard, lost most of its meaning when it reached our quiet Ohio village. My own feeling was without partisanship. If I had been pressed for an opinion, I would probably have indicated that the issues involved had little meaning for an American in the Middle West. It was simply not in even the remotest recesses of speculation that there ever would be danger of the United States being involved in the conflict.

My first impression of New York City was of what I saw from the car window, as the train entered the city and wound its way through Harlem and entered the Grand Central Station. There were the miles and miles of bleak tenements such as I had never seen in Chicago or Cleveland. The wretched inhabitants were leaning out of the windows or crowded in the streets below. This sociological bit I mentioned to Beard when I saw him the next day. He remarked that those people would never know the difference between a pig sty and a cattle corral. Harlem was only partially black at that time. It was much later that the great migration from the South scattered the white population of Harlem through the city. Indeed 125th Street was not an unpleasant shopping center for the Columbia people up the hill. In many evenings, even after I had moved permanently to New York nine years later, I used the streets down to 125th Street for evening walks and stopped in some book stores there. One of the married graduate students, whom I came to know that first year, lived with his wife in the Hotel Theresa at 125th and Seventh Avenue.

I had reserved a room in Furnald Hall, a Columbia residence building on Broadway near 116th Street. My room, a small one high up, looked over Broadway. In the second semester I moved to a room far uptown at St. Nicholas and 191st Street.

I first called at the office of Frank Fackenthal, Secretary of the University, and compromised my aversion to debt by borrowing $75 for tuition. This I paid back the next year and never borrowed again during my student year.

Then I called at Beard's office in Hamilton Hall, a building reserved for the undergraduate men. This was characteristic of Beard's interest in undergraduate teaching; most of the professors with whom I had courses were housed in the Kent Law School building across the street.

After a few preliminary comments, Beard suggested that I register for the following courses:

History of Political Theories with Professor William A. Dunning.
International Law with John Bassett Moore.
Corporation Problems and Labor Problems with Henry A. Seager.
Constitutional History and Principles of Politics with Beard.
Constitutional Law with Thomas Reed Powell.
Municipal Government with Howard Lee McBain.

Beard was to be absent during the second semester so it was fortunate that I could enjoy, in the first months, two of his major graduate offerings.

Many other courses were popular with students and I took advantage of the freedom which was allowed to visit them. Notable were James Harvey Robinson's lectures on The Intellectual History of Western Europe. This course was literally mobbed. There were some others which I enjoyed occasionally like Giddings in sociology and Felix Adler's lectures in ethics. I tried John Dewey's lectures once or twice but gave up. I could barely hear him and what I could hear, I could not understand.

What I noted at once was the complete absence of the leisurely life that had prevailed in the other higher institutions I had known. In part, this might have been due to Columbia's location in a throbbing metropolitan center. These professors were busy men, intensely concerned with their writing and research, although available to students during their office hours.

The most famous of the professors I knew at Columbia was John Bassett Moore. Moore had entered the State Department in 1885 and, after serving there in responsible positions, had been made a professor at Columbia in 1891. President McKinley summoned him to the State Department again in 1898 where he served as Assistant Secretary of the Department, the highest office at that time under the Secretary. But after a year he resigned to return to Columbia because, it was rumored, he could not endure the disorderly administrative habits of the Secretary. . . . The international commissions and conferences in which he served and the many foreign and domestic honors he had received made a long list. Despite this busy life, he had written or edited a sizable library of books and articles. In 1914 he was only fifty-four years of age but the distinctions he had won, and the appearance he carefully cultivated, encouraged me to believe he was in the twilight of his career. His lectures were little more than a few questions directed at members of the class whom he seemed to know, or interesting anecdotes gathered from his long experience in diplomacy.

He was, despite his arduous schedule of writing, generally available in his office and I had the privilege of a few visits that year. He retired at Columbia in 1924 but served as a Judge of the International Court at The Hague later. When, in some of my pieces in **Newsweek**, I was critical of Roosevelt's unneutral policies in the years before Pearl Harbor, I had several long letters from Moore who was, like Beard, very critical of Roosevelt's substantial but unofficial alliance with the Allies.

Professor Dunning's course in the history of political theories was a remarkable orientation for me, since before that I knew only a smattering of the classical political writers. He told me that he had been diverted from his research in American history by Professor Burgess, to concentrate on a history of political theories. He had already written three monumental texts on the subject. I decided that I would ask him to advise me in writing my dissertation.

After some discussion in which I told him of the awakening of my interest in national politics in 1896, he suggested that I write a history of that famous campaign. The fact that I lived in Cleveland, close to so many sources of information about Hanna and McKinley, made this seem an ideal subject. I shall tell later of why, after a year in which I gathered considerable material, I dropped the project at the suggestion of Beard and selected another topic.

The next year when I told Dunning about my change of plans, he expressed considerable disappointment. He felt, I am sure, that I had chosen another subject because it would enable me to finish my graduate requirements in less time and with less work. In this he was right. I had to admit on another occasion that he was right when commenting upon a paper I submitted that I might have exhausted myself but that I certainly had not exhausted the subject. I admitted to myself that my understanding of political theory was not one of my strong points.

Henry Seager was never counted among the leading men in the economics department at Columbia, nor have any of his writings merited much academic notice. But he was a truly remarkable teacher. His lectures in the first term on corporation problems and in the second on labor relations were simple, beautifully organized, and free from unintelligible economic jargon. A great deal of what I said in my years in journalism about the relations of government and business came from what I learned from him. He was without cant and partisanship about the relative virtues, on the one hand, of national planning, and Brandeisian "atomism" on the other. At his recommendation I read for the first time the truly great book by President [Charles R.] Van Hise of Wisconsin, **Concentration and Control**. This book, which advocated Federal incorporation of interstate corporations, was, I am sure, the inspiration of Theodore Roosevelt's ideas in his campaign in 1912.

Two junior members of the Department of Public Law with whom I had classes were Howard Lee McBain and Thomas Reed Powell, both associate professors. Powell followed the case system in teaching constitutional law. He never lectured but rather staged a sort of inquisition in which the reasoning of the Court was subjected to a searching analysis mostly of a critical nature. I was not always sure that either professor or student knew what he was talking about. Without a great deal of outside reading, the student in this course would get no idea of broad constitutional principles. In fact, the general drift of Powell's reasoning seemed to be that there were no constitutional principles, or if there were ideas which people called constitutional principles, they were, in the language of Mr. Justice Holmes, "Not worth a damn." But as the spring approached and my oral examination for the doctorate approached, I struck up a mild friendship with Powell. This gave the the idea that I would get on better with him in the examination if I paid less attention to my pursuit of constitutional principles and made a serious effort to study Powell's mental processes. I did fairly well in this because in the examination my answers seemed to please him and he suggested that I take the test for what was called the Tappan prize. However, I decided not to compete.

McBain had taken over the course in municipal government when the famous Frank Goodnow was made president of Johns Hopkins. He was a Virginian who, after his graduate work at Columbia, had taught a year or two at the University of Wisconsin. He had a keen, incisive mind, but his course was not a broad survey of municipal affairs but rather an exercise in reading chapters from a book he was writing on the law of municipal home rule. So far as I could tell by observation, nobody in the class understood what he was reading or, if they did get a glimmer occasionally, they dismissed it as unimportant. He was a small man, frail and bothered by a sepulchral cough. He was a most stylish dresser and extremely punctilious in all social contacts. Student gossip had it that he and his new wife traveled in the best of social circles. He was, however, at all times available to students and was kindly and helpful with their problems. His administrative talents caught the notice of President Butler and he was destined in the year to become Head of the Public Law Department and finally Dean of the Graduate Faculties.

When I returned to Columbia to serve on the faculty, McBain and Powell were the senior members of the department.

The center of my interest at Columbia and my chief reason for becoming a student was Charles Austin Beard who reached the age of forty in November, 1914. Perhaps a minor reason for feeling a kinship with him was the Middle Western origin which we shared. For despite his life in the East and abroad, his affections always seemed to go back to his native Indiana. His father was a prosperous farmer who had migrated from North Carolina before Charles was born. As a youth he attended a Quaker academy and after graduation enrolled in DePauw University. His chief interest outside his classes was newspaper writing. This passion for writing, acquired so early, seemed to be the reason for the truly massive volume of his literary production. After leaving DePauw, his family means enabled him to travel abroad. In 1898 he entered Oxford and during that first year he found time outside his studies to join in founding a decidedly liberal college which was called Ruskin Hall. He returned to the United States after a year and briefly attended Cornell University. Then, accompanied by his new wife, Mary Ritter, he returned to Europe and after a brief tour of the Continent, they settled down in England. Three years followed in which Beard worked to extend the influence of Ruskin Hall into the industrial population of the country. He not only lectured widely but wrote a great deal on industrial problems. The movement in which he immersed himself produced the Labor Party. In 1902 he returned to the United States and from then on for fifteen years his life was spent at Columbia.

He rose rapidly in the faculty and while he was kept at the level of an associate professor for a while, he attained the title of Professor of Politics. This was in the spring of 1915. In his book **The Political and Social Thought of Charles A. Beard**, Bernard C. Borning says of Beard's writings while at Columbia: "Altogether, during this decade and a half at Columbia, he produced, either alone or in collaboration with others, eleven volumes — not to mention six book length collections of readings or documents, two revisions, numerous articles, frequent book reviews, and various other writings." [9]

One of these books, **An Economic Interpretation of the Constitution of the United States**, had appeared the year before I knew the author, and the reverberations were at their height when I arrived in New York. On the one side, the younger and more liberal teachers and students of American history greeted this contribution to the New History as a milestone of emancipation from the old Bancroft school of historians. Beard, by this contribution, was placed high on the list of writers who were stressing economic and social factors in the development of American institutions such as Frederick Jackson Turner.

On the other hand, there were the conservative elements in New York which had their oracle in the New York **Times** and their intellectual leader in President Butler. Beard was arraigned as a Marxist professor who dared to portray the Founding Fathers as motivated by material gain in their labors in establishing an American heritage. As I look back over a perspective of more than half a century, this turmoil seems bizarre and unreal, for the march of political ideas and public understanding has made what seemed radical, even revolutionary, then, perfectly orthodox today. Students, even graduate students, are a restless lot, and there is nothing that excites them as much as the rumors that there is tension between faculty members on the one hand and the administration and the trustees on the other. And when the teacher who is suspected of being persecuted by the authorities is dynamic, attractive and popular, the partisanship of the students reaches fever pitch.

The trouble in my year at Columbia must be considered in its historical setting. The so-called Progressive movement which had split the

Republican Party and elected Woodrow Wilson in 1912 was reaching its culmination. The reverberations of Theodore Roosevelt's feud with the Old Guard of the Republican Party were still apparent in the press and in academic life. The war in Europe fanned old conflicts in the United States between the friends and the critics of British interests. Moreover the British propaganda machine was working with great intensity to mold pro-Ally opinion and work toward American involvement. This was bitterly resisted, not only by pro-German elements over here but by a large body of opinion which found no American interests in the conflict and no support for our involvement. All this was soon to be complicated because of the Russian Revolution and the appearance in the United States of a body of half-hidden Communist sympathizers. The New York **Times**, which was regarded as generally speaking for Wall Street, was decidedly pro-British in its editorial policy. There were constant rumors that British elements were financially interested in the **Times**. This was not true and someone said that certainly the British need not waste their money in buying the **Times** for they had it anyhow.

It was in the cross currents of this controversial climate that the Beard situation developed. He had been criticized in the press and in some academic circles for a variety of reasons which on examination seemed to involve a number of contradictions. His innocent travels on the Continent during his years at Oxford were alleged to have given him pro-German sympathies. His activities with the leftish elements in England were said to have associated him with Fabian socialism. And his writings on economic determination were thought to be Marxian in origin.

His great attractiveness as a teacher was not all based upon his caustic humor, his flashing intelligence and his feeling for words. His physical attributes helped. His emotional nature was signalized by his reddish hair and complexion. His deep-set eyes and aquiline nose gave him a mien that suggested a crusader or, as one observer remarked, a Hebrew prophet. His posture and movements suggested an age far beyond the forty years recorded in 1914. Hundreds of students, both undergraduate and graduate, knew him as Uncle Charley.

A small group of graduate students met and talked with him quite often in that half year when he was in residence. With these favorites, he seemed deliberately to instill an element of conspiratorial overtones. We thus became comrades against all "reactionary" elements in history writing, in current national and international issues, in the court and even in religion. He once said that the way to get on in New York was to consign your mind to Nicholas Murray Butler and your soul to Bishop Manning (who presided at St. John the Divine Cathedral). There was advice about discretion in proclaiming ideas of an unorthodox nature. He constantly advised us to look to our economic security before being too free with criticism of the existing order. And there were suggestions, which some students interpreted as "boring from within." But there was little in these suggestions of radical change to indicate what sort of objective was to be sought. Certainly not Socialism, for Beard had never indicated any interest in the American Socialist Party. And Communism had few, if any, spokesmen on the domestic scene in those days, before the Russian Revolution. Moreover, in Beard's discussions of economic determinism, his witnesses were Madison and certain English philosophers, never Karl Marx. But we students were swept along by the reverence we had for the man and, like the Sorcerer's Apprentices, accepted even his casual exaggerations and wisecracks as serious revelation.

Perhaps much of what seemed like radicalism had something of the dramatic in it and even a subtle humor. . . .

In that first year when I came to know Beard quite well, his interest moved beyond the recognition of the complex of interests described by Madison to the still greater complex of interests in the American society of the twentieth century. Here he made special and repeated mention of a book, which, however pertinent when it was written, is now forgotten. It was A.F. Bentley's **Process of Government**. Here the author speaks of the government's task of attempting to regulate and harmonize the vermiculate confusion of countless numbers of interests, agencies, associations, that constitute modern society. These may be allied or in conflict with each other and the individual may be a member of or allied with a great number at all times.

The complexity of this association of interests makes it substantially impossible to describe now what seemed so simple when the Constitution was ratified or even in the time of Andrew Jackson. At the moment, I ask the reader, as I have asked myself, whether self-interest allies me with the debtors or the creditors.

While Beard's book on the economic interpretation of the Constitution transcended anything else that he wrote in public interest and academic concern, when it appeared, in the long perspective of his thinking and writing, it is only a piece of evidence to prove his larger contention which he called the economic interpretation of history. He began writing and talking about this early in his years at Columbia. Later in 1922 he elaborated it in a book, **The Economic Basis of Politics**. This small book he revised and republished in 1936 and again in 1945.

In all that he said on the subject, he seemed to be trying to make clear that while in any appraisal of a historical event or movement or personality, economic factors should be taken into consideration, his view was far from the wholly materialistic economic determinism of Karl Marx. For Beard not only pointed to the ethical and even spiritual factors in the interpretation of history, but the pervading influence of personality. In this he stands somewhere between Carlyle's **Heroes and Hero Worship** and Marx.

Beard from the beginning cited for support a book that had been published in 1902 by a former teacher, Professor E.R.A. Seligman. This man was not only the most distinguished member of Columbia's economics department but a member of a renowned banking family. His view of economic determinism, with which Beard apparently fully agreed, not only took account of the economic factors which influence the course of politics but the qualifications which must be observed. This latter element is what distinguishes Beard as well as Seligman from the brutal materialism of Marx:

Thus the economic interpretation of history, correctly understood, does not in the least seek to deny or minimize the importance of ethical or spiritual forces in history. It only emphasizes the domain within which the ethical forces can at any particular time act with success. . . . It endeavors only to show that in the records of the past, the moral uplift of humanity has been closely connected with its social and economic progress, and that the ethical ideals of the community, which alone bring any lasting advance in civilization, have been erected on, and rendered possible by the solid foundation of material prosperity. [10]

The character of Beard himself, kindly, patient, and helpful to his students, and burning with passionate concern for the unfortunate and deprived, is the best answer to the charge that his belief in the economic interpretation of history has anything more than a slight acquaintance with the radical materialism of Marx.

So far as I knew, no student ever questioned him about his religious beliefs, if indeed he had any. We considered this to be a matter of only private concern. But in discussing Marxian materialism, he remarked with singular passion that he did not "believe this world to be a pig pen."

So far as I could see that year, Beard was almost as popular with the younger members of the faculty as he was with the students. Among the members of the Faculty of Political Science that I knew, there was nothing but affectionate regard.

In the second semester of that year, with Beard absent on a sabbatical leave, I seriously turned to my preparations for the oral examination required of all candidates for the doctorate. In making my plans, I carefully surveyed the ground, for it was quite unusual for a student to brave the oral examination after only one year's residence. I went to McBain first to get his advice. After asking me a number of questions about my past preparation, he advised me to take the chance. Powell was of the same opinion, and the third faculty member whom I sought out provided me with an extraordinarily strange experience. He was a Canadian named Sait who gave the course in European governments and had the title of Assistant Professor. I had only audited his course a few times and noticed nothing unusual about him. He was a big brawny man whose demeanor was rather thoughtful and serious. I had only a slight acquaintance with him since I had not registered in his course. I saw him briefly at his office to ask about taking the examination and he invited me to call at his apartment. When I called on him, he seemed strangely preoccupied and after a few casual comments told me that he had recently been afflicted with a species of melancholia. He seemed to enjoy talking with someone and became quite friendly. When I left, he asked me to call again.

Since he was to be one of the examiners and his specialty was British government, I made certain to reread A. Lawrence Lowell's two volumes on the government of England. But at the examination a few weeks later, Sait, who suddenly seemed to believe that he was substituting for Beard, confined his questions to rather recent events in American political history, ignoring his own specialty of European governments. I was quite unprepared for these questions. I was embarrassed and worried about his questions and when, after the examination, I was compelled to wait a long time to receive the verdict, I was sure I had flunked on account of Sait's behavior. Years after the examination, Powell told me what had happened while I was out of the room. Sait had protested against passing me because of my failure to answer his questions correctly. Powell also told me that what Sait had said about his melancholia was really a diagnosis of the quite common spell of remorse and discouragement that all alcoholics suffer after an excessive bout with the bottle.

In the following year Sait was given a leave of absence which he spent in the North Woods as a laborer in a lumber camp. At the end of that year he decided to resign at Columbia.

The examination, aside from Sait, was a rather pleasant and stimulating occasion. The rule is that the questioning lasts three hours with each participant having a fifteen-minute go at the candidate. The only questioners I remember were Moore, Dunning, Seager, McBain, Powell and Sait. I must have done quite well because everyone but Sait had favored passing me. But Powell told me later that in the discussion after the questioning when the candidate is absent, the discussion about the candidate is quite general. High priority is given to the impression he had made upon the members of the faculty, especially the professors in his major subject of interest. The plans of the candidate are considered and the question of his probable success is weighed. So I returned to Olmsted Falls after the successful termination of the exciting and fruitful intellectual experience of my life.

When I was in New York in the spring of 1916, I talked with [Beard] about my dissertation. As I noted earlier, I had chosen as a subject the campaign of 1896 and during my final year at West High had made some small progress. I had collected some material and had several interviews with survivors of the great contest between Bryan and McKinley, who lived in Cleveland. But after nearly a year of this, it was apparent that to complete this task would take several years if I were to carry on with it despite the demands of a heavy teaching load. Beard agreed with this and said that since it was essential that I get the degree as soon as possible, it was advisable to switch to a subject which I could complete in a year or two. He said that at the Bureau some of the staff members had already been collecting material on a notable movement in state governments designed to reorganize the framework of their administration in the interest of greater efficiency and economy. He suggested that I make a dissertation out of this material and that if I completed a report, the Bureau [of Municipal Research] would publish it as a report. This was a considerable inducement because a doctor's dissertation at Columbia must be published and if no publisher were willing to assume the costs, they would fall upon the author. When the little book was finished, it was printed as a report of the Bureau and I deposited fifty copies in the Columbia Library as was required under the rules.

So I made this decision and with the material at the Bureau, I began the collection of new material from the states themselves. Several of the state legislatures had created what were called efficiency and economy commissions and their reports were readily available. During my first and second years at Reserve I made considerable progress with my report and by 1918 completed it. The Bureau published it as one of their reports, and I easily passed the one hour's examination on the dissertation in early 1918 and received my degree that year. I have never been very proud of this little book because almost before it was completed, several more states had created commissions and the state of New York was working on a plan to "streamline" its state administrative machinery. The direction of this New York operation had been given over by Governor Alfred E. Smith to Robert Moses who had been a staff member of the Bureau after he had secured his degree at Columbia.

I found, curiously enough, that the first person in the academic world to treat the subject of public, which means government, administration was a man who was to be the President of the United States, Woodrow Wilson. In a startlingly prescient article he called attention to the fact, which should have been obvious, that since public opinion was demanding that the government do more and more things for people, and consequently that government machinery was getting larger and more complicated, there should be more systematic study of how government machinery could operate more efficiently and with a minimum of expense to the taxpayer.

13

The Beard Resignation

When I returned to New York in the spring of 1916 I found the East generally, and New York particularly, highly disturbed over American policy toward war in Europe. The Establishment, always easily identified, consisting of the press, the financial community and Columbia University, was more strongly pro-Ally than in the year before. In anticipation of American intervention, there was an outcry for greater military preparedness. Strong criticism was voiced against Wilson's unchanged attitude of neutrality. Later that year, in the presidential campaign, the President remained adamant on the subject and derived great support from the general feeling in the Middle West that we should stay out of the conflict. The slogan was, "He kept us out of war."

There was a strong pacifist element among the students, who had the best of all reasons for peace. There were meetings and forms of demonstrations, and several organizations dedicated to peace. Some of the demonstrations were on the Columbia campus. In one such meeting held in a school auditorium somewhere in the city, comments were made which were interpreted as defaming the flag of the United States. There followed heated appeals in the press for denying the use of school property for such gatherings. Beard, always stirred to action when freedom of speech was involved, made a statement, saying in effect that while he deplored the unpatriotic language used at the meeting, he deeply resented demands for suppressing freedom of expression.

The New York **Times**, ever ready to attack Beard for his alleged radicalism, took this occasion for a long editorial, dragging in Beard's famous book on the Constitution. The editorial said that it was the teaching of "such" professors which encouraged students in their radicalism.

The editorial appeared shortly after I returned to Columbia, and since I found my friends among the graduate students infuriated because of the **Times'** attack upon their beloved professor, I prepared a statement defending Beard and attesting to his strong dedication to American in-

terests. This statement was well circulated among the graduate students
where it gathered many signatures. We gave it to the press. In a list of the
publications about Beard in Borning's book, it appears that such a round
robin was published in the **New Republic**. This must have been the one I
initiated.

The obiter dicta in the **Times'** editorial about Beard's books
represented a widespread feeling about the professor among the Columbia
trustees and others, which had been current since the book was published
three years before. At that time Butler had been quoted as saying that
Beard was the advocate of a "notion" linked with the "crude, unhistorical
and immoral teaching of Karl Marx." [11]

On this occasion in 1916 Butler strongly defended Beard in a trustees'
meeting showing them the statement from the graduate students. We had
made sure that Butler had a copy.

At this point in my account, I am able to reveal some information
hitherto unpublished. This I have because of the generosity of Mrs. Alfred
Vagts, who is Beard's only daughter, Miriam. In the process of collecting
the Beard papers for future publication, she found two memoranda among
her father's papers which throw great light upon the facts which led up to
the resignation.

One of them says in substance that on May 1, 1916, Beard had been
asked to appear before a trustees' committee on education to explain his
statement about the flag incident and he was able to show that the words
attributed to him were without substance. However, to Beard's surprise, a
trustee, Frederick R. Coudert, insisted on comment upon Beard's ideas
about American history. Beard's memo quoted Coudert as saying that "in
his opinion the American revolution had been in fact a revolt against
usurpation by a German king on the English throne." Beard's memo goes
on to say that two other trustees (named) went on to make a general indictment of Beard's ideas, saying they felt that his teachings were
calculated to create disrespect for American institutions.

This paper, Mrs. Vagts says, was headed, "Statement of facts in the
minutes of the Committee of Education of the Board of Trustees of
Columbia University and Professor Charles A. Beard." Mrs. Vagts says
that this was "certainly written by father." [12]

After this annoying interrogation before the trustees, there came
another incident in which Leon Fraser was the subject of concern by the
trustees. As I noted earlier, Fraser was a part-time assistant in some of
Beard's undergraduate courses. He also had another job with the Car-
negie-supported Association for International Conciliation, the head of

which was Butler with Dean Frederic C. Keppel assisting. One of Fraser's duties was recruiting summer school teachers in behalf of peace. It seemed that in marking papers Fraser had flunked the son of one of the trustees and that the said trustee demanded that Fraser be fired. Apparently there was no inquisition before the trustees but the word went to Beard who was head of the Public Law Department not to recommend Fraser's reappointment. Beard went to Keppel and told him that he would rather "lay his dead body at the door of the trustees" than be a party to this persecution. But later by some means the trustee in question had been able to have Fraser removed. [13] Beard's memo does not mention the name of the trustee but tells of the aftermath:

I, therefore, lodged my personal protest against . . . the whole miserable affair. I then took a long walk in Riverside Park in the dead of night and made up my mind that I had to choose between the easy way of acquiescence in irregular, unjudicial, dark room methods of university administration and protest against such methods, destined to bring down on my head unpleasant notoriety and bitter criticism. I chose the latter . . . . I made the decision . . . . Then came the expulsion of Professor Cattell and Dana which complicated the issue, but having made the decision . . . I resigned my professorship.

This memorandum about how the decision was reached clears up certain misconceptions. It was the belief at the time, a belief which I entertained until I read this word from Beard, that the resignation was in protest against the dismissal of Cattell and Dana.

Out in Cleveland I learned through the papers all about the Cattell-Dana firing but nothing about Fraser. It was reported that a long-standing feud between Butler and Cattell had flared up and that Butler and trustees had removed not only Cattell but an instructor in English named Henry Wadsworth Longfellow Dana, a grandson of the poet. I had heard echoes of the Cattell affair the year before. Among other indignities which Cattell had heaped upon Butler was a letter written to the faculty, suggesting that since there was need for a new building to house the Faculty Club the beautiful President's Residence should be commandeered for the Club. He added to his letter the charge that Butler had used the house "for social climbing."

In response to my question, Mrs. Vagts has cleared up another misunderstanding. In Borning's book he says that the decision to resign was made at New Milford after consultation with Beard's wife, Mary. The story around the campus had it that Beard had acted without consulting Mary and that if he had, she might have dissuaded him. The letter to me in January, 1973, from Mrs. Vagts says:

> You ask whether CAB decided without consulting Mary. I should say, yes. He was in a high rage and never thought of consequences. He was, in fact, accustomed to making principal decisions without telling Mary. Thus he bought that big, old, gray house in New Milford on impulse, one autumn afternoon, when a real estate agent took him there for a drive. "Done," cried father. Mother never saw it until after the whole thing was settled, and she was really downcast. It looked like a monster to her, for the place was weed grown and decayed then.
>
> There is, however, more evidence. There is an article in a Southern magazine by Mrs. Dorothy Tucker called, "Charles and Mary Beard in North Carolina" (where the Beards spent several winters). She says that Mary told her that she was eager to have a new dining room set and went to Wanamakers, found one and ordered it sent home. That night she ran to the door to tell him of her surprise about the furniture. But he told of his surprise about the resignation. She then called off the purchase from Wanamakers.

Beard's letter offering his resignation permitted him to give expression to the attitude toward the Trustees which [he] had harbored for months and years. . . .

After Beard's resignation, the New York **Times** published an editorial (October 10, 1917) which was a reply to Beard's criticism of the Trustees. The tone of this editorial illustrates not only the extent of the newspaper's partisanship in the controversy within academic circles concerning Beard's break with tradition in his history of writing, but the extent to which anti-German prejudice prevailed in the First World War. . . .

The **Times**, and indeed public opinion, which on that day it summoned to its side, has come a long, long way until 1972 when it was unrestrained in its opposition to a war in which the United States was engaged. And in what it has to say in various departments of the newspapers about the writing of history. For Beard's version of the economic factors in politics is now taken as a matter of course. Also in the **Times** endorsement of Senator McGovern for President, a man who represents far more radical views than Beard entertained in his earlier years. [14]

When I read about the resignation in the Cleveland newspaper, my emotional reaction was quite forcefully shown in the letter I wrote a day or so later. I said in part: "I know that the time has not yet come to try and measure the fine thing you have done. That it was an act of fine courage shot through with enlightenment goes without saying. . . . The results will be too significant to be seen now. The teaching profession, too humble and time serving in the past, will forever assume an added importance. Your great letter has given to it dignity and independence and power."

I also impulsively suggested that I had lost interest in getting a degree from Columbia. And I asked Beard, who at the moment had my dissertation, to hold it for a while. . . .

Beard's reply was brief: "I could not take my own advice. I just had to do it. Will tell you all some day."

As I look back, the resignation of Beard was a tragic loss to academic life, for he stood foremost in American higher education in America, not only because of his brilliant scholarship but because of his inspired teaching. It seems that he might have accomplished his end by a statement denouncing the action of the Trustees without resigning, for resignation was good news for his enemies.

The real gain was the effect upon the policies of the University administration, for the Cattell-Dana action was not repeated. In fact, the Trustees after that kept hands off hiring and promoting and dismissing faculty personnel.

I learned this nearly twenty years later, when a trustee who was a good friend of mine came to me asking my help. He said that Fiorello LaGuardia, who was considering retirement after three terms as Mayor of New York, had an ambition to be employed at Columbia as a professor of municipal government. The Trustee wanted me to use my good offices to persuade the department, of which I was a member, to ask for LaGuardia's appointment. I asked him why he did not consult the Chairman of the Board of Trustees about it. He said very emphatically that that approach would never do, for if it were known that the Trustees wanted the appointment, the faculty would never agree. Perhaps this great change reflected the still-living impact of Beard's resignation. I then said I would canvass the members of the department about the opportunity to have LaGuardia as a colleague. Their reaction was negative. They did not want LaGuardia. So I delivered this decision to the Trustee and the matter died a quiet death.

After his resignation, Beard's interest in the improvement of government administration drew him closer to the New York Bureau of Municipal Research where he had been spending some of his time for a year or so working on the establishment of a training school for public service. The Trustees of the Bureau offered him the directorship of the Bureau and he held that title for some years.

In 1919 he joined several of his former colleagues, including James Harvey Robinson, Alvin Johnson, and others in establishing the New School for Social Research where he gave some lectures. As director of the Bureau he had a part in numerous projects involving government reorganization including the famous administrative reforms at Albany inspired by Governor Alfred E. Smith. In 1922, at the invitation of Viscount Goto, Mayor of Tokyo, he visited the Far East and helped establish a Bureau of Municipal Research in Japan. The next year, after his return, he was again summoned by Goto, because of an earthquake and fire in Tokyo. He worked with Goto in the reconstruction of the city.

My contacts with Beard in the 1920s were minimal but I was reminded of him constantly by the stream of articles and books which he wrote, mostly at his home in New Milford.

In 1926 he was elected President of the American Political Science Association and in 1933 he was President of the American Historical Association.

With the coming of the New Deal and my involvement in the Roosevelt Administration, our contacts revived in a series of letters which continued to the end of his life. I shall deal with those contacts in another chapter.

Since there has been reference in what I cited from Beard's daughter to her father's finances, some comment is appropriate here to that subject. There seems to be some confusion among those who have written about Beard's personal life as to his finances. Was the severance from Columbia an economic calamity? And was he reduced to something near the poverty line when he retired to New Milford and purchased certain farm and dairy properties which were not very productive? On the other hand, was he secreting large means, the basis of which he gained by speculation in war stocks in the First World War?

With reference to the latter gossip, I can offer my recollection. In 1914 when he told certain of his students, including me, about his earlier stock transactions, he had quit the stock market well before there was any money to be made in war stocks.

Perhaps his Quakerish manner of pretending penury had something to do with the rumor that he was poor. The fact is that he was always well fixed, ever since, in his college years or before, he made a small town newspaper in Indiana pay a profit. His textbooks, those which he wrote himself and those on which he collaborated with others, sold in the millions and brought in substantial royalties. His reason for telling his small circle of favored students about his earlier speculations was to enforce upon us the great necessity to attain financial security before throwing dangerous opinions around. His grandfather, John Payne, was a rich farmer who founded the bank at New Castle, Indiana. And his father, William, was always well-to-do. Also when he resigned from Columbia the salary in his new job with the Bureau of Municipal Research paid well above what he got at Columbia.

His passion in the years after his resignation from Columbia was investment in landed property and livestock. In commenting upon this type of property, he said that in a depression one could "always eat his investment." And when he died, he left the members of his family well provided for.

In Richard Hofstadter's study **The Progressive Historians**, the author gets quite confused in what he writes about Beard's investments. What Hofstadter does make clear is that Beard and other writers of dissent in the Progressive era voicing protest against the excesses of capitalistic enterprise [were not abandoning] the thrifty habits of the well-to-do.

14

West High
to Western Reserve

When I returned to Olmsted Falls that spring of 1915 after my year at Columbia, I enjoyed the profound satisfaction of having completed the most important step in the realization of my ambition to be a college teacher. I had successfully passed the difficult oral examination required of candidates for the Ph.D. In those days the doctorate was not easy to come by. To qualify for employment in college teaching at most institutions, you needed only "satisfactory" progress toward the degree. Most faculty members had attained their final degree while teaching in the lower ranges of the faculty.

The passing of the "orals" was a matter of considerable importance in the academic circles at that time, for degrees at Columbia were sparingly bestowed. A considerable majority of the graduate students who came and were registered in the graduate faculties were never encouraged to take the oral examination at all, and of those who did take it more than half were failed. The vast majority remained from one to three years and then drifted into non-academic occupations. This dropout rate was at least seventy-five per cent among the students I knew there. It was not without interest that two of my friends at Columbia did complete the requirements for the doctorate, and both were from Oberlin.

Before leaving New York I had made arrangements for summer employment. President Butler was at that time President of the Carnegie Endowment for International Peace. Most of his duties in this office were given over to Fred Keppel, the dynamic Dean of Columbia. . . . A part of the program was the financing of teachers in the summer schools of the country who were expected to give courses in international relations. Dean Keppel's assistant in recruiting suitable teachers was a very attractive graduate student of my acquaintance, . . . Leon Fraser. Fraser was as anxious to provide remunerative employment to his friends as they were to get the extra money and experience. I asked for one of the jobs and was assigned to the University of Delaware at Newark.

The job at the University of Delaware was my introduction to college teaching. It was not a large institution at that time but its nearness to Wilmington, Washington and New York made weekend visits quite possible. I spent several days in the Library of Congress doing some preliminary work on my thesis on the Campaign of 1896.

A diversion that summer was a lively "letter to the editor" bout with a man named Vallandigham. He had seen the account of a speech I made at the University on July 4. The general tone of the speech was pacifist for I realized that there was a growing sentiment in the East favoring our participation in the war in Europe. Vallandigham's letter attacking me and my speech was very bellicose. I answered in the same newspaper where his letter appeared. . . . There was a considerable exchange . . . .

The resumption of my classes at West High in September and the months that followed were without incident. The work on my history of the presidential campaign of 1896, which I had selected with Professor Dunning's approval, occupied considerable time. . . .

During the Christmas holidays I attended the meeting of the Political Association in Washington largely to meet various professors in the big institutions who might be looking for a young and exceedingly ambitious college teacher. Beard was there and he told me that Allen Johnson, Professor of American History at Yale, was looking for a man to teach a course in American government which he was carrying along with his classes in history. (Yale had no Department of Government until somewhat later.) Johnson was taking a leave of absence to edit the Yale **Chronicles of America.**

Beard had recommended me and he introduced me to Johnson. I was probably so excited about this unbelievably wonderful possibility of teaching at Yale that I probably overdid the job of selling Johnson on my virtues. He listened patiently, however, and then told me to write and tell him why I felt I would be a good teacher at Yale. I did this when I returned to Cleveland and my letter must have been quite a stunning portrait of Raymond Moley! However, it failed to stun Johnson. For he wrote a letter meaning to let me down with some tenderness. One point that he made ignited a resentment which I harbored for many years. He said that while he liked my spirit and admitted my qualifications, he believed I was not sufficiently mature for the Yale students. This I concluded then, even as I do now, was a patronizing message from the Eastern Establishment. I treasured that letter and never failed to quote from it when in later years, as something of a celebrity, I was invited to speak at Yale.

I had then, and for quite a while after I was teaching at Columbia, a keen sense of regional snobbery. I am sure that there was along the Eastern seaboard a rather condescending attitude toward the Middle West. When I was brought to Columbia and assigned the job of building a Department of Government at Barnard College, I told the chairman of my Department of Public Law that I had had considerable success in attracting girls to my class at Western Reserve. He answered that while this was possible in Ohio, I would find the students at Barnard "more discriminating." He added that his experience as an instructor at Wisconsin taught him that. I found, however, that the girls at Barnard were much like the ones I had at Western Reserve. I hope that this sort of conscious distinction has passed away in these more or less enlightened days.

As spring approached I began to feel considerable concern about getting a teaching job in college the following year. A major consideration was my location. The news about vacancies comes from the college needing help to the big graduate schools in the East and in those days Columbia was a major supplier of talent. It is best for aspirants to be there and "under foot" when the requests come in. So I began thinking about cutting my year at West High short by resigning and spending a month or so in New York. I wrote to Beard about this plan and he replied that while he saw a certain amount of risk for me in "casting my bread upon the waters," he would do everything he could to help me get the first available job.

An incident happened after I had Beard's letter in that spring of 1916 which I am sure stiffened my determination to make the gamble. One rainy day in April I had some occasion to visit the Public Library in downtown Cleveland. On my way out I noticed ahead of me a man whom I knew. He was the civics teacher at one of the high schools and the debating team he coached had roundly walloped my boys from West High. He must have been about sixty years of age and had been a respected figure at his school for many years. His encyclopedic accumulation of all sorts of facts was legendary.

There he was that dismal rainy day, clad in an ancient raincoat and flappy overshoes, carrying a load of books under his arm wrapped in an old rubber bag. While thus engaged I kept telling myself, "There but for a bit of daring goes Raymond Moley twenty years from now." I truly believe that this was the final determining factor behind my resignation.

In a day or so I told Dave Simpson of my decision. He was very sympathetic, for he knew from his experience that the longer a man remained in high school teaching, the more difficult it would be to move into higher education. His educational endowment would have graced any university if he had moved in that direction when he was younger. So in the middle of April, I left West High and sought my fortune in New York. It was interesting that this quest for a college job ultimately brought me back to Cleveland.

Professor Garner of the University of Illinois and I had a considerable correspondence that spring about a position in his department, but the opportunity fell through because of budgetary troubles.

A few days after my arrival in New York, Beard had a letter from President Penrose in Whitman College in Walla Walla, Washington. There was need of a man to teach political science there at a salary of $1500 a year, which was considerably more than I was receiving at West High. It was an excellent institution and I learned a great deal about it from a classmate at Columbia. This man was Paul Garrett, then a recent graduate at Whitman and subsequently a Vice President of General Motors. It is interesting to note that if I had gone to Whitman, I would have had as a student William O. Douglas who entered as a freshman in 1916 and graduated in 1920. I later served briefly with him on the Columbia Law faculty.

About the same time, an inquiry came from Scott Nearing, Dean at the University of Toledo. Nearing, a well known man in those years, had been fired from the University of Pennsylvania because, it was said by his friends, of his radical views. He had been invited to Toledo, a town which in those years had a really radical city government. I made a trip to Toledo to survey the opportunity and was cordially received and entertained by Nearing. Apparently he considered me radical enough because Beard had recommended me. I was offered the Professorship of History, also at $1500. But a subsequent opportunity to go to Cleveland caused me to reject the Toledo offer and to obtain my withdrawal from the Whitman position.

In late May, when I was about to return to Ohio, Beard had a letter from August R. Hatton, which was most interesting to me. Hatton was the head of the Political Science Department at Western Reserve University in Cleveland. The department which he headed had been heavily endowed by Dan Hanna, son of the great Mark, Senator from Ohio, and the dominant figure in the GOP during the McKinley years and after. He was in addition a very rich man because of his interests in the iron ore business on the Great Lakes. The chair which Hatton occupied was named for M.A. Hanna and the department was a memorial to him. Ironically, Hatton was a Theodore Roosevelt Progressive with ideas which would have horrified Hanna. The endowment provided for two instructors and considerable library facilities.

When I reached Cleveland I saw Hatton and he seemed receptive to my application. The letter from Beard and a conversation he had with Simpson at West High settled the matter, and I was employed at $1200 a year. Hatton later told me that Simpson spoke very highly of my teaching ability. He said that my students used the library more than any others in the school. I wish to add with some hesitation that in this matter of teaching ability, I was always a real success. I never hesitated to claim this as my most important talent. It was the result of my long experience in various sorts of classrooms in my Olmsted Falls days.

Thus the transition from high school to college, from West 65th Street to East 107th Street, was one of the great turns of fortune in my life, for Hatton . . . encouraged me to get into public affairs. He was always dabbling into city problems and had already made a considerable name for himself as a liberal.

My transition illustrated a point which in these recent years of college and university unrest I have made the subject of various written articles and one commencement address. One of the great defects in the administration of higher education has been the neglect of teaching. This seems ironical since the fundamental reason for colleges and universities had always professed to be to impart knowledge to a new generation. Research and other scholarly pursuits which used to be the ancillary factors in education seem to have usurped first priority. Administrators attract men and women of superior talent by offering them light assignments of teaching and much time for research and writing. Promotions are seldom based upon superior teaching ability, but on getting some kind of contribution, however unimportant, in print. The rule is "publish or perish." At Columbia, due to a reorganization that took place in the years between my student and my faculty years, there was established a system by which teachers, after a few years in one of the undergraduate colleges and the writing of a "contribution" to knowledge, were "promoted" to one of the graduate faculties with a very light schedule of one lecture and one seminar a week with exclusive contact with graduate students. This change, I have always maintained, marked the beginning of the deterioration of Columbia as a center for the training of future faculties. What happened was a lessening, not an increase, in faculty productivity.

When I was a student there in the year 1914-15, the really renowned faculty members who did so much to establish the University's reputation combined their writing with teaching undergraduates as well as graduates. They sought no relief from teaching and they produced more lasting written work than after the change. Beard himself had undergraduate classes and apparently derived much inspiration from the younger students.

Meanwhile, under the new dispensation in our universities, the undergraduates are taught by inexperienced young people whose only qualification has been a certain number of years in graduate school. There is no instruction at all in our graduate curricula in the art of teaching. As a consequence, undergraduates, herded into classes which sometimes number in the hundreds, listen to boring lectures from green instructors. It is no wonder that, lacking any excitement or inspiration in their classes, students seek excitement in the streets.

My remedy for this in the 1960s, when there was a great need for college teachers, was to [propose recruiting] the best teachers from the high schools. It was quite unfair, I contended, to have a wall erected between the high school [and the college] through which the high school teacher might never be promoted. . . .

While in New York, I again arranged with Leon Fraser for summer teaching in 1916. He assigned me to Wooster College. This liberal arts college, about forty-five miles south of Cleveland, was a first-rate institution. One of its distinctions was the fact that it produced the famous Compton family. The father, Elias, was Dean for many years. His three sons, Arthur, Karl and William, were all graduates of Wooster and two of them taught there for short periods. Arthur and Karl became most distinguished scientists and William an economist. All three were distinguished educators.

When I went there to serve in the summer school, the contrast between what went on in the summer and the regular sessions in the rest of the year was almost unbelievable.

The head and promoter of the summer session, whose name was Dickinson, was a folksy product of rural Ohio, who was regarded with a mixture of amusement and dismay by the winter faculty. He had been a perennial candidate for Governor on the Prohibition ticket. His managerial methods were something like those of a wandering evangelist. I noted when I first visited his office that the immense flood of letters he received daily were not filed. They were left in the envelopes and piled high on his desk or spilled over on the floor. The assemblies at noon had the fevered atmosphere of a camp meeting. But he was immensely popular with the rural school teachers. There were 2000 in attendance that summer. There were no standards in the courses given that I was able to discover. Everybody had a good time and everybody passed. Despite the horror of the fine and discriminating members of the regular faculty, the Treasurer of the college kept tongue in cheek as he toted up the tuition money that flowed in from Dickenson's show.

A serious decision had been made for marriage after summer school. The bride was Eva Dall whom I had known since school days in Olmsted Falls, and whom I had courted for years. We were married in Oberlin by Henry Churchill King, president of the college. During our remaining years in Cleveland we lived in an apartment near Western Reserve.

The teaching schedule at Western Reserve which Hatton assigned to me consisted of courses in American government at both Adelbert College and the College for Women (now named Mather College).

Hatton specialized in municipal government and gave two or three advanced courses. He was an extremely articulate individual whose views completely suited the Progressive trend of those years. He believed in and vigorously supported every possible political reform in a period when reform, especially in Cleveland, touched every aspect of the democratic process and swept every rational doubt before it. The remedies which most interested Hatton were the city manager plan, proportional representation, the initiative and referendum for state affairs, and public ownership of public utilities. Except for the more measured but quite liberal philosophy I had developed under the ministration of the faculty at Columbia, I am sure that I would have been swept along the Progressive path with Hatton. But a sense of discrimination, which I shall describe later, restrained me. I did, however, participate with Hatton in introducing the Hare system of proportional representation in the small city of Ashtabula, and I helped the election commissioners count the votes.

I had an opportunity to discover the practical defects in proportional representation in 1923, my first year at Columbia. Cleveland had adopted the system by that time and considerable interest was manifested in this trial in a large city. So I visited Cleveland, determined to study the results of the election. My conclusions, which were published in an article in the **Political Science Quarterly** in December, 1923 were mostly negative. The system failed, for the same reason that so many of the Progressive political reforms failed. They assumed too much knowledge, intelligence and discrimination in the electorate. Since the system places before the voter a longish list of names, it is highly improbable that more than a small minority of the voters will know anything about the candidates. Hence it was shown that the selections of the voters were based upon the most capricious and irrevelant reasons. The Irish voter would vote for all the micks and the O's. The Slav would select the skis, and the other slavic names, etc. The cream of the jest in that election was an overwhelming vote for a man named Sultzman. This man was a cigar maker and his name had been blazoned over his district for years on cigar boxes. Because of this failure of the voters to know the candidates, the system, in the brief experience it had in New York in the 1930s, enabled the Communist Party to elect a disproportionate number of Communist candidates. They accomplished this by having their voters concentrate upon a small number of Communist candidates to the exclusion of all others.

Also, in the distribution of the ballots of the candidates who were counted, the second and third and other choices counted just as much as first-choice vote given the winners.

All this, which was so easy to see in an actual test, the promoters of the plan never anticipated.

Later in 1921 Hatton and other reformers carried a vote authorizing the writing of a new city charter. In the commission elected to write this charter Hatton won election along with several other reformers. In the writing of the charter Hatton was able to incorporate in the revision the city manager plan and proportional election. This practically destroyed the old political parties, but after a very few years the charter was rewritten and the old system restored.

At the time that I joined the Western Reserve faculty, Cleveland was using still another scheme of the reformers in the election of the Mayor and other executive officials. This was called "preferential voting." The ballots presented to the voters listed all the candidates for an office without party designation. Following these names were three spaces for three choices, first, second and third. The conscientious voter (always an assumption of the Progressives) would put his x before his first choice, another x before his second choice, and so on. Then, in counting the votes, if a candidate failed to get a majority, the second and third choices were added to his first choices. Finally the election went to the candidate who had the most votes. When I explained this to my class at the College for Women, a particularly dumb girl said, "But this means that the second and third choices count just as much as the first choices." It was the case of the dog, the child, and the emperor with no clothes. Finally the voters got the point and the system was repealed.

In the spring of 1917 three things happened at Reserve which for me meant more, at the moment, than Wilson's call for a declaration of war. First, Hatton suffered a heart attack, mild but severe enough to confine him to his home. The other instructor in the department took over Hatton's class in municipal government and I carried his class in constitutional law.

While he was confined, he was offered and accepted a job for the next year with two national organizations to become a traveling exponent of the city manager plan and proportional representation. He assumed, quite correctly it proved, that his health would permit this responsibility.

Hodges, in a dispute about salary, decided to quit and return to Philadelphia where he entered business. Thus, suddenly I found myself, who had been the third man in the M.A. Hanna Department, the only survivor.

In granting Hatton his leave of absence, the faculty had designated the Professor of Sociology as the executive head of the political science department. In consultation with this professor, I brought into the department, to replace Hodges, a friend I had known at Columbia, Leyton Carter, who proved to be a congenial colleague.

I readjusted my teaching schedule for the next year and prepared to serve as the de facto head of the department. The added responsibility was recognized in an increase in my salary from $1200 to $1600. They paid me $100 for carrying Hatton's class for the remainder of the term.

During my first year at Western Reserve, I enjoyed many visits with my friend, Judge Manuel Levine. At the election in November, 1916, he had won a judgeship on the Common Pleas Court, a court of general jurisdiction superior to the Municipal Court. He almost immediately interested himself in applying his conciliation idea to the divorce cases coming before the court. After several discussions with him, in which he cited many instances in which the good offices of the judge had resulted in reconciling the parties to the proposed suit, I prepared an article to be jointly signed which we called "Conciliation in Divorce." After several instances to illustrate how conciliation had worked in Levine's experience, the article proposed the establishment of agencies or bureaus in large jurisdictions to review without lawyers all applications for divorce. I sent the article to the **New Republic** and it was accepted and published.

The bureau that Levine proposed was created in the Common Pleas Court and so far as I know is still functioning.

I had often discussed with Levine my still-active desire ultimately to become directly active in politics, perhaps as a candidate for elective office. He suggested running for the state legislature and said that while the lower house was a large body, it was possible for an intelligent and aggressive member to exercise a good deal of influence and enough public notice to win promotion to the Senate or Congress. For the moment I was receptive and Levine spoke with Burr Gongwer, the Chairman of the local Democratic organization and a power in Cuyahoga County. Gongwer had his political apprenticeship as Secretary to Mayor Johnson. He told Levine that he would put me on the slate of candidates from the County. This was wholly on Levine's recommendation. I had no direct contact with the boss. Since the County was overwhelmingly Democratic, election was assured.

This presented me with another serious decision. Attractive as the opportunity seemed, it involved getting leave from my duties at the University very soon after I had joined the faculty. While the Legislature held only biennial sessions, these absences would be difficult to get and if insisted upon would probably endanger my career as a teacher. So I decided to decline the offer, a decision which ended my dream about seeking elective office.

15

War and Americanization

Leon Fraser had arranged a summer job for me in 1917 as he had in the two years before. It was decreed that I should return to Wooster. We moved down there, expecting to spend a pleasant summer when after about two weeks I received an urgent call from Judge Levine asking me to return to Cleveland. He said that the Mayor's War Board had decided upon an important activity called Americanization and that he had suggested that I be employed to do some work of an educational nature. I knew something of the special problems which were associated with the foreign born in Cleveland, for Levine had discussed it on several occasions, so I arranged for a substitute to take my classes at Wooster and returned to Cleveland.

A bit of background is relevant, because the work to which Levine had summoned me was to occupy a considerable part of my time for more than two years.

In the first months after our declaration of war, a number of states had created "councils of defense" designed to promote and carry on war-related work on the home front. Some of their activities had been prescribed and directed from Washington, but generally states created their own programs. Some of these had to do with propaganda designed to inform the public concerning the objectives of the war as defined by the President. Measures of social welfare made necessary by the drafting of so many of the men, cooperation with Herbert Hoover's food administration, team work in the big bond selling drives, and in Ohio especially measures to expedite the naturalization of the many thousands of foreign-born industrial workers.

In Cleveland this work was carried on, under direction from Columbus, by the Mayor's War Board, a group of prominent citizens appointed by Mayor Harry Davis, and provided with a considerable budget. One aspect of the work of the War Board was what was called Americanization. At that time it was estimated that some seventy per cent of the adult population of the city was foreign born. The men were largely employed in the city's industries, and their loyalty and cooperation was essential to the efficiency of the war effort. As Levine and others interpreted the problem, it meant also the peace of mind of so many of these men whose native countries were locked in the mortal struggle in Europe where many of their relatives were located. Many thousands of these men were relative newcomers, for the last of the great waves of immigration was only a few years back. Many were quite unable to speak and write English, and few had taken even the first step toward naturalization. There were Hungarians, most of the Slavic nationalities, Czechs, Serbians, Poles, Lithuanians, and Italians.

Cleveland, since the beginning of the Johnson years, had been most proud of its "social conscience." Quite generally the community welcomed these people since their skills and their many cultures meant so much to its industries and cultural life. There was little disposition, except among a few benighted extremist native Americans, to regard these immigrants as threats to the social order. Their loyalty was taken for granted since they had come to America for what they failed to realize at home. The concern of Americans like Levine was that the immigrants be helped to understand American institutions and the reason for our participation in the war, to expedite their learning of the language and their acquisition of American citizenship. This was the problem as I first saw it. After several months of contacts with the newcomers, I realized that there were much more and more complex elements in their adjustment to our society.

It was quite understandable that these members of so many nationalities had gathered each in their little compound in the city, like little Italy in the East End, the Czechs out south near the steel plants, and the Magyars or Hungarians in the southeast. This creation of national communities was as natural as the huddling of the Irish on the west side many years before.

The Americanization Committee was headed by a prominent lawyer named Harold Clark and in the year that followed my contacts with him were almost continuous. Later when the war seemed to be winding down, he asked to be relieved and I was selected as his successor.

Through politics and long experience in the courts, Levine had the qualities which made him the most imaginative and constructive member of the Committee. The program, which he presented and the Committee adopted, consisted of three parts: many classes for adults in the school system for teaching English; special classes either in the school system or directly under the auspices of the Committee to teach the rudiments of

American government which was required of applicants for citizenship; and the creation of a bureau or center where immigrants and others could come and get legal advice of all kinds.

My first assignment was to prepare a primer on American government for applicants for citizenship. For this I was paid a reasonable fee. Then there was the organization of classes where my text could be used by applicants for citizenship. At first these were exclusively created by the Committee and were held in schools and branch libraries. Teachers for these classes were either from the public schools or the library staffs or lawyers. All were chosen because of their special knowledge of the language of the class to which they were assigned. To supervise these classes and to direct the work of what we called the Citizens' Bureau, I recruited a brilliant high school teacher who was a member of the bar, George Green. He spent the rest of his life in this service.

In the fifteen years that followed there were many editions of my little **Lessons in Citizenship**. There were not only editions for use in Cleveland but for other cities in Northern Ohio, each written to include a description of the government of the city concerned. After the Armistice, when the Americanization Committee ceased to function, Green and I charged the people in the classes enough to pay the cost of printing the book. The total number printed and distributed over the years must have been considerably more than 100,000.

The Ohio Council of Defense took note of our Americanization work in Cleveland and in 1918 I was made Director of Americanization for the state. This made necessary many trips to Columbus to direct an office there, and special visits to the cities over the state for consultation with educational officials. The teaching of English for adults was made a major activity in the public schools over the state and in certain large industries. In Ohio, Armco and Goodrich . . . did distinctive work with their employees.

When I was in Columbus my office was in the State House where James M. Cox sat as Governor. Since he decided to run for reelection in 1918 as the great war Governor, he announced that his speeches would be wholly non-political. To assist him in shaping certain speeches on the war settlement in Europe and, incidentally, to get the votes in the cities of Ohio of the many natives of the countries involved in the projected settlements, he enlisted my assistance in learning what and where these countries were. To facilitate this early "brain trusting" of mine, I set up in his office a large map of Europe and from that instructed him to distinguish between the Yugoslavs and the Czechoslovaks, etc. He had a quick but superficial mind and I never had much respect for his truthfulness or his statesmanship.

When it came to voting in 1920 when he ran against Harding, I decided to skip the candidates for President.

In 1918 I undertook another responsibility. A friend, Allen Burns, who had served for a few years in an official capacity with the Cleveland Foundation, had resigned the year before and with a grant from the Carnegie Foundation was directing a big survey of the problems of the immigrant population and publishing the findings in several volumes entitled **Americanization Studies**. Burns, who was familiar with the problems of Cleveland and with the work of our Americanization Committee, asked me to join his staff. I contributed several chapters for one of the volumes, which concerned naturalization. It had the title **Americans by Choice**. I also contributed a chapter to another study, **Schooling for the Immigrant**. This dealt with citizenship classes. These volumes were published after 1920. This job not only provided some additional revenue to our household, but the publication of my contributions was an asset in my academic record.

The reader of this account may be inclined to wonder how with all these extramural activities, I was able to care for my responsibilities at Western Reserve. By a concentration of my classes in three days of the week, I was able to have considerable free time and judged by the enrollment, my teaching was popular with the students. In 1917 and 1918 the student body at Adelbert, the men's college, was considerably reduced by the draft and enlistments. But my classes there showed a substantial rise. At the College for Women, the first class I had numbered only about eighteen. In the second and third year this class grew to about 100.

In 1918 I secured my promotion to an assistant professorship under rather interesting circumstances. A letter came to Hatton, one day when he paused in Cleveland to rest from his travels, from a man he knew at the University of Kansas and whom I had met at a meeting of the Political Science Association. His name was Clarence Dykstra. He was quite articulate. With his excellent academic record and engaging personality, he seemed to be destined for something more important than his position at the Kansas institution. Dykstra thought so too and his letter to Hatton said he was most anxious to get out of his present location and get located in something more exciting. Hatton and I were members of a reform organization in Cleveland called the Civic League, an organization whose purpose was to keep a sharp watch on community affairs, particularly the city government. The secretary of this organization had recently resigned and it was easy for Hatton to get the job for Dykstra. When the appointment was concluded, Dykstra, perhaps as a reward, sent me a telegram offering me his job in Kansas. This was a full professorship with a considerable increase in salary over what I had at Reserve. But I was unwilling to leave Cleveland.

However, the offer gave me the very tool which academic people used in those days to demand promotion. I made an engagement with the president of Reserve and boldly laid the telegram on his desk. Apparently he was quite familiar with this sort of pressure and he simply held his arms in the air and said, "What do you want?" I told him that I wanted something that would not cost him any money, my promotion to the rank of Assistant Professor. "Oh," he said, "that's just the stroke of a pen."

Such promotions at Reserve at that time must be approved by what was known as the "Permanent Officers," which consisted of the President, the Dean and the full professors. Since they recognized that there was something incongruous in a man with the title of Instructor operating a department with its real head away, I was duly confirmed as an Assistant Professor.

Dykstra's service in the Civic League was the opening to a notable career. He went from Cleveland to the Secretaryship of the City Club of Chicago, and from there to Cincinnati as City Manager. Thereafter, he was President of the University of Wisconsin and Chancellor of the University of California at Los Angeles. [15]

During the spring and early summer of 1918 the war seemed to be taking a turn for the worse and this might seriously lengthen the duration of the war. I was barely within the age limits of the draft, so I wrote to my old doctors, Peters and Sewall, asking for letters regarding my health record. They both replied saying that despite seven years of freedom from a recurrence of TB, my history made me a bad risk. I presented these letters to my draft board and received a classification substantially exempting me from service.

After the Armistice, the Mayor's War Board began the business of terminating its activities. As Chairman of the Americanization Committee, I asked the Board to let us continue our work with the foreign born. The Board gave us a considerable sum of money for our work. Some of this we used to continue the work of the Citizen's Bureau, and some went to the preparation and publishing of a series of booklets on the various nationalities in Cleveland, stressing their history, characteristics, and especially their contributions to the life and culture of the city.

During the following winter I felt that something in the nature of a text in citizenship was needed which combined simple English with information about American history and government. I enlisted as co-author an extremely gifted teacher in the classics, Huldah Cook. The book was published by Macmillan and was called **Lessons in Democracy**. The book was used for a while in the school system but in the following year, a member of the School Board whose printing business had been injured by labor troubles attacked our book because he said it was too pro-labor. The Board threw it out when Miss Cook and I refused to amend the text.

The war and the various civil activities which were continuous after the war had taken a considerable toll of people in the colleges and universities. This was especially notable in such subjects as political science and economics. Perhaps that was a major reason why I fared so well in the war years and after. With the war over, the budgets of higher institutions were loosening up and a considerable number of vacancies were appearing. In the spring of 1919 the president of the University of Minnesota, Marion LeRoy Burton, invited me to dinner at his hotel and offered me an Associate Professorship at a salary nearly twice what I was getting at Reserve. My duties would include some teaching, but mainly the development of a government research bureau where I would work closely with the legislature in St. Paul. Without asking for time to weigh this attractive offer, I accepted then and there. After the appointment had been confirmed, I resigned at Reserve and began making plans to move to Minneapolis. I had serious regrets about leaving Cleveland but the promotion in rank, the larger salary, the larger institution and the quite remarkable opportunity to work with the government were conclusive reasons, I thought, for going.

One of the more serious reasons for my regret at leaving Cleveland, and the ultimate reason why after a time I changed my mind and decided to stay, was my interest in the lively and colorful population of Cleveland. . . .

It is true that other midwestern cities had mixtures in their population similar to those in Cleveland, cities like Chicago, Pittsburgh and Buffalo. But none of these had the enlightenment over the twenty years since Johnson which made possible an attitude toward Americanization which distinguished our work.

It is true that a great many Americans, and some of them lived in Cleveland, understood Americanization to mean a quick job of transforming these "foreigners" into people who would be indistinguishable from native Americans, same language, same citizenship, same dress and habits of living. This pattern of assimilation would have been undesirable, even if possible, for there were just too many immigrants and their national character was too deep-seated for sudden change.

The task of Americanization as it came to be understood in Cleveland was to create a new sort of society by bringing together in every relationship in life the two elements in the population, the highly enlightened and sophisticated portion of the native population, and the great mass of unassimilated and partly assimilated foreign born, the new and the old in one community which was greatly enriched by what the immigrants brought to its culture because of their diversity. This meant amalgamation rather than mere assimilation.

To be sure, the creation of better communication between the new and the old meant the stepping up of efficient means of teaching English and for giving aliens the means of attaining American citizenship. But beyond that there were immensely serious problems of adjustment. These newcomers needed help in solving the legal problems they encountered in their daily lives; those who had relatives abroad, sometimes their immediate families, needed help after the Armistice in establishing communication. There were problems of establishing closer contact with their employers, their fellow workers and the labor unions. Their financial affairs often created problems in which they needed help. And it was immensely important to create machinery either in the government or through private agencies to protect them from the exploiters with which they were surrounded, often members of their own nationalities. All these matters came within the term Americanization.

A great part of my efforts in Cleveland and as an officer of the Ohio Council of Defense, both during and after the war, was to get these considerations over to the people through the spoken and the printed word. This meant many speeches over the state, especially in the industrial centers, and the publication of literature designed to inform both native and foreign born.

It is difficult for this generation to comprehend the immense problem created more than half a century ago when the onset of the war and the great flood of immigration came as it seemed all at once, for in the years since the children and grandchildren of those immigrants have moved up the ladder to important positions in the political, economic, and cultural life of the cities. In political life this new influence is most easily seen in the names of those who hold high office in all branches of the government. To take a single example, there was Frank Lausche, Mayor of Cleveland, Governor of Ohio, and United States Senator. He was born of immigrants from Yugoslavia.

These immigrants lived out their lives, mastered the difficulties with which they were surrounded, and raised their families to grace the city of their choice. It might not be inappropirate when we toast the early settlers who came from England, Germany, Scandinavia and Ireland to bear in mind these immigrants of the years before 1920 who in the industries of our great cities faced vicissitudes just as formidable as the wilderness and the Indians.

16
The Cleveland Foundation

A decent gesture of modesty requires me to offer an exception to the cliche that wars profit no one. The exigencies of the war effort in Cleveland had already rescued me from summer school teaching in Wooster and gave me profitable work in the Americanization movement. My participation in this patriotic undertaking brought to me a prominence in Cleveland in a very few months that I might not have attained in ten years of teaching the boys and girls at Western Reserve.

I cannot remember the exact connection of the Minnesota offer with the war, but it was no doubt the heavy manpower demands for war work that thinned the ranks of eligible men of my age and education and put me high among the eligibles for the vacancy offered. So many in my age range were drawn into the vast emergency in Washington that for a few golden months the market for college teachers turned in favor of qualified men. And it was surely the prominence of the work I was doing that brought me sharply to the notice of Belle Sherwin, to whom I was indebted for my employment by the Cleveland Foundation.

In several respects that institution was unique. It was the creation of Fred Goff, whom we met earlier when he was selected by the Cleveland street railway interests as their representative in final negotiations with Mayor Johnson. Shortly after the creation of the Tayler compromise, he was induced to leave the practice of law to become President of the Cleveland Trust Company. As he settled into the duties of a bank executive, his earlier reputation as a lawyer followed him. And despite the rules, regulations and prejudices that limit a bank's legal work, a number of elderly men of property continued to consult Goff about the ultimate disposal of their property.

In these consultations he noted a lack of constructive ideas of many testators when, after providing reasonably for their families, they had surplus wealth to dispose of. Goff's reflections on this were sharpened when he read a notable book, **The Dead Hand**, by an Englishman, Sir

110

Arthur Hobhouse. This book, in which Goff made many penciled notes, told of the many capricious bequests in England which were not only unwise and wasteful but, as they stood over the years, positively against the public interest. One passage which Goff heavily underlined was this:

> The grip of the dead hand shall be shaken off absolutely and finally; in other words, there shall always be a living and reasonable owner of property, to manage it according to the wants of mankind. This again must be a public tribunal charged with the duty of adjusting to new objects all foundations which have become pernicious and useless. [16]

Goff's thinking went far beyond Hobhouse in that he sought a means by which the ultimate disposition of surplus property should be made by some living agency attuned to the needs of the present. He wanted the property to return to the benefit of the community in which the wealth was created and which was responsible for it. Perhaps this was a version of the philosophy of Henry George as expounded by Tom L. Johnson.

The device created by Goff for eliminating the "dead hand" by providing a living agency with discretion to dispose of the residual wealth was the use of the foundation idea. In his law practice, Goff had enjoyed considerable familiarity with the foundations which played so large a role in spending Rockefeller's money. But, as he told me on one occasion, he had never agreed with the Rockefeller plan of self-perpetuating boards. Therefore, in setting up his foundation he provided that a majority of the members of the Committee should be appointed for rather short terms by public officials; one by the Mayor of Cleveland, one by the Federal Judge of the district, including Cleveland, and one by the probate judge of the county. The two remaining members of the Board were to be appointed by the Cleveland Trust Company. Thus there was assurance of adequate representation of the public interest and also sound management of the funds by the bank acting as a trustee.

The stated purpose was made very general but so stated as to assure tax exemption, and the grants and operations of the Foundation were limited to the City of Cleveland. [17]

Since in the early years of the Cleveland Foundation the income would be relatively small, Goff suggested that the Committee should begin by conducting surveys of certain social problems in the city which might serve as its guide in distributing larger sums later. In short, the Foundation sought in these surveys to acquaint itself as well as the Cleveland public with information about the city, its institutions and its needs. To finance these, Goff himself, as well as certain friends, contributed the funds necessary for operations.

As an executive, the Foundation Committee selected Allen T. Burns, who had enjoyed considerable experience in social and civic affairs in Pittsburgh and Chicago.

The first survey conducted by the Foundation was about public welfare. To conduct this study Burns brought to Cleveland Sherman Kingsley, who had been a prominent social welfare worker in Chicago. This study recommended the creation of a Cleveland Community Fund. This included an annual drive to raise funds for all social welfare agencies of all religious groups. The funds collected went into a fund which was distributed by what was known as The Welfare Federation. Kingsley was the first director of this super agency. Provision was made for donors to have the right to specify, if they so chose, the particular agency to which the donation should go. But so far as possible the public was encouraged not to put strings on the gifts.

Thus the Foundation, which itself was a new and unique institution, had brought into being another which was widely adopted over the nation. These have various names but the distinctive feature copied from Cleveland was the merging of all drives and solicitations into one master collection.

The Foundation's next survey was a comprehensive examination of the public school system and of the education problems which faced the school administration. To direct this, the Foundation employed Leonard Ayers, a specialist in education and statistics with the Russell Sage Foundation. The reports of this survey were printed in twenty-five small volumes and were mostly presented in public meetings. These reports were mostly critical of the schools. Perhaps as a result of the stir created by the survey, a new Superintendent was brought to Cleveland and under his direction there was a general shaking up of the personnel of the system.

Greatly encouraged by the success of the education survey, the Foundation in 1916 decided upon a survey of recreation in Cleveland. This was placed under the direct supervision of Burns. He associated with himself as a technical advisor Rowland Haynes, a social worker from Chicago. The work of the various divisions was well along when in early 1917 there came a clash of personalities which threatened the Foundation's explorations into the city's affairs.

One of the aspects of a division of the survey called commercial recreation was an investigation of prostitution. Burns, who would probably call himself an independent liberal, was apparently seeking to show a connection between prostitution and official, mostly police, corruption.

Now, more than sixty years later, we may with impunity enjoy the hilarious comedy that shook the special welfare structure of Cleveland and lost to the city a most colorful leader, and also paralyzed the Foundation.

Picture the enemies of vice, the well known pastor of a large fashionable Euclid Avenue Church, and a nationally famous leader in social welfare affairs. Both, rather portly middle-aged men, hawking about, snooping into the affairs of assorted bawds to see if they were in any way associated with city policemen. Real cloak and dagger stuff! I am not sure that the amateur operatives used ladders to give them visual access to what was going on in houses of ill repute (as happened in a similar case later), but apparently they saw and heard enough to prompt Burns to issue a blast at the city government for allowing the fair city which it governed to go down the primrose path to a haven for vice and petty corruption.

It must be noted that this came soon after the big survey of the schools which had received high public approval. And when Burns embellished the story of public licentiousness as having been uncovered by the Cleveland Foundation, the story rated front-page news.

I have always had a critical word for reformers because of their lack of a sense of humor. As proof, this episode of the two do-gooders and the irate banker rates high.

But at the moment nobody in Cleveland thought the episode was funny. After Burns had made public some of the gleanings which he and the preacher had discovered, together with some critical remarks about the city administration, Goff immediately reacted by denouncing Burns for prematurely revealing the findings of a Foundation survey before the complete reports were officially issued. Burns, incensed by this reprimand, resigned and left the city.

Perhaps the impulse to defend the Mayor came from Goff's outrage at the misuse of the Foundation and also because he had conceived a liking for Mayor Harry L. Davis who had been elected as a Republican in 1916, ending the fifteen years known as the Johnson era. [18]

At the time that the Goff-Burns tiff appeared in the newspapers, I could not have been more neutral. I knew Burns slightly. Goff I knew only as I read of him in the press. Indeed the affair was of only slight interest to me and I did not then or later feel any partisanship. I knew Belle Sherwin through other connections and only later as a member of the Cleveland Foundation Committee.

When, because of my interest in the Foundation, I came to a better understanding of the facts behind the quarrel, I was still neutral. I disapproved of the action of Burns which, in my judgment, was a violation of the proper procedure in conducting a survey. And I also felt that Goff had been unnecessarily aroused about a matter that should have been handled privately, perhaps with a conference with the Mayor.

Four members of the Foundation Committee, including Miss Sherwin and one of the appointees of the Cleveland Trust Company, supported Burns after the outbreak. They resented Goff's interference with the survey which was properly the exclusive concern of the Committee.

The Committee, after the departure of Burns, discontinued the survey, locked up the partially completed reports, and suspended all operations. They gave the Declaration of War as an excuse for the suspension which was regarded as a valid reason for dropping the subject of recreation. For it would have appeared foolish to be concerned with how the people were spending their spare time when the war effort demanded full employment and full activity.

In the spring of 1919 when the city and country were returning to peacetime pursuits, a colleague of mine at Reserve, an instructor in sociology, came to me and proposed that I approach the Foundation Committee and suggest that the recreation survey should be rescued from the dust and completed; also that the men to perform this salvage operation should be Moley and Coulter. The idea appealed to me for several reasons. A chief one was the prospect of remunerative summer employment. Another was the advantage to both of us through the academic credit it would bring. The members of the Committee, appointed by various public officials, were Thomas Fitzsimmons, a liberally inclined retired steel manufacturer, and Malcolm McBride, who had inherited from his father a large wholesale drygoods business. He was also a famous Yale football star of a few years before.

The third public member was a formidable figure, Belle Sherwin, daughter of one of Cleveland's pioneer industrialists who founded the Sherwin-Williams Paint Company. She had given her life to social service and was, through her dominating character and her prominence in Cleveland's social life, easily the strongest member of the Foundation Committee. I had some acquaintance with her because of a speech I had made at her request at a Columbus meeting of social workers.

One appointee of the Cleveland Trust Company was Dr. James L. Williamson, a venerable and respected figure in Cleveland who had been pastor of the leading Presbyterian Church for many years. Since his retirement from the ministry he had served as Executive Vice-President of Myron Herrick's Society for Savings Bank. Despite his banking connections and his appointment by the Trust Company, he had gone along with the majority in suspending the operations of the Foundation after the Goff-Burns affair.

The Foundation's Counsel was James R. Garfield, son of President Garfield, and a close friend and Secretary of the Interior under Theodore Roosevelt. He was a powerful name in Cleveland.

As I appraised the situation, it was Miss Sherwin with whom I should conduct negotiations. I have often said that no speech of mine, except those delivered by someone else, ever did any good for anyone. But the one I had delivered in Columbus not only won me the most important job I had ever held, but in a very important way influenced my whole career.

I had prepared it with great care. It was an appraisal of what the war had taught about the importance of a strong Federal establishment, of a wider consideration of social objectives in the plans of governments, and the necessity that governments exercise a new and enlarged role in industrial life. I also called attention to the rising power of unions and the benefits which this might bring to management, the workers, and the public. Toward the end of this speech, I quoted something from a recent manifesto of the British Labor Party.

Apparently the sentiments I expressed found a most sympathetic listener in Miss Sherwin. She was quite liberal in her political and economic views and in later years, when she was National President of the League of Women Voters, she was something of a maverick in her class.

She listened to my plan for reviving the recreation survey and for reactivating the Foundation. She said she would talk with the other members of the Committee. As a result the Committee at a meeting decided to become active and to employ me to direct the completion of the recreation survey.

My situation in this revival of the Foundation's activities called for great tact on my part in dealing with Goff, for the Committee had acted without consulting him. But his cooperation was most essential as the resources of the Foundation were so limited that dependence must be placed upon him to find the money for the survey. I immediately had an interview with Goff at which I was accompanied by dear old Dr. Williamson. Since Williamson had been appointed by the Cleveland Trust Company and enjoyed such moral stature in the community, his presence as my sponsor did much to dissipate old differences. However, Goff had every reason for seeing the Foundation reactivated. It was his baby and its future depended upon its acceptance as a going concern by the community and especially by potential contributors.

When I examined the material in the files, I found that the survey had been planned to have six reports, each written by an appropriate specialist. The titles of the reports were: Delinquency and Spare Time; School Work and Spare Time; Wholesome Citizens and Spare Time; The Sphere of Private Agencies; Public Provision for Recreation; and Commercial Recreation. I found that the first three of these reports had been completed. They had been done by recognized authorities who had been imported for the purpose by Burns, and were designed to show the area of need for some provisions, either provided by the city government or private agencies or commercially operated.

It was obvious that Rowland Haynes, who had been employed by Burns, would be necessary, not only because of his technical knowledge but because of his unfinished work on one of the reports. We immediately engaged him to come and, in addition to advising us generally, to complete the reports of private and of public agencies. I decided to take charge of the report on commercial recreation, the one which had been involved in the explosion.

I began the work in May and hoped to complete the survey by September when I was scheduled to leave for Minnesota. When I had a moment to think about the size of the task, I realized that even if the reports could be completed in four months, the task of organizing meetings to present them to the public would still remain. I realized that this would involve an emormous effort on my part to manage all that from a distance of several hundred miles. However, as we shall see, Providence intervened to save me from what might have been a civic and personal catastrophe.

I had accepted the Minnesota appointment without ever having seen the Minnesota campus. All that I knew was that it was a big institution and that some of the faculty whom I had met seemed congenial. So in June I decided to go to Minneapolis and survey the situation.

The Chairman of the Department of Political Science was a very friendly and cooperative man named Cephas D. Allin. He was not a well known figure in the academic world but his ideas about building up the department seemed sound enough, and President Burton had assured him a generous allotment of money.

Allin introduced me to the members of the department who were in residence and to other faculty people and the Dean. At dinner at his home he had as a guest a well known professor who had been recently appointed to a position at Harvard.

With this brief test of the atmosphere, I returned to my hotel room and had a sleepless night. Despite the cordiality of everyone I had met, misgivings rose in my mind. I have always attributed these doubts to the contrast in the atmosphere in Minnesota with that of Cleveland. I had become accustomed to the colorful and varied cosmopolitan life there. On the other hand the atmosphere in Minnesota, which permeated the University, was that of the cold, prosaic, Scandinavian Northwest. The question which tortured me was whether I could ever be happy there. I concluded that I could not.

So in the morning I sent a telegram to the faculty member who was acting in Hatton's absence, asking that my job be kept open pending possible reconsideration.

My meetings next day with more members of the faculty partially quieted my doubts, but not completely. When I returned to Cleveland, I learned at Reserve that my job had not been filled and that, due to a new schedule of salaries, my pay, if I returned, would rise to about the same as I would get under the arrangement in Minnesota. So with the assurance that I could return to Reserve if I so decided within a reasonable time, I was in a state of uncertainty for two or three weeks.

Meanwhile, with the help of Haynes, I had made progress with the survey. Goff was most friendly and cooperative and a mild friendship developed, for I grew to admire this vigorous, aggressive, and extremely intelligent man. My reports of progress to the Foundation Committee encouraged its members that the Foundation might soon resume the place in the community that it had held before the interruption.

Our success so far with the Recreation Survey encouraged my belief that if I played my cards right I might get the Foundation Committee to offer me the position vacated by Burns. So I arranged a meeting with Miss Sherwin to discuss matters which I hoped would lead up to the big question in my mind. She was well pleased with our progress in finishing the work on the Recreation Survey. And she was especially impressed with Rowland Haynes, whom I had brought back to Cleveland to work on the finishing touches, and gratified by my success in keeping Goff happy after the differences of two years before.

Then I tactfully brought up the question of what should be done with the Foundation after the Recreation Survey was disposed of. Whether I bluntly expressed interest in the job of Director I do not recall but I am sure that my hints were quite obvious. She said that she would consult with the other Committee members and see what they thought.

This was characteristically Belle Sherwinesque. For such was her prestige in the field of social welfare and such was the dominance of her personality that, while pretending to consult her colleagues on the Committee, she was really making up their minds for them. The result was that at a meeting of the full Committee shortly after, I was offered the position of permanent Director (not Survey Director, Burns' title) at a salary of $5000 a year. I said I would accept if I could get my release from Minnesota.

Whether the call of war-connected work had so depleted the ranks of men with my special qualifications, or because of circumstances applying exclusively to me, I had enjoyed a dizzying rise in salary over a period of two months. My salary at Reserve had been $1600 in May when the offer from Minnesota came with a salary tag of $3200. Now in July I was offered $5,000 by the Foundation. [19]

In late July I wrote to President Burton and Professor Allin saying that I had been offered the position at the Foundation and that I would like to have my release from Minnesota. I said further that while the opportunity at the Foundation was exceedingly attractive for the short run, ultimately I intended to return to university teaching. Perhaps this suggestion gave them the idea of giving me a leave of absence at Minnesota with leave to go there the next year if I so chose. This was a most generous action which I always appreciated. During the Christmas holidays, the Dean from Minnesota called on me in Cleveland and I told him that I had decided to remain at the Foundation.

So far as my interests were concerned, it was exceedingly fortunate that I remained at the Foundation, for I am sure that it was on the basis of my record there that the people at Columbia decided to invite me to come to New York.

When it was announced that I had been chosen as Director of the Foundation, a friend asked me how it felt to be the social work "boss" of the city. When I asked him what he meant, he said that my predecessor, Allen Burns, had been so regarded. I replied that I had no such ambition, that I was there to get the surveys done competently, to pick the subjects for the next study, and generally to promote the prestige of the Foundation in the life of Cleveland.

And yet, as I settled into the job, it became apparent that the expectation that ultimately the Foundation would be distributing large sums for civic and charitable purposes gave me a prominence and attention far beyond my merits as an official or a personage. Perhaps I have in the preceding sentence used the word that distinguished the Ray Moley who had been appointed Director from the Assistant Professor at Reserve. I was a personage because of the position I now occupied.

In approaching the task of public relations, I worked on the principle that characterized my conduct as an editor in later years, that whatever was good for me was good for the institution I represented. When September came I gave up my old office at Reserve and moved to a suite of Foundation offices which I rented in an office building next to the Cleveland Trust Company.

My personal situation was favorable to the responsibility I had assumed. I had been a good friend of Allen Burns and I was favorably known to his many friends as a moderately liberal individual in matters political, economic and social. Burns remained my friend after I assumed the office he had held, for he regarded the independent action of the Committee in reviving the recreation survey and choosing me without consulting Goff as a personal vindication. He was still proceeding with his Americanization studies, the printed volumes of which were coming out in 1920 and after.

I felt it to be wise to move into the life of the community by joining certain clubs like the City Club which was an organization which had a Saturday luncheon forum; the Advertising Club; the Automobile Club, which was very important because of its legislative influence; and the Chamber of Commerce. The Union Club, founded, I believe, by Mark Hanna, I did not join, first because the dues and prices were beyond my means, and [second] because I was not asked.

My liberal instincts were in those years quite opposed to the class distinctions in Cleveland. At Reserve I had been quite critical of the fraternity and sorority systems. My comments on the subject were based on the usual argument against them — discrimination on religious lines. But my views had little impact against the vested interest of the alumni and the strong traditions behind them.

However, I carried my views on the subject when I moved to New York and have never joined a club which excluded Jews from its membership. At the end of my working days the only club of which I was a member was the Chicago Union League Club which offered the great convenience of lodgings between trains and during political conventions.

In Cleveland, to a degree seldom found in a big American city, there was a distinct power structure. Whenever any project was considered which concerned the city as a whole, there were a dozen or so individuals who could be summoned to assure its success. This power structure by its support of the annual drives had practically eliminated the jealousies and rivalries which had existed in earlier years. I always thought of the power structure when I noted the "wax works" on the speaker's dais when some special dignitary was being entertained. Always lined up for all to see, there was someone from the various religious groups, the Chamber of Commerce, the Welfare Federation, the University, the newspapers, and the public schools. I often wondered when the poor editors of the papers ever got their work done because of their constant attendance at some luncheon or dinner. I noted that, as our Foundation activity got better known, I was invited up there too.

Our labors on the recreation survey extended into the fall and winter of 1919-20. In this the assistance of Rowland Haynes was most important. He was the expert. I was the manager, although I appeared as author of the report on commercial recreation. When the reports were finished, I had them attractively printed in formats identical with the reports of the education survey. There are seven volumes, for we decided on a final volume summarizing the lessons of the other six special reports. And when the printed copies were ready, I arranged a series of Saturday meetings at the City Club where the authors stated their findings and submitted themselves to questions. Very considerable newspaper publicity flowed from these, and the community received a useful lesson about the needs and problems of the people of the city who, after all, spent far more hours of the day in recreation than they spent at work or school.

Cleveland was a city of organizations and for almost every activity or problem it had its reflection in some sort of agency or committee.

As I have indicated, the result of the earliest survey of welfare agencies resulted in the Welfare Federation. In dealing with the recreation survey, I followed this pattern. At meetings of the pertinent people there was developed the Recreation Council which should be supported by the Welfare Federation and should devote itself to the implementation of the recommendations of the survey. Rowland Haynes had made a most favorable impression upon my Committee and he was the choice for the job of secretary of the new Recreation Council. He came to Cleveland permanently and after a few years became the Director of the Welfare Federation, succeeding Sherman Kingsley.

During my first year with the Foundation, I gave considerable thought to what the Foundation might do after the completion of the recreation survey. There was no lack of suggestions, all of which I carefully appraised, and some of which I discussed with Belle Sherwin and others. Some of these were of minor importance and certainly were not of a character to challenge the attention of the community. Some came from matters which momentarily challenged the interest of the public nationally and locally. One of these was a study of teacher training which was suggested to me by Ambrose Suhrie, who was head of what was then known as the Cleveland Normal School. Suhrie was a most ambitious and hard-driving individual who wanted the status and size of his institution to play a larger part in the educational system of the city. There was nothing really challenging in such a survey but I agreed that if Suhrie would get the money from the Board of Education and recommend someone to direct the study, I would give it an independent character by having the Foundation sponsor it. The report was made, an enlarged program was recommended for his school, and the name was changed to the Cleveland College of Education.

I made no special effort to publicize the content of this small study. It dealt with a matter of almost routine procedure for action by the Board of Education and would have inconsequential interest to the people of Cleveland. Its sponsorship by the Foundation was merely to give its recommendations some weight with the Board of Education.

Meanwhile another matter came to my attention which I believed might suffice as a stopgap while my search went on for a really important concern to occupy the attention of the Foundation.

17

What Was on
the Immigrants' Minds

In late 1919 and early 1920, just as I was winding up the Recreation Survey, two political developments sharply challenged the rational, humane concern which had characterized the Americanization movement. These developments turned my mind to the question of whether there was anything the Foundation might do to help.

One of the political developments was the launching by the Soviet Union of a systematic invasion of the Western nations for the purpose of exporting Communist doctrine and methods. . . .

The Soviet inspired and directed campaign of subversion and espionage was well exploited by a press still hungry for news after the glut of the war years. American servicemen were returning in great numbers to their home communities and their excess of patriotism, rapidly being mobilized into units of the American Legion, resulted in several violent clashes with radical groups, mostly in the Western states. One such clash, at Centralia, Washington, growing out of a fight with members of the I.W.W., resulted in serious shooting and some casualties.

This excess of unspent patriotism among so many who remained unemployed after shedding their uniforms had its inevitable impact upon politics at home. . . . Among the candidates for the Democratic nomination for President . . . was A. Mitchell Palmer, Attorney General, who took advantage of the "red scare" to launch official raids on organized groups because of their alleged Communist sympathies, with countless arrests of individuals. His efforts were plentifully aided by vigilant citizens' groups who sated their zest for invading the privacy of their fellow citizens by hunting for alien propaganda.

I found myself agreeing with many of the friends with whom I had been associated in Americanization activities that the hysteria of the "red scare" could do great damage to the ties of understanding we had built up between the native and the foreign born in the city. It seemed to us that the antagonism to radicalism, which people quite naturally associated with immigrants from the Communist-infected countries of Eastern Europe, could seriously impair the structure of confidence so essential to the immigrants' assimilation.

I wondered what the Foundation might do to counter the effects of the hysteria which seemed to threaten even the relatively quiet foreign-born population of Cleveland. It seemed that while I was searching for a large project to occupy our attention, I might try an experiment which had been in my mind for a long time, something which was within the limited means of the Foundation.

It seemed to me that the best way to keep an anti-alien feeling from spreading would be to go directly to a considerable number of immigrant workers in the industries of Cleveland and, through sympathetic questioning, learn something of their attitude toward their adopted country. We would seek to find out what they liked about their new environment; what they did not like; what their attitude was toward their jobs, their employers, their fellow workmen, their home life and such social contacts as they had beyond where they worked and lived; and, above all, their understanding of and attitude toward the American government, local and national, and American politics.

What I hoped would come from such a survey of opinion was a picture, however limited, of the immigrants' problems of adjustment and thus, by communicating such information to the city power structure in industry, government and social life, to promote attitudes and action to correct what was wrong and promote a better relationship all along the line.

We are now in the 1970s and are so accustomed to polling and opinion analysis that my plan will seem the most natural thing to do. But it must be remembered that in 1920 such sampling and interviewing was quite unusual. And I was to discover, from the objection made by Leonard Ayers, that it was frowned upon in academic life.

I remembered that a young economist from Seattle, Carlton Parker, had stirred up a national convention of economists by a paper which called for more examination of the psychological elements in labor relations. In the course of my planning, I went to New York and talked with Walter Lippmann who was then one of the editors of the **New Republic**. He was encouraging and suggested that I get a book recently published in England which, I believe, was called **What's on the Worker's Mind**.

To help enlist the interest of Fred Goff in what I was going to propose to my Committee, I talked with him about my idea. He looked a bit puzzled . . . and I sensed a bit doubtful of the quality of my thinking. He said nothing for a long minute and then left his desk and looked down at the busy street below. "Yes," he said slowly, "let's find out what they think. And then do what we think is good for them."

I am quite sure that this was a concession far greater than I would have heard from most Cleveland businessmen. One of them, a director in Goff's bank and a big employer, had said a year earlier, when I asked the Mayor's War Board for Americanization money, that we ought to make the immigrant worker happy, because if we did not, he would go home to Europe. He did not want that to happen because we might have a shortage of workers and that would raise hell with the unions. I got the money but certainly not for the reason he had in mind when he gave it.

With Belle Sherwin in agreement, I had no trouble winning the approval of the Committee.

To make such a study we needed someone who was experienced in the art of interviewing and who had a command of some of the languages of Eastern Europe. For not only were the Slavs and Hungarians predominant among Cleveland workers, but any trouble with Communism would be more likely to come from that region. Hungary had a Communist government for a while after the war and, of course, the great Communist "threat" was in Russia.

With rare good fortune I had a friend who exactly fitted the requirements. He was a young Hungarian newspaperman, named Joseph Remenyi. He had been employed by the Hungarian newspaper called the **Szabadsàg**. The word means "liberty" but the newspaper, while prosperous, was generally won over to the side which offered the largest sum for political advertising. Peter Witt called it the "sand bag." Remenyi was unhappy working for the paper and eagerly accepted my offer.

He had been born in Pressburg, Czechoslovakia, of Magyar parents and received his education in Budapest, Paris, and Munich. He had an excellent command of the Hungarian language and also most of the various versions of the Slavic. He was a friendly, disarming individual which made him an ideal interviewer. He was also an accomplished student of the literature of Eastern Europe and he later wrote a novel . . . in his native Magyar. After his year with the Cleveland Foundation, he was employed by the Cleveland Trust Company as a business and public relations man among the foreign born. Later he was added to the faculty of Cleveland College as a professor of comparative literature.

In my discussions with him I made sure to determine whether he actually had any political predelictions which might impair his objectivity. I found nothing more than might be found in any lover of human nature and fine literature. He had been in the United States long enough to understand like most of us the weaknesses and strengths of our ways. Fortunately he was singularly free of the ideological baggage which is brought here by so many Eastern Europeans. A strong individualist himself, he was mainly interested in the people he interviewed as individuals with their own special interests, problems and prejudices. He was also free from the cursed habit of generalizing about every particular, which is presented as a substitute for wisdom. He did not try to see the forest. He saw the trees and the leaves and the insects on the leaves and the bark, and the special characteristics of growth which distinguished one tree from another.

In preparing for his interviews, he prepared a lengthy questionnaire which he checked over with my friend Gehlke. With the limited number of interviews, the statistical work was comparatively simple.

Remenyi's method was far from that of a census taker. On his evenings and on Sundays he mingled with the immigrants in their communities. He talked informally with them in his role as a newspaperman in their homes, in coffee houses and saloons (dry), and in the streets. He did not interview anyone at his place of employment. To avoid any hint of formality, he never took notes while conducting an interview. He had a good reporter's memory and the next day he came to my office and wrote down the results. He spent the better part of 1920 on his interviews and on the text of his reflections. This was most helpful to me in my own interpretation. Our aim had been 500 interviews, but we found the final number of usable reports to be 390. They were of assorted nationalities.

Since Remenyi was more familiar with the Hungarian people and their language, the greater number of cases were of that nationality. But there were also Slovaks, Bohemians, Polish, Ukranian, Serbian, and a very few Germans, Croatians, Russians, Rumanians and Bulgarians.

All except a very few were employed in Cleveland's industries. Remenyi had made contact with about a hundred more than these but we rested our analysis upon the 390.

His reports included all the routine facts, nationality, age, date of arrival in the United States, religion, membership in union if any, literacy, marital status and family information. But the more important part of the reports was what the people said about their attitudes and reactions concerning their life in this country. For we were seeking something which was far more important than mere statistical information. We were concerned with these people as individual human beings, each with his own special prejudices, problems, and ideas.

After the reports had been classified and reduced to tabulations, I asked Remenyi to write his own interpretation of what they had said. Then

I studied the individual cases for myself and with some reliance upon Remenyi's summary conclusions, I wrote my own interpretation.

Because of the public interest in Communist influences, my first effort was to deal with that. I could find no evidence in the reports that there had been any systematic process or "apparatus" through which these people had been indoctrinated by agents of international Communism. That sort of thing appeared much later when Lenin had been able to give his whole attention to the international aims of the regime. It is true that a few of the men interviewed had brought Marxist ideas with them and to a limited degree, these individuals, who were mostly the better educated, had talked Communism with their fellow workers. But they were not inspired by any foreign organization and were wholly unsystematic in their contacts. Such radical ideas, which he found among about twenty per cent of our interviewees, had been picked up here and there, from speeches in their communities, from literature they had been given, or what they had read in the newspapers. Above all, we found that wherever these views appeared, the people who expressed them had already formed an unfriendly opinion of their life in America because of resentment arising from experiences in their living and working relations, from real or fancied injustice, from simple homesickness, and disillusionment in what they found in their adopted country. Thus, at that time, the problem of dealing with radicalism was almost entirely a matter of social and economic adjustment.

In short, our little survey confirmed what has been true in every revolution and internal upheaval since civilization came along and kept records. The spark, ignited by the more sensitive and intelligent, finds fuel in the vast majority which, physically, mentally, or both, is unhappy within the environment. The "red scare" of the time I am writing about was unusual only in the influences at work from abroad and the converts here in our midst who had the intelligence and eduation and the malign intentions born of some grudge against our particular society.

I asked myself and I asked Remenyi if this conclusion which we reached could be rooted in a predisposition. For thus our report would be a mere massing of proof behind what we already believed and which my experience in Americanization work had taught me. And so we went over the reports carefully to determine what the real evidence revealed. We were then satisfied in our conclusions and from here on our effort was to portray [through] many quotations from the interviews exactly what, in their contacts with American life, were the roots of their unhappiness.

One outstanding fact which was overwhelmingly supported by the interviews was that **among the illiterate there was not only no radicalism**

but no vestige of any political idea. An illiterate could understand a king, or a governor, or a boss, but he could never envision such a thing as organization within the social order. And the degree of radicalism increased according to the amount of education these people had received.

My own conclusions, which I fully recited in the text of my report, were based upon my examination of the interviews, upon Remenyi's interpretation and several interviews which I had with experienced social and political workers who were themselves of the nationality of some of the people interviewed. I shall set down these conclusions of mine under captions which I used in my long report. [20]

The Scrapping of Craftsmanship

A root cause of unhappiness was the lack of industrial adjustment. A skilled worker abroad came to America. He found no market for his trade, so that being obliged to take some job in the great industrial machine, he no longer respected his work, indeed he could not see his own contribution in any finished product on which numerous others had a hand. The joy of creative craftsmanship was gone. He brooded over his fall in the social order, for we must never forget that a true aristocracy may reside at the point where management leaves off. He was just like innumerable other fellow workers. There was no one to respect him.

The fact that he must perform work which he does not respect led him to think that his employer did not respect him or his skill. He decided that his status could only be regained when all society was overturned.

A Bulgarian shoemaker, not the cobbler who resoles your shoes but the truly skilled craftsman found only in Europe, says, "I was a respected shoemaker in Varna. I hear of America and came. I got a job in a coal mine in West Virginia. There I am put to work with the pick and shovel with hundreds of other laborers. Then I came to Cleveland and still must live and work with common laborers. I don't feel at home. I am going back. I never spoke to an American gentleman. I am inclined to Socialism because I am not satisfied."

Denial of Family Life

A considerable number of the men interviewed seemed to have no cause for complaint except the lack of family ties or unhappy home conditions. Some of those had been separated from their families since 1914. Some had not heard of them. They were drifting from one miserable boarding house to another. Americans should remember, I said in my report, that the life of boarders in a foreign district is the most abnormal state that can be imagined. Accustomed, perhaps, to rural life, they live under crowded urban conditions. Accustomed to the friendly life of a village, they spend their leisure hours in talking with a fellow countryman about the past. If they are normal single men, they live without association with decent respectable girls of their own type. "Single men in barracks," said Kipling, "don't grow up to be plaster saints."

The Impact of Prejudice

Another group seemed to feel that their strangeness, "foreignness," made them marks for sneers and condescension. There was a feeling that America did not welcome them, that a foreigner was not considered equal to an American. A Polish workman said, "Whenever I speak Polish on the street, people look at me as if I were a murderer." Another said, "My friend and I talked loudly in the street and a policeman came by and called us Bolsheviks." Another said, "My girl is eleven years old and goes to an American school. Now she is more prejudiced against foreigners than even American children."

The Barrier of an Alien Language

This should be fairly obvious as a cause of unhappiness. It hardly needs comment. The individual before he learns English is locked in a world without communication, either through speech or the written word. And the illiterate in their own language are the most isolated of all. They find it much more difficult to learn the rudiments of English.

The Rivalry of the Past

In their daydreams, in their waking hours, or the dreams that attend their sleeping hours, the immigrant lived in his native past. In contrast with his unhappy present, these glimpses were glorified. One of the people interviewed told Remenyi that on his days off he had a habit of loafing around the livery stable on another street. "It smells like home," he explained.

The Exploitation of Loneliness

Surrounded by strangeness and tortured by homesickness, the immigrant was an easy prey of a species which has plagued newcomers from colonial days. In the generation we are considering, these birds of prey were members of the immigrant's nationality who had arrived some years before and, equipped with the English language and a superficial sophistication and a familiarity with the tricks which are practiced upon the ignorant and unwary, offered friendship and comradeship to the bewildered newcomer. Too often this seeming friend became the custodian of the immigrant's savings, the seller of dubious insurance and of other items which the immigrant thought he needed. Too often the immigrant lost track of his alleged friend and found himself despoiled. Our Citizens' Bureau cared for many of these people but only in those cases which came to its attention. These exploiters traveled from city to city to escape discovery.

Failure of the Appeal of American Institutions

Independence Day orators would have been surprised, when addressing a group of newly enfranchised, at the number of listeners who took their gaudy tribute to American political institutions with several grains of salt. For these people, who waited several years to win their citizenship, were quite familiar with American life. Among those who came later, and are removed several years from the crown of naturalization, the distrust of American institutions was already a reality.

The interviews we studied revealed that there were many who could see no connection between the claims and the reality of American institutions of government. And of all Americans for whom the immigrant reserved his greatest contempt was the American politician. We Americans should awaken to the bitter truth that it is too often our more unseemly characteristics that the newcomer notices before he realizes that we are not all cast in the same mold.

Disenchantment

The overall conclusion which I reached after an examination of the material gathered by Remenyi was a story of disenchantment. Busy with the prosperity that the country had enjoyed in the past two or three decades, before and after the Wilson recession in his first year, and with the excitement which attended the war, Americans had forgotten the great additions to our population which every ship from Europe brought to our ports. The labors of our American workers which I have described was only scratching the surface of the problem. Granted that the stories of the promise of American life which had reached those countries of Eastern Europe and had induced the great emigration had been overstated, the reality of our life in America was not what we had been taught in our schools. The fact that some of these immigrants, mostly the better educated and the skilled, had turned radical was not the real problem. It was the failure of the promise of American life when the reality was faced.

Before I had finished my report of the immigrant study in mid-1920, the "red scare" had begun to fade as an issue. Palmer had failed to get the Democratic nomination and, as the campaign proceeded to the Harding landslide, it became evident that we were moving toward a period when a wearied public would show little interest in reform. I completed my report but did not show it to the Foundation Committee, for by this time my whole attention needed to be concentrated on the preparation for the vastly more pretentious survey of criminal justice. So the report and the materials upon which it was based were laid aside until more than two years later.

At that time when I had already been officially appointed to the Columbia faculty and my resignation at the Foundation was imminent, I brought the immigrant study to the attention of the Committee and made its results public with certain consequences which I shall describe in a later chapter.

18
The Cleveland Crime Survey

In the summer of 1919 as I was approaching the end of my thirty-third year, I was elected Director of the Cleveland Foundation. I was old enough and had lived long enough to have made the acquaintance of a considerable number of the leading citizens of the city and had identified myself with several rather important community affairs. But as I look back at the Committee's decision to hire me, I wonder if my state of maturity justified the risk the members were taking with the potentially important institution for which they were responsible.

While the four men on the Committee, Williamson, McBride, Fitz-simmons and Swasey, were important and well known members of the community, the truth is that Belle Sherwin was such a dominant and prestigious figure in that phase of the city which was concerned with humanitarian causes, and her family name was so important in Cleveland and throughout the nation, [that] the male members placed complete faith in her judgment of my capacities and judgment.

The Foundation at that moment was not an active institution with policies well fixed and with a substantial body of public prestige behind it. For Burns' indiscretion and Goff's ungoverned temper had dealt it a crippling blow, and the memory of the sensational stuff that had been printed about the row had not died out in the public mind.

Obviously the job I faced was to present the image of the Foundation to the city in such a favorable light that the past would be forgotten, or, if remembered, forgiven. This was a formidable job for an assistant professor for the ink was scarcely dry on the signature of Nicholas Murray Butler on my Ph.D. diploma.[21]

However, I took up my responsibility with the self-confidence which had characterized my behavior in previous turns of fortune. This time, however, I was more aware of the risks involved and I decided to take plenty of time before deciding on the next major Foundation project. The overhaul of the schools several years before had been an ambitious undertaking, but the direction it took was fairly obvious for the system was reeking with inefficiency and obsolescence. The recreation survey really involved nothing about which there could be more than one opinion. Burns' adventure into prostitution was totally unnecessary.

I wanted time to assess all the considerations involved in any new project which was large enough and sufficiently interesting to the public to bring the Foundation back into the headlines, and constructive enough to win the support of the more responsible people of the community.

I took some time in winding up and publicizing the recreation survey and fending off several proposals to plunge the Foundation into small and unimportant community affairs. Certainly I was convinced that the recreation survey would be the last venture into social uplift, for however important children's playgrounds and settlement houses might be in building character, they were not matters which the whole community would get excited about. And the terribly long drawn out discussion over the school survey, which had been directed by an uninspiring Dr. Ayers, was about all that the community could stand for a long time to come. I shared much of the feeling said to be expressed by Lord Melbourne, "I am tired of hearing about education. I am tired of talking about education. I am tired of being educated."

I realized that the Foundation must do something sufficiently interesting to excite the minds and emotions of the whole community and sufficiently comprehensive to dominate the news for a considerable number of months, and sufficiently constructive to be of lasting benefit to the city.

A clue to the answer came when my friend Charles Elmer Gehlke, who taught sociology and statistics at Reserve, told me one day that the Foundation might make a major study of delinquency, meaning juvenile delinquency. This led to an answer to my quest, for my mind immediately moved beyond juvenile delinquency to the broader field of crime, police, prosecution, the courts, and law enforcement generally. The subject fascinated me in part because of my earlier interest in studying law, and because of the research I had conducted in writing my essay on the Cleveland Municipal Court. Also, through Levine, I had measurably kept informed about the courts and other related matters in the years since 1913. Above all, I realized that crime and the law were subjects which were sure means of attracting public attention. The newspapers had learned that long ago.

The most important reason that this subject appealed to me was the dreadful conditions which had prevailed in Cleveland's agencies for law enforcement during the past three years. [22]

I realized that if I got the Foundation into the cockpit of law enforcement, we simply must succeed. There had already been at least three
efforts to do something about the mess and nothing had resulted. In approaching the decision provoked by Gehlke's suggestion, my feelings must
have been dominated by considerations which my hero Edmund Burke had
put into a famous passage long ago and which Professor Massotti had
quoted in what he wrote about the Cleveland survey:

It is an undertaking of some delicacy to examine into the causes of
public disorders. If a man happens not to succeed in such an inquiry,
he will be thought weak and visionary; if he touches a true grievance,
there is a danger that he will come near to persons of weight and
consequence, who will rather be exasperated at the discovery of their
errors, than thankful for the occasion of correcting them. If he should
be obliged to blame the favorites of the people, he will be considered
as a tool of power; if he censures those in power, he will be looked on
as an instrument of faction. But in all exertions of duty, there is
something to be hazarded.

In my case, there was everything about my future to be hazarded.

The situation in Cleveland in the year or two after the Armistice is the
best illustration of a rule in social behavior which has been noted over and
over. It is characteristic of human beings in the mass that while the
capacity for moral indignation is very great, its staying power has rather
short limits. Put in other words, moral indignation is too often followed by a
failure of moral endeavor. The most famous example of this syndrome was
the reaction after President Wilson's idealism to the election of Harding
and the scandals that followed.

Cleveland, after the brilliant Administrations of Johnson and Baker,
elected in 1916 a Republican politician, Harry L. Davis, as Mayor and soon
an assortment of long-quiescent rascals slipped into the public service. The
same laxness affected the county government when a weak county
prosecutor came into office. Another manifestation, which was later noted
in the report of the survey, revealed itself. This was the perversion of the
humanitarian policies of the Johnson years, first into permissiveness and
then into that sort of laxness about crime and delinquency which is used by
crooked officials to mask political mischief. This clearly came out in the
statistics of the survey.

Thus Cleveland suffered a severe breakdown in its public service in the years after 1916, which, because of the war, was not noted until after the Armistice. Prior to 1920 there had been investigations and reports by the Bar Association, the City Council, and at least two grand juries. Also a continuous outcry by the newspapers and numerous appeals to the Mayor, the courts and the Governor. But nothing much was done in the way of reform. Finally, Mayor Davis in early 1920 resigned to run for Governor, and also to escape the intensifying heat from the press and the public. He was succeeded by an equally weak and mediocre man, Law Director William Fitzgerald. It should be noted that the Harding sweep carried in Davis as Governor, although he failed to carry his home county. I watched things closely in 1920, especially since moving the Foundation into the dangerous water of law enforcement was being considered. There was plenty to watch, for the crime statistics kept rising and the newspapers continued their crusade. Then an almost incredible thing happened. The Chief Justice of the Municipal Court, William H. McGannon, was indicted and tried for murder. [23]

While this trial, which had thoroughly aroused the people of Cleveland, was under way, I decided to lay the groundwork for action by the Foundation. I spoke with several lawyer friends about the practical problems that such a survey would involve and the manner in which it might be launched and conducted.

Finally, late in the year, I spoke with Goff. He was, as I have indicated, essentially a reformer. He listened attentively as I unfolded my plan, and after a short time for reflection, he approved. He said that his first step would be to speak with Mayor Fitzgerald and get him to urge the Foundation to make a comprehensive examination of the entire system of law enforcement in the city and county. I had already arranged with the officers of the Bar Association to make a similar request. This they did following Fitzgerald's letter. Several other civic organizations added their requests. In a short time Goff assured me that he would raise the necessary money for such an undertaking and all seemed ready for action by my Committee. I felt sure of strong newspaper support, for the editors and, more important, staff members were friends of mine and I had hinted to them that the Foundation might undertake the survey if we could be assured of strong public support. Moreover, I had long ago secured the approval of the members of my Committee and of Garfield, our Counsel. Everything was ready for an announcement in December, 1920, but because I learned that the McGannon case might be declared a mistrial, I decided to wait. On the last day of December the trial was discontinued because of the disagreement and I decided to ask the Committee to announce its intention to make the survey. This it did on January 4, 1921.

In this announcement, as in the Mayor's letter, the resolution of the Bar Association, and my explanation of our intentions which I gave to the newspapers, a single theme was stressed. Our concern in this survey was not headhunting. Whatever might exist of official misconduct was the job of the appropriate government authorities. The Foundation was not a prosecuting agency and it lacked the powers essential to unearth official wrongdoing. The problem was not individuals, I said repeatedly; it was the system which simply did not do what it was intended to do. The study, we promised, would be by authorities whose competence and objectivity could not be questioned.

Since the Cleveland Bar Association had been intimately involved with the problems of law enforcement, I felt it to be of the utmost importance to keep this professional organization close to our work. Consequently the Foundation announced the formation of an Advisory Committee composed of lawyers with an outstanding attorney as its Chairman. Again, after consultation with the President of the Bar Association, we invited Amos Burt Thompson to serve and he accepted. Thereafter, we kept him close to the operation, meeting with the Committee throughout. Thompson was a member of the firm of Thompson, Hine and Flory, which in the legal profession occupied a middle ground between the majority of personal injury lawyers and the big firms representing large corporate clients.

Thompson was a Vermonter who spoke in the peculiar idiom of his native state. He was an independent in every one of life's relations. Keenly concerned with the integrity of the government's services, he was shocked and saddened by the deterioration he had seen in the courts and was willing to give us as much of his time as was demanded. He probably kept as close to every aspect of the survey as anyone on my Committee, and he was always helpful with his vigorous comments. Since we had almost continuous luncheon sessions at which Thompson was always present, I well remember over the years his regular order, "Half and half with graham crackers." He lived beyond ninety and was present at the office every day. Years later, possibly in the 1940s, I used to get long letters from him complaining about the practices of some of the banks.

From the time that the survey first came under consideration, I had been mulling over names of possible directors. In line with Foundation policy, established by Goff, there was to be a permanent Director, or executive, working with the Committee in Cleveland. And for each survey someone with a national reputation as an expert usually was brought from outside the city. ... In the case of our Criminal Justice Survey, circumstances demanded a large part of the direction by me. ... [The] general director ... obviously ... had to be a highly respected lawyer, distinguished enough to have the full confidence of the Cleveland Bar and the citizen leaders. The list that I first presented to the Committee had several names which for one reason or another were crossed off, and the final choice was between John H. Wigmore and Roscoe Pound.

My familiarity with Pound's writing came from the writing of my essay on the Cleveland Municipal Court, in which I included a sprinkling of quotations from Pound's article on the administration of justice in the modern city. But I knew enough of Wigmore and of lawyers' opinion of him to prefer him over Pound. Almost every lawyer I consulted preferred Wigmore.

Wigmore, Dean of the Law School of Northwestern University, was best known for his towering masterpiece, **Wigmore on Evidence**. This was beyond doubt the foremost American product of legal scholarship. Lawyers everywhere were familiar with it and judges had written it into the prevailing case law. In my statement to the Committee, I took note of his high qualifications but added that "he lacks tact."

Pound's reputation beyond the Harvard Law School, where he presided as Dean, rested on his legal scholarship, his facility as a writer and his popularity as a speaker at gatherings of lawyers. Wigmore had brought Pound from his native Nebraska to Northwestern as a professor. Later Pound had moved on to Harvard as Dean. Wigmore acknowledged Pound's legal and historical scholarship but strongly disapproved of him as a candidate for the Cleveland assignment. Incidentally, the range of Pound's interests is suggested by the office he held in Nebraska. He was State Botanist.

After several trips to Chicago and much discussion, Wigmore finally ruled himself out. He was needed, he said, to raise money for his Law School.

So I turned to the task of interesting Pound. I developed a great liking for him largely for reasons which I felt sure would make him popular in Cleveland. He was a true son of the Middle West. He never belonged to the New England tradition. He was a salty, good humored man, full of funny stories and exceedingly shrewd. While he had expressed views concerning the administration of justice which were rated liberal, he was as solidly Republican and as conservative as William H. Taft. In my final contacts with him in the 1950s, he had hardened in his opposition to the radical views of the times. One of the oddities for which he was outstanding in

Cambridge was his habit of disdaining an overcoat in the cold New England winter. In 1921, and I assume later, he was completely devoid of teeth. He told me that this was the result of an accident. But his capacity for adaptation prevailed and he had no trouble eating and speaking. He also told me that he owed his prodigious memory to training, for in his younger years he had weak eyes. Despite these handicaps, he lived to be ninety-four. His sister, a distinguished scholar and writer, was the first woman to be elected to the Nebraska Sports Hall of Fame. She was Western Woman's Champion in both tennis and golf. . . .

Pound was most interested in the idea of the survey, for he saw it as a way to confirm his ideas about the problem of law administration in large urban communities. He said he would rather do this than anything he could conceive of but he was afraid that his absence from the Law School would subject him to severe criticism. So he proposed that he accept the nominal directorship of the survey, work on the plans, review the reports, and make a speech in Cleveland launching the survey. He would also contribute one of the individual reports. For the actual management, he suggested that we associate with him as Co-Director Professor Felix Frankfurter who had joined his faculty in 1914. I considered this arrangement far from ideal, especially since in conferring with Frankfurter I found that he would promise only fortnightly trips to Cleveland.

But since it seemed the only way to bring the great prestige of the Harvard Law School behind our undertaking, I recommended the appointments to the Committee. At the same time I made clear that I would have to strengthen my Foundation staff and do a lot of the managing myself.

When the selections were announced, I had my hands full for a time quieting the opposition to Frankfurter. Garfield strongly objected, quoting what Theodore Roosevelt had said about Frankfurter's actions in labor disputes during the war. TR had regarded Frankfurter as an irresponsible radical. But when the Committee accepted my recommendation, Garfield subsided. There was plenty of protest from lawyers and from some businessmen. Some were based upon his radicalism and some, I suspect, on racial grounds. The latter objection had always had a singularly irritating effect upon me, largely because it seems so irrelevant in choosing someone for a purely secular job and partly because I felt such a sense of obligation to Manuel Levine.

I selected a letter from Harold Clark, my old friend on the Americanization Committee, as a suitable occasion to answer at some length these objections to Frankfurter. I argued that Frankfurter's views were no more radical (or liberal) than had been evidenced by the Cleveland electorate at repeated elections; they were, indeed, no more liberal than those of Tom Johnson or Baker or Witt, and that certainly Frankfurter had the qualifications necessary to evaluate the agencies which would be under investigation. Wigmore, who had questioned the suitability of Pound, objected strenuously to Frankfurter in a letter to me. As a matter of policy the selection of the topical divisions of the survey and the prospective authors of the reports was a responsibility of the two directors, but Frankfurter consulted me before inviting any of them. The divisions seemed to be quite logical:

Police. Raymond Fosdick, whose two books on European and American police systems were standard works on the subject, was a lawyer with close relations with the Rockefellers. Subsequently he served as President of the Rockefeller Foundation. He was a brother of Harry Emerson Fosdick, long pastor of Rockefeller's Riverside Church in New York.

Judicial Administration. Reginald Heber Smith was nominal director of this study but the major work in Cleveland was done by a junior in his law firm in Boston, Herbert Ehrmann. Smith had earlier made a survey which was embodied in a book written by him titled **Justice and the Poor**. This was done under a grant from the Carnegie Foundation.

Prosecution. Pound selected Alfred Bettman for this. Bettman had been City Solicitor of Cincinnati and had served for a time as an Assistant U.S. Attorney General. He was assisted by Howard Burns, a brother of Allen Burns and a lawyer in the Newton Baker law firm.

Penal and Correctional Institutions. Burdette Lewis was Commissioner of Corrections in the State of New Jersey. A bit later the directors selected Herman Adler who was State Criminologist of the State of Illinois to make a study which was called, when completed, **Medical Science and Criminal Justice**. Later still, Albert M. Kales was selected to report on **Legal Education in Cleveland**.

Meanwhile I had selected a staff of my own which was housed in my office. We had temporary quarters for the survey directors in a hotel near the courthouse where the out-of-towners had sleeping quarters when they were in town.

Since the statistical work would be a major component in all the reports, I selected Gehlke, who secured a leave at Reserve. He was a tower of strength in the survey and his "mortality tables" were the most strikingly original contribution of the whole investigation. I had him with me in surveys with which I was connected in later years in Missouri, New York, Illinois.

To handle all publications which we issued later and to keep in touch with the press, I was able to get a respected newspaperman named John Love who had been writing a business column for the **Plain Dealer**. My secretary, Helen Chew, who had been my student at Reserve, had an assistant, also my former student.

While I was scrupulous about keeping my hands off the methods used by the people who were responsible for the various divisions of the survey, I kept in close touch. Indeed, since these people were strangers in Cleveland, they were most anxious to have my help. I arranged all the necessary contacts with the officials concerned.

I maintained cordial relations with the volatile Frankfurter during his fortnightly visits to Cleveland. While I realized that he and his surveyors were there to tell the people of Cleveland about their government, I found that Frankfurter needed plenty of guidance about dealing with the people.

In that year of the survey, Frankfurter's age was thirty-nine. Despite his cosmic pretensions, his knowledge of the United States and its people was limited to the Eastern seaboard. Indeed I doubt if he had ever been west of Chicago until he made his trip to Bisbee, Arizona, during a labor crisis during the war. [24] Clearly he felt in Cleveland that he was in a new and strange country.

When the survey was about half finished, he proposed to the Committee that there be a division of the survey which would deal with the influence of the newspapers in the administration of justice. To this suggestion Garfield, Thompson and I objected. We held that since we depended upon the press to publicize the survey and to help bring about the adoption of its recommendations, it would be poor policy to antagonize the newspapers by criticizing them. But after some discussion, the Committee authorized the study and, probably on the recommendation of some of Frankfurter's friends on the **New Republic**, he secured a man named M.K. Wisehart to come to Cleveland and undertake it. I bowed to the decision of the Committee, and delegated my staff member, John Love, to give Wisehart all possible cooperation. [25]

When the Wisehart report was finished and before the Committee for approval, the argument was resumed. This time the opposition argued that not only was it unwise to publicize a criticism of the newspapers, but the report itself was a poor piece of workmanship and unfair in its conclusions. For its thrust was wholly negative. It gave the press no credit for developing the public opinion which made the survey possible.

There was a long and heated discussion in a Committee meeting in which Miss Sherwin defended the report and favored its publication. Frankfurter was present and when we left and returned to my office, our talk became highly personal. He said, obviously in a state of great irritation, "I am getting tired of educating your people out here." I replied with some heat that he was a snob. Other pejorative words were exchanged. The next day he sought aid and comfort from Belle Sherwin, throwing into his approach the sort of flattery which he could use when it served his purpose.

Garfield, Thompson and I sought the opinion of Newton Baker, who replied as follows: "I am satisfied that we ought not to print the Wisehart report as a section of the final report of the survey for two reasons: First, it seems to be inadequate, and, second, we are now at a place in the Cleveland Crime Commission's work where we will need cooperation at every point from the newspapers. This sort of cooperation we can better secure if we do not start out in the attitude of criticism." (Baker, in referring to the Crime Commission, meant the follow-up organization which had already been formed and of which Baker was one of the directors.)

Despite this opinion of Baker, Frankfurter won the day and the Wisehart report was ordered to be printed.

I had the last word, however, for I did not issue the report as a separate document. There was no public meeting to publicize it and I buried it at page 515 in a 700-page comprehensive report. If any of the editors saw it, they were smart enough to keep it out of their newspapers. [26]

Considering the immense area covered by the survey, the reports were completed before the year-end deadline. That this was accomplished was due to the constant reminders which I gave to the authors for expedition, for public opinion is short of breath and moral indignation soon fades. Surveys are all notoriously slow in completion. The survey of Springfield, Illinois, about which Vachel Lindsay wrote a book, was ten years in the making. And an alleged survey of criminal justice in Boston, for which Frankfurter got some money from the Rockefeller Foundation and started some years after his Cleveland experience, was, so far as I know, never finished. We in Cleveland in 1921 could not afford to be leisurely. The first of the reports was given to the public at a meeting on September 13, 1921, and there followed five more at intervals until the next year. We used the City Club Saturday forum meetings for most of these reports. This Club, which I have mentioned from time to time in this story, was a popular institution in Cleveland. It prided itself on the catholicity of its acceptance of all sorts of opinion and the freedom which was allowed the audience to question speakers after their performance. The meetings, generally attended by from 200 to 500, were most lively and were occasionally very spirited indeed.

It seemed wise, however, to have some subsequent meetings by other organizations for discussions of some aspects of the survey. The report on Medical Science and Criminal Justice was released at a meeting of the Academy of Medicine.

At these meetings I had to provide printed copies of the printed report with the author as the speaker. In his detailed account of the survey, Professor Massotti says: "The results of the Survey were not confined to Cleveland. Moley and several of the survey's project directors spoke to professional and reform organizations all over the country. Moley spoke before the Ohio Welfare Council Conference in Toledo, to the 27th Annual Meeting of the National Municipal League in Chicago, before a large city slum symposium in Philadelphia, a meeting of the Louisville Bar Association, and many other civic groups." In Nathaniel Howard's book **Trust for all Time**, a history of the Foundation issued on its 50th birthday, he says that there were sixty-seven speeches made in Cleveland, and twenty-five in other states and cities. I am not sure where he got the statistics but the figures are believable, and I probably made most of the out-of-town appearances.

It seems that, due to the industry of Frankfurter, other speeches were delivered by eminent people. In one newspaper account it was noted that Harlan F. Stone, then Dean of the Columbia Law School, ultimately Chief Justice of the United States, made a speech before the Toronto Bar Association, in which he said that the Foundation survey had blamed the troubles in Cleveland on the "inferior bar" of the city. Also some people attributed the upset in Cleveland which resulted in the adoption of the new city charter and the election of a reform mayor to the survey.

The big book **Criminal Justice in Cleveland**, which was widely distributed to publications for review, [received] a great deal of favorable comment. Frankfurter had it sent to various individuals and newspapers in England where it had a good review in the **Times** of London. Lord Haldane wrote, saying that the reports "would be studied exhaustively in many countries."

John Love practically monopolized an entire issue of the **Survey Graphic**. The report received good reviews in several law school reviews. Dean Stone of Columbia reviewed the survey in the **Harvard Law Review**, especially praising Pound's summary report.

One of the most important contributions of the survey was the pattern it set for the measurement of the competence of law enforcement agencies in other states and cities. Wherever, after this, bar associations or other civic bodies sought to improve law enforcement, the studies they made were patterned after the Cleveland survey. As we shall see later in this narrative, I was associated with several of these.

However, I was not alone in the feeling that by far the most important contribution of the survey was what it did for the Cleveland Foundation. I had literally underlined the importance of the Foundation as one of Cleveland's great institutions. This claim is fully acknowledged in Howard's account, published on the Foundation's half centenary and forty-two years after the survey. I had taken a great risk, not only to my own career but to the Foundation, and had succeeded in escaping the pitfalls on every side.

The survey was in the process of completion when I consulted with various lawyers about some sort of a permanent follow-up organization, a service which might act as the community's eyes and voice in watching the agencies in law enforcement. Here we borrowed an idea from Chicago where its famous Crime Commission had been operating for some years. I interested a brilliant member of one of Cleveland's law firms in serving as chairman of the new organization. At my suggestion he went to Chicago and made a thorough study of the operation of the Crime Commission. When he returned, he drew up the plans for a similar organization in Cleveland. We called it the Cleveland Association for Criminal Justice.

This organization was duly installed with offices near the courthouse. As the first executive director, we selected a former agent in the Department of Justice with a staff which included two individuals who substantially spent their whole time in the felony court. The key to its operation was a card index file of all felony cases to be kept up to date with everything that happened as they passed along the production line. When information seemed necessary, the Association sent questions to the officials concerned. The governing board was a small committee which met with the Chairman and Director every week. The most eminent member of this committee was Mr. Baker. Others were well known lawyers and businessmen. This organization continued its work until the 1950s.

Some readers may wonder why, in this long account of the origins, operation, and results of the Criminal Justice Survey, I have not included at least a summary of its findings and conclusions. Among the reasons for this omission are the following:

1. It is not the purpose of this narrative to produce an anthology of all the writing with which I have been associated. Such an omnibus would be deadly dull as well as useless because so much that was written years ago is dated and specialized.
2. The content of the reports of the survey was not written by me and reflects the views and facts gathered by several specialists. Much of what they found to prevail in Cleveland has changed with the years. Also their conclusions and findings were of conditions prevailing quite generally over the United States which were commented upon in many writings at the time, and since.
3. The large comprehensive volume containing all the reports was widely distributed at the time and must be available in many libraries, especially law libraries. Moreover, in 1922 I wrote a summary of the survey which was published in a single volume which also must be available. Pound's summary report was published in substantially the form in which he wrote it, and it must be among the books of his authorship. Moreover, my two books published in 1928 and 1930, **Politics and Criminal Prosecution** and **Our Criminal Courts**, have many of the findings uncovered in Cleveland. The latter book has just been reprinted for libraries.

The really distinctive things about the surveys I managed in Cleveland were the manner and devices I employed to use them in educating the community and in securing community cooperation in putting the findings into the institutions involved. Also, my job involved the creation and mobilization of public opinion and the use of the city's power structure to get reforms accomplished. In these respects I made a distinct and somewhat original contribution which was quite generally recognized at the time. Indeed, it is what I learned about creating public opinion and in organizing the research of many people that prepared me for the larger assignment I had with Roosevelt ten years later.

Also, the survey was effective as contrasted with the various investigations that had preceded it because I was careful to make it known that we were not criticizing individuals but a system. As I indicated at the time the survey was started, we were not "headhunting."

19

Last Year in Cleveland

The year after the Criminal Justice Survey was completed, which covered 1922 and some more, was one of almost unbroken idleness. Several small writing tasks occupied a part of the time and served to remind my Committee that I was doing something to earn my increased salary. There were several out-of-town trips involving speaking engagements in which I told of the survey and its results. There was a paperback summary of the survey to write and distribute, likewise a monograph summarizing the results of earlier surveys. I also initiated two publications which were supposed to appear annually, a Cleveland social work yearbook and a directory of social and civic agencies. For help on these I retained Professor Gehlke part-time. And in the summer months I spent a good deal of time at the ball park, a habit I developed when I was writing the report on commercial recreation.

More important, there was plenty of time to think about myself, my future, and the future of the Foundation. I felt no compulsion to find another big survey in the realm of local affairs as it seemed to me that Cleveland needed a long rest from self-examination.

Therefore, so far as my future was concerned, it did not rest with the Foundation. Beyond the making of surveys or special investigations, the job of such a Foundation as the one established by Goff would be doling out money to worthy and qualified charities, and generally keeping track of the way the Foundation's money was spent. With increasing bequests coming due and rolling into the treasury of the Foundation, that sort of thing would go on year after year. My days would be occupied with interviews with hopeful donees, hour after hour, day after day, interminably. A horrible prospect of well paid boredom. This surely was not the way I intended to spend the prime years of my life.

I could view the time already spent with the Foundation as well spent. The surveys had captured the interest of the public and the Foundation's destiny was secure as a popular local institution. The Committee's

144

relations with Goff were cordial and while he would not interfere with their important decisions, he would hover over the Foundation's affairs like a loving mother-in-law in the home of a newly married couple. However, I made a guess that so active and vital a spirit as his would not long retain interest in children's nurseries and rest homes.

I was particularly appalled at the prospect of days full of office interviews. One sits there while the visitor tells his story, thinking up ways to pass the buck to somebody else. This occupied a fair part of my time when I served in the government with Roosevelt and it was the least exciting part of that very eventful year.

Beneath and behind my unease that year was a desire to get back to teaching where meeting young people every day is a perpetual challenge to complacency, and the man behind the teacher's desk is enjoying the flattery of a listening, although captive, audience.

In the year and a half after the crime survey there was an additional small cloud on the otherwise bright surface of my life with the Foundation. [With] the end of the war and the mustering out of civilians and other participants, two individuals who were to figure in my calculations were released from positions which they had filled in the War Department with Secretary Baker. They came to Cleveland and took positions made for them by Goff.

One was Ralph Hayes who, as the Secretary of the City Club, had attracted the attention of Baker. Baker called him to Washington to serve as his secretary. Goff, having great confidence in Baker's judgment, took Hayes into his private office as a sort of assistant.

Release from the War Department also made it possible for Goff to call Leonard Ayers to the Cleveland Trust Company as a sort of economic prognosticator, in the belief common to many businessmen that a man with a slide rule can tell you anything you want to know. Ayers and his slide rule had measured education in the Cleveland survey [and] then, working for Secretary Baker, had condensed America's war effort in a small book with all sorts of charts and tables. What next but to portray business trends in a monthly bulletin of the Cleveland Trust Company? I suspect that Goff had another task for Ayers in mind when he brought him to Cleveland. This was to watch things at the Foundation to make sure that the Committee, which had shown such independence in making me Director, was not doing something of which Goff disapproved. At any rate, the Trust Company made Ayers secretary of the Foundation and later a member of the Committee.

Ayers and Hayes were bachelors and lived together.

Allen Burns, whose shoes I was selected to fill, on his various trips to Cleveland, made sure to put me on guard against Ayers. He told me that Ayers had told him in New York that the Committee had mistreated Goff by its independence.

In addition to these evidences that Ayers was a potential critic of my policies after the big survey was my personal feeling toward him. He was one of the coldest human beings I ever had encountered. Hard as I tried to ease our relations, I never could make them cordial. About the only good word I had from him because of the generally acknowledged success of the crime survey was a comment he made to the effect that my judgment of public opinion was excellent. I assumed that he and Hayes had discussed the possibility of Hayes taking over the directorship of the Foundation if for some reason I left. This I determined to prevent at all costs and, as we shall see, I succeeded.

Meanwhile, Ayers' early career as a prophet had a severe jolt. In one of his bulletins he was very bearish about the automobile manufacturing industry. Looking at all the cars on the road and coldly figuring their future years of service, he stated that the car market was "saturated." Nothing could have been more unfortunate because by a change of body styles about 1922 or 1923 the crafty car makers had car owners rushing to the dealers for one of the new models and a boom set in that was to last until the Great Depression.

Like George Gallup, when his political predictions fall on their faces, however, Ayers was unperturbed. The following month he discussed another subject. In his calculations he failed to understand the human element in the car market. Customers seem to be perpetually happy with the wastefulness of their economic management. For despite their old car's serviceability, the owner will trade it in for a new gadget or style change.

I have always believed that part of Belle Sherwin's reasons for wanting me in the Foundation, made in the years after the end of the war, was my professional capacity in the teaching of government. For she was gradually shifting her interest in social welfare to the work of the League of Women Voters. She had risen in that national organization to the point where she was made President in 1924 and to facilitate her operations she moved to Washington. Since I had joined the Foundation she had frequently consulted me about the educational work of the League, and in 1922 I had written at her request a small textbook on American politics and government, and in 1925 I brought out a revised edition. Our relations continued rather close after I went to New York, and in 1923 I directed and lectured at a big educational meeting given by the League at Columbia

University. [27]

In September, George Baer, a judge of the Common Pleas Court, enlisted me as Chairman of the County Grand Jury for the autumn term. I enjoyed the opportunity to have an official position so near the center of the law enforcement system, and the human problems that came before us were fascinating. I had been interested by the great potential of the venerable Grand Jury inquest, powers that have survived from antiquity, for under its legal mandate, its authority could go far beyond the routine responsiblity of bringing in indictments. Some of the ancient language is still preserved in state law, such as the famous words in the prescribed oath of the Foreman, who "shall diligently inquire, and true presentment make of all matters and things . . . touching this present service." In short, it might summon and interrogate under oath almost any public official and make a presentment of what it had learned. I made pretty good use of the the powers, especially in investigating the bad practices of county officials in enforcing prohibition. [28]

At the end of the judicial term in December, the Grand Jury was required by law to inspect the county jail. We found conditions there to be very bad, chiefly because the old courthouse that housed the jail had long outlived its usefulness. The Sheriff, officially the jail keeper, went with me to Judge Baer asking him to call a meeting, and I was able to get Fred Goff to be the main speaker. Goff, ever the reformer, made a spirited speech, calling for a bond issue for a new building. Within a year the bond issue had been carried and the new building was being built.

This proved to be my final contribution to the civic life of Cleveland, for I was to leave within the next year.

It happened that Goff's speech was destined to be his last, for he died in the spring of 1923 at the age of sixty-three.

One morning in December on my way to the courthouse I opened and read a letter from Professor Howard L. McBain at Columbia. I probably stood for some minutes attempting to collect my thoughts amid the crowd of workers hurrying through the snow. I'm afraid that the thoughts I collected were irrelevant for rash emotion quite overwhelmed me. Despite icy December air, birds seemed to be singing on the ledges of the office building below which I stood. And heavenly music came through the barred windows of the bank before me. The theme in my ears was that this message in this little letter solved all my problems. He, without warning, came to rescue me from my doubts and problems in Cleveland. Once more I would be free to do what I loved best of all, teach.

McBain, in his capacity as Chairman of the Department of Public Law, said that the members of the department and Dean Virginia C. Gildersleeve of Barnard College had agreed to recommend me to the Trustees for appointment as Associate Professor of Government. It was a most cordial letter which said that everyone concerned hoped that I would accept. This was especially good to hear for my relations with every member of the department had always been pleasant. It is true that the position was less than a full professorship and the position would be financed in the Barnard budget, but the official appointment was like that of a Professor in Columbia University and the tenure was permanent. Moreover, this appointment would open the door to a career in the one university which I would have preferred above all others.

McBain, in another letter, asked me to visit Columbia in January to meet Dean Gildersleeve and President Butler, and enjoy a reunion with all my friends on the faculty. During that visit I learned more about how the appointment came about. The Dean at Barnard, in keeping with the new status of women in political life, was anxious to establish a department of government in Barnard where only one course had been given over the years, usually by someone whose main job was in Columbia College or the Graduate Faculty. So my main responsibility would be at Barnard for the first year or two. I was not sorry about this arrangement for while I intended ultimately to develop a graduate course, I would be relieved to spend the next year getting reoriented in the routine of teaching. And my success at Reserve in teaching women gave me every confidence about creating interest in government in the college.

The wheels turned at Columbia and my appointment was confirmed in a matter of weeks.

The matter of salary, which hardly concerned me at that time, was briefly discussed with the Dean. It would be $4500 for the first year. This was quite a drop from what I was earning in Cleveland, for I received $7000 from the Foundation and fees for lecturing on Americanization for the State of Ohio of about $2000 more. But we had never permitted our standard of living to control our lives and there were some savings.

For reasons which I shall presently explain, I kept the Columbia appointment secret and private until May of the new year. There were several matters which I hoped to clear up at the Foundation.

One was the final disposition of the study of immigrants. I completed my report and distributed it to the members of my Committee. Also I arranged to deliver a summary of my conclusions at a Saturday luncheon meeting of the City Club. This went well enough and the newspapers gave it good coverage. But when the question of publishing it under the auspices of the Foundation came up, Ayers, who had just been made a member of the Committee, said he had some reservations. His point was that I had generalized from too few samples. This was the typical statistician's gripe. I admitted that I was only partially resting my conclusions upon a statistical count of the interviews. That would have been an absurdity for many reasons: First, who was to say what number of samples would be enough? Also, since the account of the interviews covered so many facts about each interviewee, it would involve something like a crossword puzzle to make a statistical count of the many facts. I explained that my report was an informed opinion, my own, based upon several years study of the immigrants with the help of Remenyi, and my conclusions were presented for the purpose of contributing to a public understanding of a serious community problem. I hardly needed to tell Ayers and the Committee that at least half of the divisions of the Ayers Survey of Education had been the presentation of experienced opinions of the experts he had imported for the purpose.

But when this discussion took place I had already told the Committee of my Columbia appointment and, for reasons that I shall presently explain, Ayers was not really concerned about the "scientific" nature of the immigrant study. His real gripe at the moment was the fact that I had withheld the news of my projected resignation so long because I wanted to eliminate Hayes from directorship of the Foundation. Anyhow I was not interested in publishing the study through the Foundation and an argument with Ayers on that subject would be a waste of breath.

So I proposed that the Committee give the completed report and the supporting documents to me for later publication by a publisher of my choosing. This was agreed to.

It was destined to remain unpublished to this day. After I moved to New York I became so busy with my new responsibilities that doing anything about the immigrant study remained on the back burner year after year. I still believe, as I noted earlier, that it was the finest piece of writing I had ever produced and the subject should still be of interest even though all of the people interviewed are probably dead. Remenyi is dead and no doubt the children and grandchildren of the unhappy and distracted strangers in America have in many cases taken their places in the life of Cleveland and are not concerned about the problems of their forebears.

As I indicate above, I still believe that by delaying the news of my Columbia appointment I frustrated a plan long conceived by Ayers and Hayes to promote the election of the latter as my successor. For considering the prominence he had enjoyed during the war, he was certainly not planning to spend years of his life as a faceless assistant to the President of the Cleveland Trust Company. Something happened at about the time of Goff's death to remove Hayes from Cleveland. He received an offer from Will Hays to join him in the motion picture association and he accepted.

It was quite natural that in leaving a position which had been so congenial and so stimulating that I should want to name my successor. I had two possibilities in mind. One was Leyton Carter, who came to Cleveland some years before, at my invitation, as an instructor in my department at Reserve. Subsequently he had moved into a job with the Civic League. I was very fond of Leyton but I felt that he lacked the drive and imagination that the Foundation needed. So, although he wanted the job, I threw my influence to another friend who had also graduated from Oberlin and had spent some time at Columbia. He was Carlton Matson, a **Plain Dealer** reporter for a while, and later advertising manager of the Cleveland Trust Company. He had also done some writing for me in the recreation survey.

I secured an agreement from a majority of the Foundation Committee that Matson would be appointed when he would be available in the following year. He was appointed in 1924 and served four years. But the boredom of routine work moved him to resign and join the Cleveland **Press** as an editorial writer. Thereupon Carter was appointed Director of the Foundation, where he remained until his death many years later. [29]

When the news of my resignation was announced in May, 1923, there were many heartwarming indications of friendship and congratulations from people I had worked with in Cleveland. Belle Sherwin spoke of my "distinguished service," and Malcolm McBride gave a dinner which was attended by many of the civic leaders and other notable people of the city.

In my farewell speech, I commented on what I believed should be a great future project with which the Foundation should associate itself. I said that Cleveland, in addition to the remarkable record it had made in building civic and social institutions, needed a physical setting appropriate to its distinction. This it lacked because its greatest physical asset had been neglected, its frontage on Lake Erie. While Toronto, Milwaukee and Chicago had made their lakefront beautiful and at the same time useful to people of the city, Cleveland had permitted commercial enterprise to litter the shore of the lake with unsightly docks, buildings, and railroad tracks. The cost of such a tremendous development, I said, should mainly be a charge upon the public purse. But the inspiration to bring it about and the planning and some of the cost might be something to occupy the Foundation for years to come.

This was a dream never to be realized.

20
Return to the Classroom

The sharpness of my recollection of what happened during the first months after my return to Columbia and New York is suffused by the memory of the unhappy emotions I entertained during that time. My final half-year in Cleveland had been in anticipation of attaining what to most teachers is the top of their profession. But the reality proved to be a drastic let-down. Over the perspective of years I can remember with considerable feeling certain of the specific reasons for my unhappiness. These were real and they were not anticipated. But overall, there was the sensation of a great change in all the relations of my life. And that change was not to my liking.

In Cleveland my position as Director of the Cleveland Foundation made me a somewhat notable person in the life of the community. I knew almost everybody who was regarded as a person of consequence and, so far as I could tell, I was well regarded as a useful citizen. My circle of friends was large and included the people I knew at Reserve and others associated in some way with my work downtown.

Beyond Cleveland I had, in the course of my trips promoting the Foundation, enjoyed flattering receptions and accumulated more friends in many of the large cities of the country. Now suddenly in New York I was a nobody, a faceless pedagogue like hundreds of others who made their living in the city's many schools and colleges. At Columbia I was somewhat below the average rank and, beyond the members of my own department, was a stranger in the Faculty Club. I should add in fairness that my colleagues at Barnard were most friendly and, except for the differences in our academic interests, quite congenial.

Curiously, I noted from the first that the brilliant galaxy of famous men in the humanities which I knew when I was a student nine years before was missing. During the years in between, death and retirements had carried away many of them and those who were left and the people who took their places were not inspiring.

151

After consulting with McBain and Dean Gildersleeve at Barnard, I was assigned two sections in beginning American government, one of them at Barnard and the other consisting of boys at Columbia College. The classes numbered about twenty-five and at first glance they were not an inspiring or challenging lot. The girls were strange and I was strange to them, and their concern seemed to be to size up their teacher. The boys, they were called men, of course, seemed to me rather nondescript. They were gabby, not very courteous, and argumentative. From that time forward I never cared for the male undergraduates at Columbia.

I was, however, appreciative of the light schedule of teaching. Undergraduate teachers were mostly assigned nine hours of classroom instruction. Mine was only six, thus giving me time to reorganize my courses and otherwise orient myself.

My arrangements at Barnard were very satisfactory. I was assigned an attractive office in Milbank Hall, which housed all the administrative offices and most of the classrooms I used. The Comptroller at Barnard was a retired physician, [Henry A.] Griffin. He and I enjoyed pleasant relations and, as a mark of friendship, he had the desk and other furnishings he had used in his practice installed in my office. The office was large, centrally located, and easy for visitors to reach. What made it most attractive was that it was warm in the winter and cool in the summer. I used it for many years, even after my promotion, rather than move to the graduate quarters across the street at Columbia. During the 1932 campaign I held most of my small political conferences there and most of Roosevelt's speeches were drafted and dictated there.

In the first year we lived in an apartment in a building similar to every other building on 149th Street, a short steep incline running down from Broadway to Riverside Drive. The next year I found better accommodations near Columbia.

After classes had been meeting for a week or so, I took the opportunity to ... appraise my situation and try to analyze the growing feeling of unhappiness that was creeping over me. The organizational pattern of the university was simple enough. Several educational institutions were included within the university, some of which had a measure of self-government, others none at all. Barnard had its own Board of Trustees, its own budgets, and the Dean had a good deal of independence even in the years when the autocratic Nicholas Murray Butler was President of the university. In recent years the traditional office of Dean at Barnard has been changed to President. The Teachers' College also exercised a great deal of self-government. Details of organization varied in the professional

schools. The graduate part of the university, apart from the graduate
professional schools, was divided into three "faculties": Political Science,
which included all the departments of what are commonly called the
"social sciences"; Pure Science, which is self-explanatory; and
Philosophy, which included the languages and fine arts. The three
graduate faculties had an overall Dean.

My status as an Associate Professor was membership in the
university-wide Department of Public Law and Jurisprudence which extended into Barnard, Columbia College, and the Faculty of Political
Science. Also I was a member of the faculty of Barnard College. But this
gave me the title of "Professor in Columbia University, subject in tenure to
the pleasure of the trustees."

Election to the Faculty of Political Science was a sort of honor
bestowed upon faculty members who taught graduate courses, and I was
told with great seriousness by Thomas Reed Powell that for me that
distinction was "all in the future." I was willing to wait for I was certainly
not ready to give a graduate course and I assumed that promotion to a full
professorship and graduate teaching would come when I was ready. But
Powell's comment made me quite aware of the distinctions which were
observed in the institution. I was, of course, a member of the Barnard
faculty.

As I have indicated, McBain was chairman of the department. He was
strictly a graduate teacher at that time with the title of Eaton Professor of
Municipal Science and Administration. . . . McBain was small and frail and
a Virginian who regarded social distinctions very seriously. But he had a
keen intelligence which I found to be quite devoid of anything in the way of
constructive ideas. He was a strict and efficient administrator and in a few
years he became Dean of the graduate faculties.

Powell taught Constitutional Law and although he was a member of
our department, his course was attended by Law School students and for
that he was accorded a place on the Law School faculty. His teaching as
well as his conversation was totally negative. He called his political
philosophy "futilitarianism." Mostly the discourse in his classes consisted
of dissecting Supreme Court opinions. Never in all the years I knew him did
I hear him utter a constructive idea. In 1937 when he had been a member of
the Harvard Law Faculty for more than a dozen years, he refused to take a
position on the Roosevelt plan for packing the Supreme Court. This I
regarded as a shocking evasion of a responsibility which, as a specialist, he
owed the public. He also had a heavy streak of sadism in his character. He

delighted in humiliating students to whom he had taken a dislike. I got on well with him, however, and when he spent a year at Berkeley, his letters to me were delightful.

The department was sorely shaken by the retirement of John Bassett Moore. And Dunning's course in political theory was sadly missed. Arthur MacMahon, who had been a student when I spent the year 1914-15 there, was an Assistant Professor who still had not finished a thesis for the Ph.D. He was in charge of the classes in government at Columbia College. There were two or three very green instructors helping at Columbia College. So I found the once formidable Department of Public Law quite an emaciated affair, and at that stage in my career I was useful only as a good undergraduate teacher. There had been an effort to bring Charles Merriam of Chicago to Columbia when I came, but he decided to stay where he was. There was, in addition to the people mentioned above, Lindsay Rogers who had joined the faculty in 1921 and taught a graduate course in European governments. He soon took on the character of McBain and Powell, mostly regarding students as annoying impediments to the even and mostly unexciting tenor of faculty life. Rogers and McBain were very close socially and, in the course of the 1920s, collaborated in writing a book about the post-war governments of Europe.

I realize that this appraisal of my closest colleagues is not flattering to them, but I have no alternative but to describe them as I came to know them at the time. I had not realized until I came to live in Columbia what a terrible decline there had been since I saw Columbia as a place of brilliant and constructive scholars before the war. But something in the tradition which made us the unworthy successors of the masters maintained a friendly association with only an occasional flare-up. With McBain especially, one could not become critical, for with all his shortcomings he was a warm friend and as fair an individual as I had known in my years of academic life. There was just something anemic about the place which made me sad rather than angry.

It was Dean Gildersleeve at Barnard whose budget had made room for me, although it was members of the department who made the selection. She was that year in her middle forties and had been Dean for ten years. She was a tall, handsome woman, in whom a certain shyness had been overcome by her projecting a somewhat challenging presence with a sort of explosive voice. In all my years of association with her, which lasted nearly twenty years, I never felt entirely comfortable in her presence. I believe it was said that Gladstone overcame his hesitation about conferring with Queen Victoria by making speeches to her. I found myself doing that with the Dean. I never risked a familiarity with her, although a young man who taught history who came after I did was soon on first-name terms with her. But in building a department of government on a par with the older disciplines such as history, sociology and economics, we had a common interest. I think she was rather proud of the place I had in national politics after 1932, partly because it was in behalf of the Democratic Party and mostly because it showed that Barnard was contributing something to the public service. She was an outspoken Democrat, as was her father who was a judge elected by the Democratic organization. He was also famous as an international champion rifle marksman. Miss Gildersleeve was rather prominent as a leader in women's educational circles. She had been an ardent worker in the women's suffrage movement. And her national prominence reached its climax when Roosevelt appointed her, along with Harold Stassen, a delegate to the 1945 international conference in San Francisco.

Despite our common political interests, I am quite sure that she personally disliked me. This, however, was not exceptional for a great many people in those years resented my activities and views. After I broke with Roosevelt, she liked me even less and would, on our infrequent meetings, omit even the bare amenities. I never knew the reason for her aversion but it was probably the result of gossip mongering which was common in the political life of those times.

On her retirement she was succeeded by Millicent McIntosh, who was most friendly on our occasional meetings, and when I retired in 1953 she signed a glowing tribute to my services as a member of the Barnard faculty.

I found, when I met my class of about twenty-five at Barnard in the fall of 1923, that there had been considerable trouble during the year before because of two or three students from Teachers' College who had secured permission to register in some courses at Barnard. One of these students from Teachers' College was a girl who had been heavily indoctrinated with some of John Dewey's permissive educational philosophy.

She was very quiet during the first weeks but in early November she had her opportunity when I was absent for a trip back to Cleveland. . . .

Since Barnard operated under the honor system, I left a question to be answered in writing to serve as a test. Inasmuch as I had been discussing city government and the relations between New York City and the State of New York, in short, home rule, I asked the class to state the provisions that should be embodied in a state constitutional amendment giving the city home rule. We had been over the subject in class and had discussed all the facts. But the variation from a straight memory test was that my question asked them to put the answer in the form of an amendment to the state constitution. I had often put such questions in tests at Reserve and never experienced any trouble.

When I returned to a meeting of the class after my visit to Cleveland, I was surprised to find that, instead of the customary "blue books" from the members of the class, there was a single page in the form of a petition with the signatures of the class members. It said, in effect, that the members of the class considered the test question "unfair" and that they therefore had declined to respond.

In the class discussion which followed I permitted the Teachers' College girl to do most of the talking, using the time she gladly occupied in her exposition of the Dewey educational philosophy to do some thinking about how to stop a revolution.

When she finished I had a plan to propose. I did not reveal the slightest degree of irritation about the petition and its implied charge of unfairness. I said that I would withdraw the question and cancel out the test. I further stated with all sincerity that I respected the judgment of the class and would not argue. But with tongue in cheek I said seriously that I came to Columbia and Barnard at the request of the authorities because I was an experienced teacher who was supposed to have something important to say about my subject. I may have slipped in the comment that I was not a beginner in the art of pedagogy.

So, I proposed a deal with the students. If they would let me lecture the rest of the term with reasonable chance for interrogation, I would appoint a committee of the class to take careful note of the content and method I used and write a critical report at the end of the term, embodying what they liked and what they did not like. I would take the report as a directive and do my best to conform to it in the next semester. They could hardly reject this offer for they were "stuck" with me for this fall term in any event. So I made my Teachers' College student chairman of the committee of criticism.

In the conduct of the class for the remainder of the term I met the challenge to my capacity as a lecturer. I used every teaching skill I had practiced at Western Reserve, every item of information not in the text, and every bit of personal experience I could to illustrate my points; also a bit of humor where it was appropriate. I also kept my office door open and welcomed conferences with students. And, like a good politician, I turned up at every tea and other social event given by the college. The result was a good report by the committee. The only constructive point it made was that the class liked my personal reminiscences of my life in Cleveland. When the new registrations for the course came in, my enrollment went up from about twenty-five to sixty-five, and we had to have a larger room. The girl who made the trouble dropped out and I presume went back to Teachers' College. I never after had any problems with Barnard students and, despite my depression about the life at Columbia, my life at Barnard was happy. [30]

Despite the pleasant life I found at Barnard, the months before the Christmas holidays were generally unhappy. I experienced a total let-down from the euphoria of the spring and summer. One, quite naturally, was change from the busy public life I had so enjoyed in Cleveland, where I had considerable prominence as an individual and civic leader, to my new role. In short, my ego suffered severe aches and pains.

Another source of unhappiness was the character of my associations at Columbia. McBain, Rogers and Powell were cordial enough but I conceived a revulsion against what seemed the shallowness and futility of their lives.

Luncheons at the Faculty Club consisted of small talk, almost wholly negative and supercilious. I watched the effect on the spirits of some of the young instructors who occasionally sat with their elders at lunch. They hardly dared express a personal idea or tell of a personal experience lest they be made the object of some contemptuous wisecrack or silly joke. I was old enough at that time to keep fairly quiet during these experiences, and learned to speak when spoken to, but I felt something quite alien in this atmosphere.

These members of the department, where presumably I was to spend the rest of my life, seemed totally uninterested in serious research or writing, and evinced nothing but indifference to important political or economic issues. Cynicism was the blue haze which permeated the whole establishment. I began to believe that I was an alien, not only within the small group, which was the limit of my acquaintance, but also in New York and the East. I felt so keenly the absence of the vibrant climate of the Middle West.

Eve and I went to Ohio to stay with various relatives for the holiday season, and in the week after Christmas I attended the annual meeting of the Political Science Association at Columbus. I decided to explore the possibility of getting another job in some Midwestern university, so I talked with Arnold Bennett Hall of Wisconsin, Henry Spencer of Ohio State, and Charles Merriam of the University of Chicago. I told them I did not like the climate I found in New York and that I would welcome an opportunity to move. I had reason to know that due to my expressed availability, I was seriously considered at the University of Michigan and ultimately there came offers from Ohio State and Oberlin, which I declined. There was a very serious offer from the University of Chicago four years later which I shall discuss later, but perhaps it was my good fortune that no offer for my services came at the time of my solicitations.

When we returned to New York after the Christmas holidays, things began to happen which immeasurably helped to dissipate my depression. The students in my courses seemed to be picking up more interest in the mysteries of government. And when the large increase in registration came in, in a week or two, I was immensely cheered. The year before, when I came to New York to look around and be looked at as a prospective member of the faculty, I made a comment to McBain about my success in teaching at the College for Women in Cleveland. Always a cynical fellow, he replied that I would find things quite different at Barnard. He had taught at Wisconsin, he said, before he came to Columbia and found the students there flocking into his courses. But it was quite different when he came to New York. "You will find the students in the East more discriminating," he said. I did not answer but I remained unshaken in my opinion that the young women in New York were no different than the ones at Madison and Cleveland.

And now I had the proof in my enlarged registration for the second semester.

Other than my work at Barnard, which I was beginning to enjoy very much, there was little at Columbia that excited my interest. The only graduate course in party politics that attracted my attention was given by MacMahon and therefore closed to me. (I later inherited it.) And the small talk at the Faculty Club by McBain, Rogers and Powell grew more and more stifling.

So in the new year I decided to expand my activities beyond New York and profit by the reputation I had enjoyed because of the Criminal Justice Survey in Cleveland. A few well placed letters brought me several speaking invitations, of which two or three were in Cleveland. And every trip out of town, and the subtle flattery that these invitations implied, gave my spirits a big boost. As I have already said, the invitation of the Foundation conveyed by Malcolm McBride to return in the summer to my old office was a pleasant prospect.

During that summer in Cleveland I had a letter from a St. Louis lawyer named Arthur Lashly who asked me to meet him in Chicago and talk about a prospective survey of criminal justice which the Missouri Bar Association was planning. I had a talk with Lashly which was the preliminary to an invitation to join him as research director of the survey. This opened what was to be a major series of outside engagements which I shall presently describe, for when the Missouri survey was drawing to a close, Lashly was called to direct a similar survey in Illinois with me as Research Director. This lasted until 1928, and in 1926 I was appointed Research Director of the New York Crime Commission.

The progress I was making in building up a Department of Government at Barnard proceeded rapidly. Four years after my arrival in New York, when a sort of crisis came in my relations with the department at Columbia, I added new and more advanced courses which required the appointment of an instructor.

In my fourth year it was apparent that the department needed still another addition. So I negotiated with the History Department for the transfer of an assistant professor who took over the courses in European governments and international relations. This man, Thomas Peardon, who became my fast friend over the years, was a superb teacher and scholar, although he was content to limit his writing to his doctoral thesis. Later I made a fight to recognize his teaching competence by promotion. Despite the opposition of Rogers, the Dean supported me and he became a permanent member of the department. When I became absorbed in politics, I turned over the chairmanship of the Government Department to him. Ultimately he became Dean of the Faculty.

In 1926 I decided to offer a new course of my own invention. I intended it to be a history of American politics and parties. But noting the success of the famous Billy Phelps with his course on the English novelists rather than the English novel, I used for the first year the title of Political Personalities. This I changed in a year or so to American Political Life. It soon became one of the largest elective courses in the college. When I reduced my teaching to one course, once a week, I kept this course and its title until my retirement in 1953.

In 1926 I was finally permitted by the trio who were running the department at Columbia to offer a graduate course. Presumably this was a step toward admission to the graduate Faculty of Political Science, although that distinction was denied me for four more years. The course I offered was called Public Opinion which was only moderately successful and dropped after a year's trial. I substituted a course on the Administration of Criminal Justice which was very well attended.

In the spring of 1927 I decided that the time had arrived when I was entitled to promotion to a full professorship. I had seen several examples of what was called "freezing" a faculty member at a rank below a full professorship but high enough to merit permanent tenure. In such cases, when for one reason or another the members of his department will not recommend his promotion, he must reconcile himself to an undistinguished teaching career at Columbia or get an appointment at some less prestigious institution at a higher academic rank. The fear that this might happen to me was very real, for the standards of scholarship vary.

Some administrators and department heads are disposed to give little credit for teaching ability and public service, and let the whole decision rest upon printed pages in a book or an article in a reputable academic journal. Also in some cases purely personal likes and dislikes prevail. Beard himself was held up at the Associate Professor's level because, it was rumored, some of the trustees and President Butler distrusted his "radicalism."

I had no idea how McBain and Rogers, who seemed to be running things in our department, would rate my extra-mural activities. I was soon to learn.

My reasons for believing that promotion was due were, I believed, quite ample. I had enjoyed complete success in building up the interest in government at Barnard. I had seen the Missouri Survey completed and published. I was at work on the Illinois Survey and had the appointment on the New York Crime Commission. Moreover, the people at the Law School had appointed me, among several other non-lawyers, to their faculty.

The manner in which this appointment came about was the plan of the Law School Dean to reorganize their curriculum to meet what was conceived in those years to be the need to introduce more economic, sociological and psychological material in the courses. An economics professor, [Herbert C.] Marshall from the University of Chicago, had been employed to preside and advise the law faculty in their work on the curriculum, and there were long meetings every week. I sat in on these and while I learned a great deal from the discussions, I had not contributed many suggestions.

Marshall was quite familiar with my work in the criminal justice surveys and in one of our personal conferences, he suggested my going to Chicago for a year to lecture and discuss with the faculty the substance of the surveys and the methods employed by those who had worked as staff members. I understood quite well what was motivating the Chicago people in wanting my assistance, for the importance of improving law enforcement was growing so fast that a good deal of Foundation money would be attracted to any university which manifested an interst in doing something about it. At any rate, the offer was made and I had the chance to go there for a year after which I believed there would probably be a permanent appointment.

This offer gave me what I needed in asking some assurance from Columbia about my promotion.

McBain had been on leave that half year in Europe and Rogers was acting chairman of the department.

Rogers, when I discussed the Chicago offer with him, told me that there was a rule observed from time immemorial at Columbia that promotions were never made because of an offer from somewhere else. McBain, when he returned from Europe, reminded me of the same rule and mildly chastised me for pressing the matter of my promotion. I was convinced that Rogers and possibly McBain had other reasons than this alleged rule for putting me in my place. I wondered whether there was such a rule, but if there was, I was sure that it was more honored in the breach than in the observance. For in all the institutions I knew the traditional pattern of seeking recognition at home was to be wanted somewhere else. And I determined to give it a test just as I had at Western Reserve some years before.

The Department of Public Law would have to make the recommendation but Dean Gildersleeve would have to provide the money in the Barnard budget. So I turned to her for an opinion. She heartily favored the promotion since I had amply fulfilled her desire to create a Department of Government at Barnard. She told me to speak with President Butler.

As a result of a long conversation with this remarkable man, he said that he would speak to the parties concerned, the department, which meant McBain and Rogers, the people at the Law School, and Gildersleeve, and let me know whether I should stay at Columbia. In a day or two I had a letter from him, saying in part:

Following our conversation of Friday last, I have had the opportunity to consult Dean Gildersleeve, Dean Woodbridge (of the graduate faculties), Dean Jervey (of the Law School) and Professor Rogers, acting chairman of the Committee on Instruction of the Faculty of Political Science. They are all of one mind in expressing satisfaction with your plans of work and in the belief that your new association with the Faculty of Law and its members opens the way to your carrying forward your scientific and scholarly projects to excellent advantage.

We all hope you will permanently throw in your lot with Columbia University, resting on the assurance which the University's traditions and history so amply support, that no earnest and productive scholar in our ranks long fails to gain suitable recognition and reward.

This was exactly what I wanted. I replied that I intended to do exactly as he suggested, to remain at Columbia as an assured member of the family. So I rejected the offer from Chicago.

After this, I decided that to clinch my case for promotion, I would press on with all deliberate speed and produce a book summing up the essence of what the various surveys had revealed about the administration of criminal justice. One of the incidental results of such a production would be "to throw the book" at McBain and Rogers. Although they were not old men — Rogers was four years my junior and McBain only six years my senior — they were obsessed by the academic tradition that academic rank should be accorded only on the basis of publication of a scholarly product in "hard covers" or as articles in scientific or scholarly periodicals. Administrative direction of the researches of a staff did not count in their scale of values.

My first concern was to get the money necessary for the work necessary to the writing of the book I had planned. To that end, I secured a grant of $10,000 from the Columbia portion of the Rockefeller money distributed by the Social Science Research Council. In the summer of 1927 I made an extensive trip, visiting several important cities from coast to coast and in Western Canada. During the next fall and winter I completed a considerable part of the book I planned. Then, since it was running long, I decided to divide the material and make two books, one on the subject of police and prosecution, the other on the criminal courts. The book on prosecution I was able to show the various interested people in the spring of 1928 and with this evidence the promotion was granted. The publication date of **Politics and Criminal Prosecution** was January, 1929. The publication date of **Our Criminal Courts** was July, 1930. The reviews accorded these books were favorable and in some cases quite laudatory. My new title, Professor of Public Law, was agreed to by Gildersleeve and McBain.

I should note in this account of my first seven years at Columbia-Barnard that I was finally admitted to the Faculty of Political Science in 1930.

I should add here also that despite my feelings about the Columbia administration at the time of Beard's resignation, and the differences I had mostly with Rogers, and my depressed feeling about the relative sterility in the Department of Public Law, that in the long range of my active life, Columbia has a substantial and enduring place. I should rather say that

Columbia and Barnard have a place, for the teaching responsibilities there with the young women students was a tremendously happy experience. In my early years in the 1920s I always preferred to have my name associated with Columbia rather than Barnard, perhaps because of my snobbish belief that the name Columbia lent the more prestige. But my love of teaching triumphed and I continued my Government 7-8 course at Barnard for all the years until my retirement in 1953.

I owe a great deal to the policy inaugurated by President Butler and now embedded in the Columbia tradition of permitting faculty members wide latitude in their extra-mural activities. Otherwise, I might have had to choose between politics and later journalism and academic life. Columbia enabled me literally to have the best of two worlds.

21
Sabbatical Interlude

When the year 1930 dawned, I felt that I had reached one of those quiet periods when serious thought must be given to what interests I should pursue for the immediate years ahead. I hated to let circumstances make these decisions for me, although in previous periods in my life that is exactly what happened. And, as it chanced, that is exactly what was to happen then.

I had just passed my forty-third birthday which I had regarded as the gateway to middle age. My academic position was secure for I had received what I believed to be my final promotion. I had spent the better part of a decade specializing in criminal justice. Several important surveys had occupied my time and what talents I had managed to develop, and I had published two books summarizing what I had learned about crime and law enforcement. I realized that I had not exhausted this important subject but I had certainly exhausted my interest in it. I had gained a moderately good reputation in this field but I had realized all along that my fundamental interest was in a broader field of politics. And while I expected to develop a graduate course in contemporary politics, I realized that a good deal of preparation would be necessary, including some experience in practical politics.

The thought occurred to me that I should for a year or so take things easy, go on with my big course at Barnard, do some lecturing outside, and write some political essays. Another factor added to my perplexity as 1930 dawned. I was qualified to have my sabbatical after several years on the faculty. Under the rules, I could take the whole academic year off on half pay or half a year at full pay. I decided to take the latter which stretched from September, 1930, to February, 1931.

It was not an especially happy period for reasons other than indecision about what I proposed to do with the rest of my life. The market crash of the previous fall had not only shaken my nerves, as it had those of practically every other American, but it had cost me most of my remaining

164

savings. This loss was not all in October and November, 1929. I had indeed gained a few dollars then while most others had been losing their shirts. My losses had been steady since 1927, for I had so firmly anticipated a big decline in stock prices that I had been cautiously playing short with continuous losses. I simply did not have the temperament to play the market, and well before the crash I had decided to quit the market entirely and hold only a few remaining securities.

Along with this financial malaise which gave me no comfort, I found myself worried about my health. Our two sons (twins), Malcolm and Raymond, Jr., were, in November 1929, five years old. The welfare of my family, if ill health should incapacitate me, haunted me. Nearly twenty years had passed since my experience with TB, but it is not unusual for former victims of that ailment to worry after several years about a return of the ''bugs.'' At any rate, in 1928 and 1929 I had a bad case of psychological torment about the possibility of a recurrence. However, in 1929 I had finally found a doctor who demonstrated that I had no reason for further worry. What is most important, I had confidence in his judgment. [31]

There were other things at the crossroads in 1930. The great wave of Progressivism which arose out of the decay of Populism at the turn of the century had practically died out in the prosperous years of the 1920s. As I have already demonstrated, some of the ideas which it had generated had been tried and were a part of the business-government order, but some of the political reforms had been tried with indifferent results. At any rate, as a viable movement, it had vanished and now with the great business upset it seemed to me that something new was needed, within, not outside, of the two-party system. Certainly by 1930 it was apparent that the days of the great business boom were ended. It was a year of pause and redirection, and as it happened when the Depression set in, of a lot of reconstruction.

An incident in the previous autumn proved to be interesting in the light of what happened later. A young man named Wayne Morse had appeared at my office and told me that he was enrolling as a graduate student in the Columbia Law School and wanted me to advise him about a subject for his doctoral thesis. He had, after his undergraduate career at the University of Wisconsin, taken a law degree at the University of Minnesota, supporting himself meanwhile by teaching a course in public speaking in the college. He seemed like an ambitious and promising student and, as it happened, I had just the subject for him.

I had secured a small grant from Columbia to make a study of prosecution, specifically to concentrate on the two alternative methods of initiating a prosecution, by indictment or by information filed by the prosecutor. I had a considerable amount of material but had lost interest before finishing the study. During the academic year that followed, I had very pleasant relations with Morse who finished his thesis, took his degree and departed for Oregon where he became Dean of the University Law School at Eugene.

I had several speaking engagements that spring. One was at Cornell, others were at the Universities of Iowa and Minnesota. And sometime during the next year at the University of Oregon where my former student, Wayne Morse, was my host.

A visit later that spring from Samuel May, a political science professor at the University of California at Berkeley, determined what I would be doing during my half year's sabbatical, beginning in September, 1930. He had some money from a foundation and contemplated establishing a sort of institute at Berkeley for the study of public administration. He wanted me to go to Berkeley and help with the job of organization, and I accepted. It would be a pleasant way to spend a few months, the work would not be difficult, and the pay would supplement my modest income from Columbia. Incidentally, this assignment led to many contacts with Earl Warren who was District Attorney at Alameda County with his office in Oakland. He was greatly interested in developing some training work in the Law School at Berkeley where he had graduated only a few years before.

When classes adjourned in May of that year and all arrangements for Berkeley were completed, I felt much in need of a change of scene and some relaxation. So I decided to indulge myself in a short visit to Europe which would be my first. Eve and the boys were spending the summer in Berea, Ohio, and, since they were still short of their sixth birthday, were, we believed, too young for Europe. So I engaged second-class passage on the **Mauretania** for mid-July. When I landed at Cherbourg I went to Geneva where a summer school was in session and my Barnard colleague Tommy Peardon and his wife were spending the summer, he having been engaged as one of the instructors. . . .

The European visit was uneventful except for one rather amusing episode. After a week in Geneva, I decided to visit Munich, Vienna and Budapest. In Munich, which I reached on the first part of my trip, a young man introduced himself in the American Express office. He was a Columbia student, Otto Kinzel, who had seen me when I lectured to one of his classes. He then introduced me to his mother and I introduced them to a young woman, a student at Geneva who had been in the train that morning on her way to the Passion Play at Oberammergau. While we four Americans were having lunch, Mrs. Kinzel made a most extraordinary proposal. It seemed that her husband, who was a music teacher in New York, had been taken ill when they arrived in Madrid at the beginning of

what was to be an automobile tour of Europe. . . . Mrs. Kinzel and Otto
had taken a car, a fine Packard touring model, on this trip to Munich. She
was very anxious to return to Madrid and care for her stricken husband,
but she was puzzled about what to do with Otto and the car. Believing me
to be a responsible Columbia professor, she suggested that I take custody
of Otto and the Packard, go wherever I chose for as long as Mr. Kinzel was
not movable, and enjoy my European vacation with the advantage of this
form of transportation and a chauffeur. He was a good driver and could
speak German and was to be wholly subject to my orders as temporary
parent. With no particular plan of my own, I agreed to make this
arrangement, at least for the trip to Vienna and Budapest and back to
Munich.

"Oh, goody!" said the girl from Geneva, whose name was Virginia.
"May I go along as a passenger?" I had seen enough of her during my
week in Geneva to have a fair appraisal. She was from Seattle,
Washington, and was a student at the University of Washington. She was
extraordinarily cheerful and bouncy and, because of her indulgence in
sweets, a bit on the heavy side. I agreed to include her for the trip provided
she was willing to be subject to my discipline for I knew enough of students
to realize that with two such as these, I would have to exercise pretty tight
control. She wanted to use her ticket to the performance at Oberammergau, however, and we told her we would pick her up there. For some
reason, I had no inclination to visit the Passion Play myself.

So Otto and I met Virginia at Oberammergau and set forth on the
strange journey. We traveled through Linz to Vienna where we had a day
or two, and then Budapest, in my judgment the most beautiful city in
Europe with the Danube and the hill and the castle. But it was desperately
run-down and poor, since it had no sooner started to recover from the war
than the great depression which originated in Vienna had added a crushing
blow. Vienna, too, was only a shadow of what it had been.

Keenly aware of the precautions necessary when one takes two twenty
year olds on a tour through three European capitals and the countryside of
three national jurisdictions, I insisted upon propriety so that at all hotels
and guest houses Otto and I occupied the same room and Virginia had her
room. I was somewhat puzzled about how she got along for she had
brought nothing but an extra shirtwaist and a toothbrush.

They had a wonderful time dancing at the Gypsy places we could
afford in the cities, and singing college songs en route.

But by the time we returned to Munich I had had enough of such a
responsibility and I sent Virginia back to Geneva on the train and Otto on a
tour through Bavaria. Otto, however, found his way back to Geneva where

he had a pleasant time with the students there. The elder Kinzel died in Madrid. All talk which might embarrass me about abducting Virginia was for all time answered by her later marriage to Otto's brother. They settled in New York and I had a very pleasant dinner at their home.

I returned to Geneva for a week and then spent my remaining weeks in Paris and London.

When I returned to the United States in September, I rejoined the family and we traveled by car to Santa Barbara where I had the use of a house owned by a political friend in New York, Mrs. Caspar Whitney. I spent the weekends there. During the week I lived at the Durant Hotel in Berkeley and kept rather irregular office hours at a building close to the library where May had the offices of his planned Department of Administration and his proposed Institute of Criminal Justice.

Progress was slow, for Sammy May had a great many problems about finance and the hiring of personnel. There was considerable opposition to May's plan by some of the professors and deans who were rather dubious of May's talents and the introduction of his practical plans into the pattern of scholarly research, which they conceived to be the purpose of higher education. But I had fruitful discussions with the people at the Law School, with Earl Warren in Oakland, and with Berkeley's Chief of Police, August Vollmer. Chief Vollmer was an extraordinary public official. He was a real student of police science, and had read widely, traveled a good deal, and had introduced many innovations into the department over which he had jurisdiction. It seemed that with Warren heading up the work in judicial and prosecuting administration, and Professor Kidd in the Law School considering criminal law, and Vollmer in police, a very useful and respected training school might be created for law enforcement officers. We prepared a rather elaborate plan which I submitted at the end of my term of service.

22

Seabury, the Reformer

Late in November at Berkeley, I was suddenly confronted with a serious decision, and what seemed at the time a most attractive opportunity for a new adventure in my specialty of law enforcement. A telegram [asking for assistance] arrived from Judge Samuel Seabury in New York, who had been designated by the Appellate Division of the Supreme Court of the First Judicial Department. This means the Boroughs of Manhattan and the Bronx. Dreadful conditions in the Magistrates Courts had been revealed earlier in 1930 by a grand jury report which stirred the Governor to ask the Appellate Division to act. As a result, Judge Seabury was called from retirement and charged to conduct an investigation into the Magistrates Courts "and the magistrates thereof" and to report to the Appellate Division. . . .

The investigation, which had been underway for some months before I received Seabury's telegram, had revealed serious conditions which had resulted in the resignation or removal of a number of magistrates. The procedure for removal was simple. The Appellate Division had general supervision over these lower courts and after the charges were made by Seabury the Court had the power of removal.

Seabury had excellent qualifications for his task. As a considerably younger man, his rise in the court system had been remarkable. He had been a city judge, Supreme Court judge, and judge of the elective Court of Appeals which in New York is the highest tribunal in the state.

During political upheavals in 1912 and 1913, he had presided at the trial of the infamous Police Lieutenant Becker, and as a result of the notice he had received was given the Democratic nomination for Governor in 1914. His loss . . . was largely attributed to knifing by Tammany. [In consequence] he had conceived a lasting hatred of the machine and, having the mind and temperament of a reformer, took on the assignment with a zest that knew no bounds.

After I received his invitation, I replied saying I would come East to

169

confer with him. On the train I sketched out the part of the investigation which I might helpfully contribute, for his purpose was not to ask me to contribute to the unearthing of misconduct but rather to propose reforms in the whole court set-up to prevent these conditions from reappearing. This I was well prepared to do since I had encountered the problem of the lower courts ever since my study of the Cleveland Municipal Court eighteen years before, and had seen the operation of many of them in all the surveys with which I had been connected. I learned from Seabury when I reached New York that the idea of summoning me had come from reading my book **Our Criminal Courts**, a copy of which had been given to him by Basil O'Connor, Roosevelt's law partner. That was one instance where one of my books brought me large returns.

After I conferred with Seabury at his home in New York shortly before Christmas, it was decided that I should return to Berkeley, wind up my work there, and return some time in January to take up my work with Seabury.

I will not describe here the nature of the Seabury investigation, or my part in it. It ran until some time in 1931 and the fat report, the constructive part of which I wrote, was published and submitted to the Appellate Division. A complete description appears in my book **Tribunes of the People**, which was published in 1932 by the Yale University Press. I also wrote an article for Wilbur Cross, editor of the **Yale Review**, and contributed several articles which were published in the New York **Times**.

As soon as Seabury was clear of the investigation of the Magistrates Courts and while the report was being written, charges against the New York County District Attorney were filed on the basis of some facts which came to light in the Magistrates investigation. [Governor Franklin D.] Roosevelt, using what was called the Moreland law, appointed Seabury to investigate and report to the Governor. The District Attorney was a rather elderly former Supreme Court judge named Thomas Crain. He was a completely classical Tammany type, perhaps personally without sin but a subservient tool of the machine. He also was an ostentatious Protestant church attendant. (It was a custom based upon religious and racial considerations that while a Tammany ticket generally had a Catholic candidate for Mayor, the District Attorney should be a Protestant.) Crain's office was incompetent, overstaffed by political appointees, and was quite generally regarded as harboring a certain amount of corruption. Crain himself was far beyond the age when he could give vigorous direction to his heavy responsibility. Moreover, in those days the ties between Tammany, the City Administration and the Archbishop's house on Madison Avenue were very close. Indeed the Archbishop-Cardinal's place of abode was, in political circles, called the "power house."

When Seabury started this new assignment which derived directly from the Governor, he told me to prepare a series of charts and diagrams designed to show the inefficiency of the District Attorney's office in the prosecution of felony cases. This was a procedure which had been developed by Professor Gehlke, first in the Cleveland survey ten years before, and repeated in every survey with which I had any connection since. This time it was unnecessary to have Gehlke do it. I assigned the job to my assistant, Celeste Jedel, and two other former students from Barnard. Then, having assembled the statistics, I had a good draftsman make the charts.

Crain had engaged as his defending lawyer the well known Samuel Untermyer, a redoubtable figure for years in the New York courts. The day when I presented my charts and delivered my testimony and later when Untermyer delivered his defense were lively and newsworthy in the extreme. Untermyer, a veteran of scores of famous court battles, and one of the most flamboyant figures in New York, made every effort to break down my case, but according to the press reports I held my own. In his rebuttal, he employed some magazine man to prepare a set of charts that looked like mine. These were designed to present the record of Crain favorably in comparison with earlier district attorneys. In the course of the duel, we established friendly relations and posed for press photographs. Our show dominated the front pages of the **Times** for three or four days.

It should be noted that to establish gross incompetence sufficient to justify the removal of the District Attorney, two methods of proving the case are available. One is to show by a number of specific cases that the Prosecutor's office had been guilty of malfeasance. The other is what I adopted, which relies upon cold statistical facts. Seabury, having tried both, submitted a report which, while it severely chastised Crain, failed to recommend his removal. I always felt that I had been let down in this verdict.

With the completion of this task and the final report on the Magistrates written and published, my relations with Seabury ended.

He was immediately appointed as chief counsel for a committee usually referred to as the Hofstader Committee because of its sponsor and chairman. The purpose of this committee was to investigate the entire government of the City of New York. This meant that the main objective would be to "get" the Mayor, James J. Walker. Seabury asked me to serve as a staff member but I declined.

My reason for not wanting to be involved in such a hunting expedition was my general appraisal of the political situation and of Seabury in particular. The tremendous publicity and general praise which Seabury had received in his investigations had implanted in his mind the idea that with his anti-Tammany record, he might very well qualify as an attractive candidate for the Democratic Presidential nomination. There was ample historical evidence that opposition to Tammany was the best of all claims for national favor. Consider, as he no doubt did himself, Tilden, Cleveland, Wilson, and to a degree Hughes. A newspaper reporter named Chambers set to work to write what might be interpreted as a campaign biography of Seabury and asked me to write the introduction. For the same reason that I avoided any connection with the new investigation, I declined. About that time, a nephew of Seabury asked me what I thought of "Uncle Sam" as a candidate for President. Therefore, it appeared quite clear what was going to happen in the rest of that year of 1931 and the first months of 1932. After several of the small Tammany fry had been disposed of, Seabury would concentrate on Walker and thus throw the burden on Roosevelt to decide whether to remove him.

The scenario I had anticipated appeared on schedule. After a long and sensational confrontation with Walker on the stand, Seabury presented his charges to the Governor and demanded his removal. Roosevelt set hearings on the charges for after the Democratic Convention, thus blocking the way for Seabury to make his pitch for the nomination and gambling on getting the nomination himself. Later I shall discuss the final disposition of the Walker case. Suffice it to add here that whereas Seabury had, during the time I was with him, been utterly contemptuous of Roosevelt, he changed suddenly to worshipful praise when in July and August it appeared that Roosevelt intended to be very rough with the Mayor.

I am sure that I greatly displeased Seabury when in 1933 he became the chief backer of Fiorello LaGuardia for Mayor, and I chose to join Farley and Flynn in support of an independent Democratic candidate, John V. McKee. My reason for believing that Seabury regarded me as a lost soul for failing to support LaGuardia was something he said about me in one of his speeches. He said that when he employed me in his investigations he thought I was a professor but it turned out, he said, that I was only an assistant professor. This not only shows to what lengths a reformer will go to smite the backslider, but his careless way with his facts.

23
Relations with Albany

My ruminations that winter were broken into by a letter from Albany. There had been serious prison riots in the previous year and wise observers had convinced Governor Roosevelt that something had to be done, not so much about the prisons, but [about] the laws and practices governing the sentencing of the people who had been convicted of crime. I had served for some years as Research Director of the State Crime Commission largely because of my friendship with two of the members who had been appointed by Governor Alfred E. Smith. They were a minority of the Commission which was headed by Senator Caleb Baumes, who a few years before had sponsored the Draconian Baumes laws. Jane Hoey and William Butcher, the two Smith appointees, had very enlightened ideas about crime and sentencing and I shared their views. So, indeed, had Governor Smith.

In one of our sessions, Smith told us that convicted felony offenders should not be sentenced for fixed terms but for indeterminate incarceration. Then their cases should be subject to the determination of a parole board of really distinguished individuals, fully equal to the judges who had pronounced sentence. He regarded the Baumes law, which provided for a life term for people convicted of a fourth offense, as likely to create not only riots in prisons but murderous shootings at the time of arrest by potential fourth offenders.

Miss Hoey and Butcher had convinced Roosevelt of the wisdom of Smith's idea and he consequently appointed a commission of six to revise the parole laws and their administration. Miss Hoey and I were appointed as members of this Parole Commission. Our chairman was Sam Lewisohn, the energetic and public spirited son of the very rich philanthropist who gave great sums to City College. Sam worked us very hard and our report, the main feature of which was a provision for a parole commission of well paid and, we hoped, high grade men, was passed and we were thanked.

Some of my time that spring and early summer was taken by the activities of Louis Howe, who was struggling with the job of Secretary of

173

what was known as the National Crime Commission. This largely paper organization had originated in the crusading spirit of Chester Rowell. ... The letterhead of the National Crime Commission was most impressive. Among the big names among its officers and directors were Charles Evans Hughes, Newton D. Baker, and Governor Roosevelt. However, it had no staff except the frail and unimpressive Louis Howe — no program and not much money. Roosevelt saw making Howe secretary, or perhaps he was assistant secretary, with a salary of $400 a month, as a way to relieve him of the burden of supporting Howe. It also provided Howe with an office in downtown New York from which to carry on his political correspondence in behalf of the Presidential ambitions of FDR.

I was a frequent visitor at Howe's office in the Equitable Building that year. Sometimes he would have large piles of the Governor's stationery, dictating letters constantly, letters to whom, I could never fathom, but always with a purpose. He had two dictating "teams" somewhere in New York City, and handwriting experts who were writing good imitations of the name of Franklin D. Roosevelt. Also there was an assistant secretary in Albany, also dictating and signing endlessly. Once I asked this Albany man to have two photographs of Roosevelt autographed for my two sons. I said that he could sign them himself. But he protested, "Listen, I'll get his nibs to sign them himself. I'd just as soon fool some hick out in Montana, but I wouldn't fool little boys."

Providence knows what commitments, what absurdities, were made in these dictating operations. It seemed to me that if the opposition were smart, it would try and find some of those irresponsibly written letters and embarrass the candidate. But apparently this was never done, and the thousands of letters went far and wide. No doubt today in some benighted states, worthy rustics have on the wall of the parlor a letter written and signed by one of these stooges, the hallowed signature being appealed to as an amulet to protect the owner against warts, bee stings, or athlete's foot.

However, when Howe had a moment to spare from politics, he would talk with me about a program for the National Crime Commission. There were a few rather hastily composed pieces of propaganda issued to the press and signed by one of the luminous names on the letterhead. The one real solid piece of work was a report on payroll robberies which I prepared. It was a discussion of the subject with statistics as to the number of such depredations, the amount of cash stolen, and the casualties involved. The remedy recommended was to pay by check. Howe collected a small sum of money for this plug by some bankers' organization. I collected some return from Howe for this unpaid work by having him up to talk about his political adventures at meetings of my class at Barnard.

EDITOR'S NOTE

With this brief chapter, Moley brings his account to the point where he was about to become head of Roosevelt's famous "Brains Trust." The sequence of events was rapid. He drafted Roosevelt's order removing Sheriff Thomas M. Farley, and prepared a speech on judicial reform, both well received. Moley has written in **After Seven Years** (pp. 6-7) that he thinks the work "illustrated a technique no one else then around Roosevelt possessed. It seemed to help crystallize his own ideas and inclinations, reflect them accurately, extend them where necessary, and present them congruously — in brief, to relieve him of a good deal of personal drudgery." Roosevelt, swamped, and needing to develop national programs, called upon Moley to help assemble a group of advisors. "I moved into a vacuum in his scheme of things," Moley has said. He assembled a small number of Columbia University faculty who submitted memoranda for speech drafts and debated possible courses of action. Their views were both to the left and right of Moley's; some were useful and some were not. By the time of the Democratic Convention a cohesive and effective inner circle had evolved. Beyond it were countless figures called upon for occasional advice. It was this inner group, mostly professors, that newspapers began to call the "Brains Trust."

The Brains Trust, Moley always said, came to an end with the victory at the polls in November, 1932. Nevertheless, Moley continued as coordinator and chief figure among those helping Roosevelt. During the spectacular "Hundred Days" he became renowned for his key role in launching the New Deal. By the fall of 1933 he was back in New York, editing **Today**, but making frequent visits to the White House.

Gradually by 1936, Moley came to a parting of the ways with Roosevelt. Slowly, too, he began to reappraise some of his earlier progressive views. The two chapters that follow illustrate these changes. In "Beard Revisited," Moley, quoting from letters and conversations with his long-time mentor, shows how they came to have second thoughts about both progressivism and Roosevelt. The final chapter is Moley's ultimate appraisal of progressivism, socialism, and the role of business in modern America. It is a look backward at the long intellectual path along which he had come.

24
Beard Revisited

During the 1920s and until 1933 I had scarcely any contacts with Beard. About all of the correspondence I have dating from that period is a note of congratulation in response to a notice I sent out announcing the birth of my twin sons. But with the coming of the Roosevelt Administration and my participation in it, a rather brisk correspondence began which continued until his death in 1948. I am quite astonished at the number of these letters which I have deposited with my other papers in the Hoover Institute at Stanford University.

Many of Beard's letters are in longhand and others are typed by his hand on his old machine in the house in New Milford. His daughter, Miriam, calls my attention to the fact that his reluctance to change typewriter ribbons produced some problems of legibility. . . .

After the campaign of 1932 and [when] I found myself in Washington in the spring of 1933, my contacts with Beard were revived. I must have had some correspondence with him earlier, letters which have been lost, but a note from him in late March indicates the enthusiasm with which he greeted Roosevelt and the early New Deal. He said:

> Mrs. Beard and I wish to express to you our greatest satisfaction in the course thus far pursued by the Administration. To have enlightened and human people in the White House is a privilege to be deeply appreciated. In case there is anything which you think I can do in my capacity as a private citizen, I hope you will call upon me. If you find occasion to command me, pray do so. I like the Far Eastern policy — caution with enlightened cooperation in League deliberations, reserving final judgment.

There was nothing I could suggest at the moment for him to do, but I thanked him cordially. But what he said about the Far Eastern policy of Roosevelt suggested that he would not be so enthusiastic if he knew what I

176

did, for I had already learned enough of Roosevelt's anti-Japanese bias to disturb me. For he had only a month or so before heartily endorsed the hostile policy of Stimson.

While I was unable to suggest anything which Beard could do at that busy moment, I was able to help with one of his concerns. For under date of March 24 he wrote again, asking me to lend a hand in getting his son-in-law, Dr. Albert Vagts of Hamburg, Germany, admitted to the United States as a non-quota immigrant. Sometime before, Dr. Vagts had married Beard's most attractive daughter, Miriam, and the couple were in London awaiting permission to cross to the United States.

Armed with my new authority as Assistant Secretary of State, I was able to facilitate the desired result. Another communication in March had an enclosure in the form of a memorandum on war debts submitted by Professor William Y. Elliott of Harvard.

In 1934 I asked him for an article which had been suggested by Roosevelt himself. I thanked him for his prompt reply and published the article in **Today**.

But in 1935 his early enthusiasm about the Roosevelt policies seemed to ebb. For the most part, his doubts were about international policies, but some concerned national affairs which were in some disarray because of the Supreme Court's rejection of the National Recovery [Administration Codes]. In a letter dated October 18, which I believe was in 1934 (he seldom noted the year), he said that two weak points in the administration were finances and the railroads. "In both fields chaos seems to reign and a blow is likely soon, especially in railroads, unless some policy is adopted soon and followed."

About that time he sent me a memorandum about railroads which I passed on to Roosevelt. Nothing happened in Washington about railroads, incidentally, because the real way to help them was to cut down the number of lines and employment, and the big brotherhoods were adamant against anything which would lose jobs for their members.

In 1935 he returned to the concern about railroads and wrote this:

Glad you are looking into railroads. My dear friend, Max Lowenthal, who is working for Wheeler (Interstate Commerce chairman) simply cannot see anything but soaking the crooks and will not listen to anything constructive. I fear that the Wheeler committee will make another big scandal, add to confusion, and bring nothing constructive to pass. I may be wrong, but that is my fear. In the circumstances I think you should take counsel with the best type of RR man (like

Willard or Ralph Budd) and get something constructive out of the
experience of the last few years. Jesse Jones seems fair enough on
the surface, but he strives to please the boys in trouble. That gets
nowhere.

There is in this comment about Lowenthal and his call for constructive
action a growing impatience with a Harvard legalistic school of young
protégés of Frankfurter and Brandeis which were guided by two fixed
ideas. One was that there was something inherently evil in big business
that needed probing and exposure, and the other that bigness in business
was uneconomical and bad for the country. This reaction of Beard was
precisely my own. And I was close to the scene and on intimate terms with
some of the Brandeis-Frankfurter boys in Washington.

Beard, ideologically, was dead against the trust busting philosophy.
His comment in a letter in November 1935 makes this clear:

Thanks for your note on Felix. You are absolutely right. It is not a
personal matter, but a matter of fundamental interpretation of the
task before us. Brandeis is firmly convinced, as you say, that bigness
is an evil, and that men are little, if not dishonest. This is his right. I
dissent flatly. That is my right too, and implies no reflection on his
character or lack of affection for him personally. I fear that his crowd
will deliver the government over to the big fellows with no restraints
upon their predatory interests. If forty years of trust busting cannot
change Brandeis' mind, I am sure that my arguments can't.

What seems wrong with Beard's reasoning is his assertion that trust
busting would turn the government over to the predatory big fellows. I
don't think he meant exactly that. He meant that a program of anti-trust
prosecution of the type pursued by Taft against the Standard Oil Company
neither regulates nor destroys bigness. And the old concentration of
economic power goes on under different forms.

Thus his attitude, like mine at that time in late 1935, was ripe for
reaction against the anti-business scare which Roosevelt launched in his
message of January 1936.

The fact is that Roosevelt's crusade against big business was all
oratory and no substance and was merely projected to hide the fact that he
had run out of constructive ideas. In the years after 1935 when the Brandeis
boys were so important in national policy, there was no substantial increase
in the number of anti-trust prosecutions by the Department of Justice.

Earlier that year of 1935 (I am not clear about the date on the letter) Beard voiced his fear about our policy in the Far Pacific, especially as it affected our relations with Japan. He wrote:

> As I have often said to you, I consider the foreign implications of our domestic policy and the hazards of a futile and idiotic war in the Far Pacific more important than old age pensions [the Social Security legislation was passed in 1935] and all the rest of it. Next year is a critical year in our history and here is a pamphlet by a naval officer that contains more sense on sea power than all of Mahan's tomes. I wish you would read it, comment on it in **Today** and send the marked copy to President Roosevelt.

In December, 1935 I had a letter from my old professor John Bassett Moore voicing grave apprehension about Roosevelt's belligerent temperament and our partisanship in European affairs. I had copies made and sent them to several people, including Key Pittman, Senate Foreign Relations Chairman, Bob La Follette and Beard.

Beard was constantly putting fundamental issues of freedom above considerations of liberal or Progressive policy. This is shown by his reaction against the action of the La Follettes in dismissing Glenn Frank, President of the University of Wisconsin. He wrote a letter to the **New Republic**, vigorously condemning the action of the La Follette-dominated regents of the university for not consulting the faculty. After reading the letter, I wrote the following to Beard:

> You said in [the letter to the **New Republic**] what a good many of us have been thinking these days, and for once some of our palsy-walsies down in Washington won't be able to say that he who speaks a word against a La Follette is a tool of the interests.
>
> I am pretty disgusted sometimes with the Felixian attitude that those you love can do no wrong, and that to be honest means to choose one side or the other and then raise no whisper of public criticism against it.
>
> I also love Felix and the La Follettes, but I am pretty outraged these days about the obvious distrust with which they greet anything I say in a critical vein.

Behind this letter there was in my mind a growing distrust in Frankfurter's judgment. He was showing such fierce partisanship that he had all but lost any real sense of critical objectivity. I remarked that when I wrote something in my magazine which favored his partisan point of view he commented that it was not only right but beautifully written. And when he happened to read something which went against his point of view, he condemned it not only for rightness and logic but style and syntax.

This comment about Frankfurter will be questioned by people who knew him only as a latter-day Justice of the Supreme Court. My answer to them is that they should have known his narrow partisanship in the years when he was keeping the bonds of affection alive with Roosevelt in anticipation of a Supreme Court appointment. If he had wavered in his partisanship for a moment, he would have lived out his life in the Harvard Law School. I was also at that point in 1935 getting all I could stand from the Frankfurter protégés who were trying to sway the Administration away from its earlier course and down the road to mere business baiting and trust busting.

Beard answered my letter:

> Thanks for your letter on the Wisconsin business. Parties must have discipline, no doubt, but I will be damned before I will tie myself with any sect. My years are too few to be spent in that racket, while the world is sick unto death with fanatical sectarianism.

The Frank dismissal was in 1937 but despite the doubts which Beard had expressed earlier [concerning] Roosevelt's foreign policy, he rushed to his support in the fight over reorganizing the Supreme Court. The struggle in the senate had been going on since February, and on May 20, Roosevelt wrote to Beard commenting upon a radio speech which had been made in March:

> I have just been reading the text of the address you made over the radio on March 29 in favor of the judiciary reform proposal. I have received comments on it from nearly every State of the Union. Its clear statements of fact are refreshing in the emotional atmosphere of the charges that have been made against the proposal, and I want to thank you for the firm public spirit you showed in making it.

Nine days later Beard answered:

> It was good of you to take the trouble to write me about my radio broadcast.... You really should not have added that burden to all the load you are staggering under, but I deeply appreciated your

thoughtfulness and am happy to learn that you found my address in accord with your thought and opinion on the subject.

Whatever may come of your proposal, it will be a landmark in the history of American efforts to preserve the balance of powers in government, as distinguished from judicial supremacy. You have already won the battle, though, although I do not mean that you should surrender the project. This is not "advice" but it may interest you to hear that your friends with whom I have talked hope that you will take a substantial victory rather than lose everything in Congress. I just pass it on. You know your business and the "lay of the land" better than any dairyman in Connecticut.

The suggestion that Roosevelt should accept the "substantial victory" and withdraw the bill came from the belief in May by many people that the new turn in the Supreme Court in certain decisions had indicated a willingness to go along with some of Roosevelt's reforms. This tactic had been engineered by the Chief Justice as a means of denying one of Roosevelt's strongest arguments which was the irreconcilable obstinacy of the old Court. In short, what was interpreted by Beard as a "substantial victory" was the change in the Court's point of view. That interpretation had some validity. However, the strategy of Hughes could be interpreted as killing the alleged reform. Both sides would have been satisfied if the matter had been left there, but Roosevelt declined to heed the advice from Connecticut. He pressed on, Senate Leader Robinson died under the strain, and the bill was killed.

I had opposed the Court bill from the outset and on March 23, 1937, I spent a whole day before the Senate Committee on the Judiciary opposing the bill. I was the first witness for the opposition and at the end of the day I received one of the finest rewards of my life. Senator Borah told me that mine was a "magnificent performance." Of even greater importance, as a treasured compliment, was what Beard said one day in the 1940s when his appraisal of Roosevelt as a statesman had suffered radical amendment. He said, in speaking of the Court fight, "You were right and I was wrong. You knew your man."

When you hear something like this you are too surprised and pleased to answer. But in the years since, my answer might have been that Beard had put his finger right on the spot. Our institutions, which are designed to check, balance and limit authority, are created precisely because it is men who need to be watched. [It is] the evil spirit which everyone carries into the world, the original sin of men who, vested with authority, turn it to their own advantage. I would have opposed court packing by any President, even George Washington, if it could be conceived that he would propose such a "reform."

In addition to my labors for **Newsweek** which consisted of preparing my weekly column and traveling through the country promoting the virtues of the magazine, I worked hard on my book **After Seven Years**. It was finished by the spring of 1939, when it ran serially in the **Saturday Evening Post**. I was very anxious to have the opinion of Beard about the book which we had discussed during its incubation many times. His letter, which unfortunately I have lost, was enthusiastic. In part it said: "This is the best book we have about the outside, inside and underside of politics."

The publisher used this in all his advertising.

After Roosevelt's election, which I regarded not only as a prelude to our participation in the war but [as] the beginning of an avalanche of inflation, I decided to purchase a place in Connecticut as a place for weekends and also as a small hedge against inflation. In fact I called the place The Hedge. It was in the town of Bridgewater, and my house was only five miles distant from Beard's. In the summers that followed from 1941 to 1948 I drove over to visit with him almost every Saturday.

As I have indicated, Beard, as early as 1935, had worried about a possible involvement of the United States in a war in the Far Pacific. But at the same time he looked with apprehension upon the danger which Hitler's rise to power presented to the peace of Europe. He said in 1936 in an article in **Foreign Affairs**:

> Turned in upon themselves, nourishing deep resentments, and lashed to fury by a militant system of education, the German people are conditioned for that day when Hitler, his technicians, and the army are reasonably sure of the prospects in a sudden devastating attack, East or West. To cherish another conception of Hitler's state [of mind] or of the aims of German education, is to cherish a delusion.

But Beard from that time on until Pearl Harbor expressed increasing determination to lift his voice against any intervention in the European struggle. Throughout those years, from 1936 to 1941, his reasons for dreading American embroilment were not only the lives and treasure which our intervention would cost, but the danger to our institutions created by mobilization for war. His predictions about what would happen to our American institutions reached pretty extravagant proportions.

After Pearl Harbor, and during the war years, he supported the war effort. A character in his book, **The Republic**, says, "Personally, I am in favor of pushing the war against Germany, Japan and Italy to a successful conclusion. Whether it is righteous in the eyes of God, I leave to the theologians.''

But his determination to fix the responsibility for our involvement upon the calculations of President Roosevelt never flagged. He laid aside all of his old theory of causation in history and fiercely embraced the concept of individual responsibility.

In appraising his feeling about Roosevelt, we must keep in mind that Beard had lived through the years before our involvement in the First World War when President Wilson had talked peace and neutrality while secretly believing that our entanglement was inevitable. He had seen the tragedy of the peace created at Versailles, the astonishment and lost illusions which came when secret archives were opened after the war. Now he noted that Roosevelt was where Wilson was twenty-five years before, and that in this instance he would, by heroic research, fix responsibility for all time to come.

The result of his labors was embodied in two books which have stirred a tumult of controversy which still continues. Old friends and admirers turned against him but this did not drive him to cover. When I saw him at New Milford a week before his death, he came with me out to my car as I was leaving and said, "I have written two books about that   . And I will write another, if I live."

I have no intention in this book to enter the controversy that developed over Beard's two books. Even if I thought I might contribute to the debate, I simply don't know enough about Beard's evidence, nor do I believe that the evidence so far revealed resolves the question of Roosevelt's responsibility. Beard talked a good deal with me on my visits and on one or two instances I arranged contacts.

I had vigorously opposed Roosevelt's lack of neutrality before Pearl Harbor, both in my columns and in my book **After Seven Years**, but after Pearl Harbor I dropped the subject because there were other matters of greater urgency. My belief is that we can never know the full story of Roosevelt's motives, not only because he carried them with him to the grave but because, from what I knew of his mental habits, I don't believe he knew himself whether he wanted to get us into the war or not. My belief is that he had pursued his unneutral policy because his sympathies were so solidly on the side of the forces opposed to Germany. With this sympathy and with the various acts, like lend-lease, and his definitely unneutral attitude toward Japan, we were so far committed that war was unavoidable. In short, **if** he had wanted war, he would have behaved about as he did behave. I find him grossly at guilt for telling the American people that their sons would not be sent into a foreign war.

I also found great wrong in the casual way in which he initialed the Morgenthau plan at the time of the Quebec conference, the Casablanca declaration on "unconditional surrender," and the concessions at Yalta.

He was also to blame for the incompetent way in which the operations before Pearl Harbor were handled. He can be blamed for the general weakness of his instruments of diplomacy. He had, against warnings, appointed an incompetent Secretary of State in 1933 who compounded his incompetence by his furious jealousy against anyone, like Sumner Welles or Harry Hopkins, whom Roosevelt called to his side to help him serve as his own Secretary of State. There is enough in the record to place a heavy responsibility upon Roosevelt for bringing on the Cold War. But the charge that he connived at our involvement consciously remains a subject of controversy and I prefer to leave it there. . . .

During the war years one of the most important subjects of [my conversations with Beard] was a sort of revision of earlier views we had entertained in our teaching years. I felt this with rather poignant feelings of guilt. And I have often said rather bitterly that I ought to return much of the salary I had received for teaching at Western Reserve and Barnard as a penalty for having conveyed so many ideas that I had rejected in later years as not so. . . .

[As for Beard], writing and publishing the little book, **The Republic**, was a wholesome relief from the passion which consumed him over Roosevelt's part in getting the United States involved. The book, whose dialogue is meant to suggest Plato, was easy to read and had a considerable sale. Beard replied to my letter which I wrote telling him I was using it in my Barnard class, [saying] that it was being used in a number of colleges. Also that it had received good reviews in the Harvard and Columbia law reviews. But what gave him the greatest pleasure was its serialization in **Life** Magazine with a fine picture of the author. I have a print of that picture on the wall of my study where I am writing.

By early 1945 he was hard at work on his book on what he called the United States foreign policy after 1928. He said that before the nomination in 1932, Mr. Hearst published a letter calling on Roosevelt to repudiate the League of Nations publicly (as apparently he had done privately to emissaries of the publisher). Roosevelt, Beard said, had complied in a speech before the New York State Grange a few days after the Hearst letter was published, but Beard was unable to find the speech in the collected works, edited by Samuel Rosenman. (This collection prudently omits many items that might be embarrassing.) The purpose of Beard's letter was to get in touch with James Farley and through his good offices secure a copy of the speech. I was glad to comply.

On a Saturday late in August, 1948, I talked with Beard about a book which I had been thinking about ever since the New Deal experience. It would have a suggestion of Machiavelli's **Prince** about it, in that it would be about the principles of politics presented as a letter to some young man who was looking forward to a career in public affairs and public office. I had made many notes, not only practical ideas but references to the three books of Aristotle which had pertinent ideas, the **Ethics**, the **Politics**, and the **Rhetoric**. I told Beard I wanted his advice about an outline I had made. He was the teacher again and I was the student. He said, "Come back next week and show me the outline."

I spent hours that week sharpening up my outline and doing an introduction.

That Saturday Beard was not at home. I was told that he had been taken to a hospital in New Haven for treatment. When I opened my newspaper a few days later it was announced that he had died.

I had seen no evidences that summer of physical deterioration. He was apparently his old self, a motor of energy, with ideas pouring out, illuminating any subject we touched on. But apparently the passion he had felt over the war and its origins had taken its inexorable toll.

My book on **The Art of Politics** was never written. The notes and outline rest in my files just as they were prepared for that meeting in 1948.

POSTSCRIPT

It was essential to Beard's thesis in his 1948 book about Roosevelt's policy to consider whether and for what reason Roosevelt back in 1933 had adopted what was known as the Stimson Doctrine on Japan's taking over of Manchuria. I had written about that in my **After Seven Years** . . . :

On January 18 [1933, Tugwell and I] spent hours at Roosevelt's 65th Street house explaining . . . why we felt that it was a tragic mistake to underwrite the Hoover-Stimson policy on the Far East. . . . I listened intently, trying to discover from FDR's reaction, what had motivated him.

We might as well have saved our breath. Roosevelt put an end to the discussion by looking up and recalling that his ancestors used to trade with China. "I have always had the deepest sympathy for the Chinese," he said. "How could you expect me not to go along with Stimson on Japan."

That was all. It was so simple, so incredible, there could be no answer.

I had, after the whole Roosevelt policy toward Japan ended in the great tragedy of Pearl Harbor, wondered, not at the irrational, capricious reason he gave that day for agreeing with Stimson, but whether Hoover himself had really approved of Stimson's policy at all. In the 1950s, when I enjoyed a warm friendship with the former President, I asked him whether he had really approved of the hostile attitude of Stimson toward Japanese actions in Manchuria. His answer was negative, "It was like sticking a pin in a rattlesnake."

Here, again, is a wry but tragic commentary on the way foreign policy is made. One President favoring an anti-Japan policy because his ancestors like the Chinese, and another President permitting his Secretary of State to proclaim a policy of which he did not approve. Among the many subjects for disillusionment in ways of governments, this takes high rank.

25
Progressivism:
The Realities and the Illusions

Providence decreed that I should spend the first thirty years of my life, after becoming politically conscious in 1896, in a national climate of active dissent, reform and controversy. This revolt, after a time, took the name of Progressivism. It took many forms and sought many different objectives so for this reason it is difficult to make viable generalizations about it. But everywhere it seemed to take the form of a revolt against the traditional party alignments. It generated a public opinion which held politics to be a more or less dirty business, and politicians a species to live under a dark cloud of suspicion. . . .

My conclusions about the political reforms of Progressivism were [by the 1920s] about what they are now. The leaders of that movement, so far as the political reforms they proposed, except the direct primary, were bound to fall far short of their expectations. For the capacity of the electorate was and is, so far as this age in our history is concerned, far short of the **romantic** notions of the Progressives. It is not true that the cure for the shortcomings of democracy is more democracy. Ignorance and apathy stand as a bar to the assumption of more responsibility in government. There are functions that the sovereign people must delegate and the nearest approach to government ''by the people'' is the republican government of our inheritance. And republican government must operate through the two-party system. Thus direct legislation through the initiative and referendum and elections without political parties is still beyond the capacity of even the best educated electorate which we have.

When I use the word ''romantic'' I am speaking of a concept which perhaps originated in the period of the Enlightenment in France and Germany. In Germany it was called the **aufklarengun**. This movement in effect in France and Germany held that the real human being, unlike the creature that was ridden with superstition and ignorance through most of the centuries before, had infinite capacity for self-development. Translated into American terms, the Progressives believed that he was capable of

187

more intelligence in political affairs than the facts warranted. It was romanticism in both cases.

I was never sympathetic when some progressives turned to socialistic reforms. I revolted against the party's alien influence as manifested in government (mostly city) ownership of public utilities. . . .

My feeling is that American socialists are generally infected with the same weakness that made so many of the political reforms of progressivism fail. It was a **romantic** concept of capabilities, not necessarily potentials, of the average run of adult American humanity as we know it, if we will take a moment to consider. If I were to coin a generality I would say that the vice that grasps the millions is a combination of fuzzy-mindedness, ignorance and apathy.

They seize upon socialism as a way of ending the defects we all see in our society. We all, with some exceptions, see all these defects and probably many more and some of us are trying to do something about them. But the socialist would sweep them all together and dump the whole civilization in which we live on something called government. They never calculate that the government is composed of men and women picked by popular selection from among people like ourselves and given the power to take our liberty and destiny in their imperfect and often polluted hands. No socialist has thought out the problems his system would create because if he ever did he would give up socialism and would in the words of Hamlet "bear the thousand shocks the flesh is heir to." To grasp socialism is like suicide: one transformation and all worries are ended. It is too simple, too simplistic a solution for burdens we were born to bear.

As an individual I come to my final point. The New Deal, as some have said, was an extension of the Progressivism that preceded it by more than thirty years. My answer is a partly qualified No!

I am uniquely qualified to elaborate on that negative answer for I was an active and integral part of the planning in the first Roosevelt term when the New Deal was created and adopted. What happened then and what scraps and pieces the New Deal was made of I have laboriously described in my book **The First New Deal** (1966). Repetition of the details here is out of the question. I will only make a few points to justify my negative answer to the claim made by some that the New Deal was but the culmination and flowering of the Progressive movement.

1. The New Deal was born in the depths of an economic depression which had only a tiny number of previous parallels, such as 1820 and 1893. It was our first responsibility to get out of a depression which had never figured in the years of the Progressive Era except in 1893.

2. It had none of the anti-party tone of Progressivism. It was wholly created by orthodox party activity within the Democratic Party with a President who was at that time a loyal and professed Democrat. And the political management was within the Democratic National Committee, of which Farley, who had been one of the three managers of Roosevelt's fortunes in getting nominated and elected, was Chairman.

3. As I demonstrated at length in my book noted above, the New Deal was not an integrated pattern of reform. It was a patchwork of many reforms drawn from many sources. It was not a monolithic body based on a single philosophy. Indeed some of the reforms clashed with other reforms within the New Deal.

4. While Roosevelt was mastermind because of his status as President, only a part of the reforms adopted by Congress came from him **or from the Brains Trust**, so-called. There was always cooperation from members of Congress and its committees. In fact some important matters were actually created in Congress, or came from outside and even from the business community.

5. Many of the reforms, especially in banking and finance, were latent in the Hoover Administration. The measures taken to solve the banking crisis in 1933 were almost wholly ready for action in the Hoover Administration. They were lifted along with the people who created them, Hoover appointees, and recommended to Congress by Roosevelt. Why Hoover did not recommend them was largely due to the fact that he feared the negative reaction of a hostile House of Representatives.

6. Perhaps the greatest reform which helped many businesses to recover was the Reconstruction Finance Corporation. It was a Hoover proposal in 1931 and masterminded for thirteen years by Jesse Jones, the greatest administrator in the Roosevelt Administration. He was originally appointed by Hoover on the recommendation of John Garner, then Speaker of the House.

7. The great banking reforms were masterminded by Senator Glass, whose cooperation with the White House showed a great deal of independence on the part of Glass. And some of the items in that bill came from enlightened bankers like Fred Goff in Cleveland.

8. The reform, called by Milton Friedman the greatest in the banking field, came from outside the White House entirely. It was the guarantee by the Federal government of small deposits. Jesse Jones pressed it, Garner helped in the parliamentary stage, and Senator Vandenberg presented the bill. It was attached to the Glass bill and passed, although Roosevelt was bitterly opposed to it.

9. Two further reforms passed in 1934 and 1935, respectively, are counted as part of the New Deal. The Securities Exchange bill was passed as a substitute for the Securities Act of 1933 which proved unworkable. Part of the idea came from English legislation, part was drafted by Rayburn's Interstate Commerce Committee with the help of Benjamin Cohen and Thomas Corcoran, protégés of Felix Frankfurter. Also many enlightened bankers from New York helped and a renowned lawyer, Samuel Untermyer.

10. In 1935 the Social Security System was adopted and was also called a New Deal measure. The concept of old-age pensions had been kicking around for years. I know because when in 1913 I was coach of the West High Debating Team, we had a meeting with the team of another Cleveland High School. I forget who won but I remember the research I did with my team on the subject. As Roosevelt told it he got the idea from Lloyd George's reforms in England. He had considerable help from Gerard Swope, President of General Electric, various labor leaders, and social workers.

This, then, is what the New Deal was and how it was created in brief form. It was, as I said in the beginning, **not** an extension of Progressivism. It was a creation of many minds and many ideas. It was a pity that Congress, in passing the Social Security bill, so mangled the original that Roosevelt had in mind. I know, because I wrote Roosevelt's Message to Congress in 1934, and I have dealt with it in my various books and later in dozens of **Newsweek** articles.

The most important and wholesome reforms in the economic world of the early twentieth century came not from laws passed or by propaganda about reforms, but from within the business community itself. As a means of explaining this, I shall, at least in the first part of this explanation, state certain conclusions of mine at the time to which the preceding chapter refers which was in the middle and latter 20s. . . .

At Barnard I succeeded in attracting a large registration in a new course I was offering numbered Government 7-8, "American Political Life," a course which succeeded beyond all my expectations, the registrations numbering the largest elective course in the college. As I developed the lectures I used as material the facts and conclusions which were the fruit of my thinking in the final months in Cleveland. Thus what I shall set down in the next few paragraphs is substantially what I told my class in the years after 1926. The final paragraphs are the more mature and experienced thinking in the half-century since.

I was and am willing to grant that what was happening in the world of business and in the behavior of men of great wealth in the period after the Civil War, which has generally been known as the Gilded Age, spawned William Jennings Bryan, the political evangelist who shook the nation with blasts from his trumpet. He was only too true in his negative attack upon great private wealth and big private business. Private profit and passion of acquisition was the order of the day. Giant capacities and visions were exploiting the land and its people while they were building the foundations of a great industrial nation. No one denies, least of all the virulent critics will deny, that they were strong men and the more perceptive realize that the builders were laying the foundation which makes us so great today.

I cannot take the time and space to go into details. That has been done in many books written either in negative, pejorative terms or apologies or balanced history and biography. But I remember clearly the joy I had in reading some of the books of Lewis Mumford, such as **The Golden Day** and **The Brown Decade**, the first of which came out in 1926. But in my 1920 lectures I gave a strong radical twist to the story and left no messy scandalous stone unturned. What else would you expect of a devoted reader of the **New Republic** and other publications of the kind?

Who were these strong, ruthless men who flourished in the period after the Civil War? I name only a sample. Some were builders of railroads, others were manufacturers, others exploited the natural resources of the earth, while others were bankers and financiers. Jim Hill, Rockefeller, California Big Four, the elder J.P. Morgan, E.H. Harriman, Carnegie, Frick, Rockefeller's partners, and hundreds of others. They flourished most resplendently before, during and later than the 1880s.

Their accumulation of wealth they carelessly left to the spending habits of their wives, families and friends. Something which came to be known as high society became a factor in some of the great cities where these men of wealth made their homes. In this, to be sure, New York City set the pattern and witnessed the full flowering of gaudy nonsensical waste. There was no lack of bitter criticism, not only of these men of business but of the way their surplus was spent.

Foremost among the critics was the embittered son of a Norwegian farmer, Thorstein Veblen. His books, especially that masterpiece of scornful satire, **The Theory of the Leisure Class**, published in 1899, had a sensational success. He had the extraordinary genius of making solid contributions to economic theory while at the same time he excoriated the business establishment, its masters and their family lives.

An extension of his genius was that the jargon he used was pure academese which was no doubt used in such a way as to satirize the scholarly world he lived in. It was remarkable that somewhat later H.L. Mencken, himself capable of highly humorous writing, should have missed the point of Veblen's use of academic jargon, not only to castigate the wealthy establishment but his own colleagues in the various institutions where he held professorships.

Thus there was no lack of bitter criticism in the years before the word Progressive was invented. The Populists had their rivals in vituperation in political radicals elsewhere in the nation, even in the politically stagnant South.

A critical press was coming to maturity which supplemented the political critics. The culmination of this press criticism was the appearance of the yellow press, with Hearst and Pulitzer as leaders. By falsifying the news and inflaming the public, they sometimes claimed credit for thrusting the United States into a war with Spain.

But an interesting phase of the activities of the yellow press was the seeming contradiction in the treatment of the rich and business masters. The editorials and news pages were bristling with attacks upon the business community and the rich, but the society columns wallowed in news about the antics of society. Hearst, above them all, sensed that the average American who hated big business and was jealous of wealth loved the juicy stuff about high society. The antics were watched with intense interest by people probably wishing they could participate.

While I kept myself pretty well informed and knew intimately many important businessmen in Cleveland, I knew in the late 1920s very little about what was happening in the business world.

Nature had had its inexorable way with the masters of the industrial revolution of the three decades after the Civil War. Many were dead, others, old and infirm, were retired. Only a few were still alive and working in 1930. But the business and industrial establishment they created lived on with all the appearance of immortal life.

But as these masters grew old they longed, as indeed most of us yearn, for a certain immortality. If they could not live, at least great benefactions forever bearing their names would assure their perpetuation in the minds of future generations. And they also nourished the thought that when as ghosts they faced judgment before the great white throne, something more tolerable would be given in their sentences to ease their life in some eternal region, maybe a place in Heaven itself! Great institutions for the benefit of humanity would be their defense at the celestial assizes.

The proportion of their surplus wealth spent on the antics of high society was only an infinitely small part of the abundance they were leaving. Thus they rivaled each other in building and endowing great institutions; educational institutions such as the University of Chicago, or great buildings to adorn other existing institutions — hospitals, clinics, research institutions, public libraries — seemed to be the concern of Carnegie and others. Great art galleries filled with the treasures their gold bought in Europe. Then there came the Foundation as a social institute to channel their leavings as the managers decreed. Thus, as the title of a section of my Barnard lectures had it, there were Uses and Misuses of wealth.

But most important, what of the great business institutions they were leaving behind, for these were the sinews of our civilization and their preservation and management meant the vitality and health of our nation. It was the solemn truth when Charles Wilson, President of General Motors, and designee for Secretary of Defense, said to a Congressional committee that "What was good for General Motors is good for the United States." But like many truths it was used for demogogic attacks upon him.

But, to repeat, who was to wield the great sword of Charlemagne? Who was to manage the great institutions shaped by the masters? In a very few cases the direct blood issue of the masters. Sometimes female issue married men who had ability. But mostly the management fell into the hands of a new managerial class, while at the same time the businesses themselves "went public," were incorporated, and taken over by investors who bought shares of stock.

Where did this management class come from? Mostly up from the ranks, sometimes snatched from smaller companies, and sometimes acquired through mergers.

These managers could not help but be endowed with a certain enlightenment denied to or forgotten by the masters. But they were sorely troubled because of the criticism of their companies. They became socially responsible. They stand at the cross-spot where the interests of workers, organized or not, consumers, investors and other interests converge. They try to keep the balance. But any description of the mechanism in which they work and of the managers themselves is beyond the province of this book. I merely want to stress that this managerial class was forming in the years of [the] Progressives. But the Progressives had no part in creating it. It came from within the business world itself.

Epilogue

In the many years after his service to Roosevelt, Moley was proudest not of his role as a presidential adviser or as a political science professor, but rather as a journalist. He took great satisfaction in his editing of **Today** and **Newsweek** and in the political column that he wrote for **Newsweek** for thirty years until he finally retired at eighty-one.

As early as the spring of 1933, he was involved in the planning for **Today** with its backers, Vincent Astor, and Mary Harriman Rumsey and her brother Averell Harriman. In the fall the first issues began to appear, at first a showcase for the New Deal. Moley brought his fame as a Braintruster to the editorship; the rival fledgling **Newsweek** had his picture on the cover of its first number, and he had been on the cover of **Time** that spring. The fame made it possible for him to command unusual talent. A fellow Ohioan, Sherwood Anderson, toured the country writing human interest stories on the local impact of the New Deal. Moley wrote editorials that attracted attention not only because of his reputation but also because of their clarity, cutting through the confusion to the heart of issues. In 1937, the backers of **Today** purchased **Newsweek** and merged **Today** into it.

By 1935, Moley, working in New York both as an editor and a Barnard College and Columbia University professor, was becoming increasingly disturbed by the directions the New Deal was taking. The first phase of the New Deal, focusing upon the National Recovery Administration, with an emphasis upon national planning in cooperation with business, was drawing to a close. Those seeking tighter regulation of business and finance were in the ascendancy, and Moley was uneasy on his visits to the White House to assist Roosevelt in preparing messages. Moley lamented the growing hostility toward business. Yet there was merely a drifting away, not a clear-cut break. Moley's last service was to work on a draft of the 1936 acceptance speech. After that he participated no longer, and by the next spring was in Washington appearing before a Senate committee to testify vehemently against Roosevelt's "court-packing" proposal. In 1939,

Moley made public his opposition to the New Deal in **After Seven Years**. As he himself recognized, it was full of fustian compared with the more contemplative **First New Deal** which he wrote a generation later. Yet the factual accuracy of **After Seven Years** was unassailable; Roosevelt wanted it picked apart, and his advisers were unable to do so.

By the 1940s, Moley had moved firmly into the conservative ideological ranks and had become one of the senior advisers to Republican presidential aspirants. In Chapters 23 and 24 he sets forth much of his ideological reevaluations and his reasons for them. It is interesting to note, as has Otis Graham, who marshals extensive data in **Encore for Reform** (1967), that a large number of old progressives became hostile to the New Deal. That was especially true of the Ohio progressives with their roots in Henry George's single tax proposals and Tom L. Johnson's administrative reform movement. Newton D. Baker and Brand Whitlock, who had been mayor of Toledo, exchanged bitter letters, expressing their abhorrence for the New Deal well before Moley broke with Roosevelt. Moley does not seem ever to have been unfair; he was too careful a scholar, too dedicated to the truth. Nor did he seem to indulge in bitterness. He once remarked at a dinner party that whenever he dreamed of Roosevelt it was that they were making up.

Tax reform ideas, growing out of Henry George's ideas, never lost their validity for Moley. The Lincoln Institute of Land Policy named its headquarters in Cambridge, Massachusetts, in his honor, the Raymond Moley House.

Moley was as staunch a Republican as once he had been a loyal Democrat. He and Herbert Hoover became firm friends. In 1938 he began to urge Republicans to nominate Wendell Willkie, and in 1940, to the dismay of Averell Harriman, backed him in **Newsweek** and campaigned for him. Moley was appalled by the amateurishness of Willkie's campaign, and felt that in the defeat of the "Indiana Lochinvar" the Republican party learned a salutary lesson. In subsequent campaigns, Moley gave some advise and wrote some speech drafts for Thomas E. Dewey and Dwight D. Eisenhower, was a strong backer of Barry Goldwater, and was especially attracted by Richard Nixon. Those intimate with Moley have said that when Nixon after his defeat in California in 1962 moved to New York City, Moley, still full of faith in him, did much to help him make the transition and begin his political comeback.

It was fitting, therefore, that Moley's highest honor came from President Nixon in 1970. At a ceremony in the White House, Nixon bestowed upon him the Medal of Freedom. The citation read, "A man of thought and a man of action, he has not only studied and analyzed the history of our times, but also helped to make it."

Notes

[1] Until 1964 the best and most objective biography of Bryan was John C. Long's **Bryan the Great Commoner**. But in that year there was published by the University of Nebraska Press a monumental study in three volumes [1964-1969] by Paolo E. Coletta of the United States Naval Academy. It is the product of prodigious research. If it is possible ever to say that a biographer has said the last and definitive word about a public figure, these volumes deserve that acclaim. As I shall show in this chapter, the Eastern press, the literati, and the academicians have had their fun and their contempt for Bryan ever since the Scopes trial in Tennessee. H.L. Mencken set the pattern back in the 1920s. But Coletta has done a national service in rescuing the reputation of a man who, however wrongheaded in specifics, set the tone for an epoch in our national life.

[2] Largely because of my Cleveland experience as Director of the Cleveland Foundation and my sympathy for the Georgist cause, I was made advisor of the Lincoln Foundation and am still in 1974 serving in that capacity. I am also the author of a biography of John C. Lincoln. The book is entitled **The American Century of John C. Lincoln**.

[3] A very interesting [study of] Johnson's business life, Michael Massouth, "Tom Loftin Johnson, Engineering Entrepreneur (1869-1900)" [was submitted as a doctoral thesis at Case-Western Reserve University in 1970]. The author discussed his project with me in the course of his research.

[4] In the chapters that follow, especially the one which deals with the Muckrakers, I have not relied entirely upon memory. Because of the importance of the subjects dealt with, I have supplemented memory with rereading some of the material referred to, and some other books and articles which were available as I wrote. However, my newspaper and

magazine reading which I followed despite my growing teaching responsibilities in those years from 1907 to 1910 covered all the subjects to which I refer. A great deal of the material was available to me at that time or a year or two later, such as Johnson's autobiography. And because the writings of the Muckrakers were widely distributed and were cheap, I actually read most of the matter to which I refer.

[5] In 1932 when the Republican New York **Sun** was desperately trying to portray [Franklin D.] Roosevelt's advisors as dangerous radicals, I was accused editorially of having been a Lecturer at the Rand School.

[6] In the years that followed, I saw a great deal of John Morrissey. His partnership of Morrissey, Mahoney and Schofield continued for many years and prospered. In 1964 when I was seventy-eight, I found myself in Denver one evening. A call came to me just as I was preparing for bed, hoping to get a good rest in preparation for a commencement address I was to give the next day, and also because the memory of that first night long ago warned me to be quiet. Morrissey had seen [in the press that I was speaking the next day] and, guessing that I was at the hotel, he called. John must have been two or three years my senior. For some reason he was downtown at his office. He suggested that we meet and have a drink or so, adding, "Let's go out on the town." I replied that the last time I went out on the town with him was fifty-four years ago and tonight I preferred to go to bed early.

[7] I did not see Dr. Sewall again until in 1932 I visited him when I was in Denver with the Roosevelt campaign party. He had returned to his home in Vine Street, but was extraordinarily happy to note my recovery. His mind was clear and he was still doing a bit of writing. He died in 1936 at the age of eighty-one, a marvellous example of longevity considering his long years of ill health.

[8] The day after FDR's nomination in Chicago, the successful candidate asked me to go to Cleveland and encourage Baker to support him in the campaign. It was a strange meeting. Baker seemed terribly depressed. This was surely not because of disappointment that he had not been nominated, for I never doubted his lack of interest in the efforts to get the nomination for him. I interpreted his depression to be a profoundly felt distrust in the man Roosevelt. Like some of the other elders in the Wilson Administration, such as Carter Glass, there was distaste in the Cabinet for

the young Assistant Secretary of the Navy from New York. They considered him a shallow opportunist and something of a playboy. Baker certainly shared that opinion.

I have learned in the years since, from close associates of Baker in Cleveland, that one reason for Baker's reluctance to seek the nomination was the state of his health. He had suffered slight heart attacks before 1932, and in 1937 another carried him away. I feel sure that he was advised by medical authority that to seek the Presidency might well shorten his life, and that if he were elected he would not have lived through the first term. In the relative quiet of private life, he lived only five years after 1932. He died in December, 1937.

[9] Seattle: University of Washington Press, 1962.

[10] E.R.A. Seligman, **The Economic Interpretation of History** (New York: Columbia University Press, 1902), p. 126.

[11] In 1913 when the Beard book came out, Albert Bushnell Hart of Harvard, revered among the older historians, was quoted as saying that Beard's book was "little short of indecent." When I read this, I was reminded that the high school in Cleveland which Hart had attended as a boy was West High where I was teaching. In discussing Hart's statement with a very old assistant principal who had been there when Hart was a student, she characterized the man who was to be a beacon light at Harvard as that miserable little Albert Hart.

[12] Coudert was the head of a very old and prominent law firm with considerable business in France. The firm had been founded by Coudert's father who was born in New York "of French parentage" in 1833. The elder Coudert was entrusted by President Cleveland with important diplomatic tasks and at one time was offered the office of Secretary of the Treasury. Coudert III, whom I knew well, served in the House of Representatives from New York's Seventeenth District for several terms and was succeeded by John V. Lindsay.

Apparently there was a very cozy relationship in those days between Butler and his trustees, the latter running to "Murray," as Butler was known to his intimates, with all sorts of gossip about the University. Some time in the 1930s, after my distressing experience at the London Conference in the summer of 1933, I had a telephone call from Butler, asking me to stop by his office. He said, courteously enough, after greeting me, that "one or two" trustees had told him that the story was going around "down town" that while I was in London on the President's business, I had made some indiscreet remarks to a French reporter which had gone back to the French Foreign Office. I answered that if he wanted to listen, I would tell him several much worse stories about me which were going around in the "whispering gallery" called Wall Street, and that they were just as false as the one he heard from the trustee or trustees. He laughed and said that it all sounded to him "like E. Phillips Oppenheim" and that he would so report to the trustees in question. It all seemed to me like the cackling of old men and I thought no more about it.

[13] The irony of the whole thing is in the subsequent career of Fraser. After getting the sack at Columbia, he enlisted and was immediately given a responsible position in the Judge Advocate General's office. After the war he became President of the International Bank of Settlements and finally President of the First National Bank of New York City.

[14] It is interesting to note that in Beard's class in politics which I attended in 1914 there was also enrolled the daughter of Adolph Ochs, owner of the **Times**. Her name was Iphigene and she married Arthur Sulzberger who succeeded his father-in-law as President and Publisher of the **Times**. She has in the years since been a strong but unseen influence in shaping **Times** policy. Indeed, it has been reported that in the controversy within the **Times** family in 1960 about the endorsement of a presidential candidate, Mrs. Sulzberger threw her weight to John F. Kennedy over Richard Nixon. Perhaps the long shadow of Beard had something to do with that decision.

[15] In 1942 when I was the guest speaker at some function in Los Angeles, I was the luncheon companion of Dykstra. In discussing old times, I referred to the time twenty-four years before when his telegram from Kansas brought me a promotion at Western Reserve. He suggested that we make history repeat itself. He noted that the new branch of the University of California at Santa Barbara was looking for a Chancellor and he said that from his present position he might get in a word to the Regents that I might be a suitable choice. I assured him that I had no interest in and no qualifications for an administrative position, however splendiferous, that writing for **Newsweek** completely satisfied me. "There are some situations that we can't live over," I added.

[16] This is quoted in a book about the Cleveland Foundation called **Trust**

for all Time by Nathaniel R. Howard, which was issued on the 50th Anniversary of the Foundation.

[17] From the beginning the actual authority of the Foundation was known as the Committee, although it may have been in the resolution creating the Foundation designated as the "Distributing" Committee. This designation was apparently carried through its subsequent history. When I became Director I dropped the title which seems to have been used by Burns, Survey Director. In the publications of the Ayers Survey of the Schools, the Committee bears the name, "The Survey Committee of the Cleveland Foundation." In my time the Committee, being the people who were appointed by the public officials and the Trust Company with authority to distribute funds, was the effective authority of the Foundation and I was simply Director of the Foundation, not director for the Committee.

In 1962, when Howard's book appeared, there had been 180 similar community trusts established in the United States. Thus the idea born in Cleveland had become a standard form of philanthropic giving over the nation. Mr. Howard estimated the assets of those community trusts to be about 423 million dollars. The Cleveland Foundation was the largest of these with assets of 65 million dollars. Its annual distribution was in excess of two million. Since then it has been estimated that the Cleveland Foundation's assets have exceeded $100 million.

[18] Davis was an amiable politician who came of a family long engaged as employees of the big steel mills on the south side of town. His election over the formidable Peter Witt was interpreted by most people I know as a reaction from the high tensions of virtue which had characterized the Johnson era. Under Davis the city settled down to the comfortable misgovernment and corruption it had enjoyed before Tom L. Johnson came in 1901. With the charming but mediocre Davis at the head to beguile the public, the real political machinery was managed by a shrewd boss named Maurice Maschke. Later, with a sweeping Republican year in sight, Davis resigned, ran for Governor, and was elected in 1920. He left behind as a mark of his complacency the mess which brought on the Crime Survey in 1920. Davis served only one term as Governor and then vanished for a decade, when in 1930 he reappeared to become Mayor in another wave of reaction.

[19] Hatton, whose responsibility it was to find my successor in his department, selected and secured the acceptance of a graduate of Penn

named Harold W. Dodds. On his removal to Cleveland he lived near us and we saw a good deal of the Doddses during the year 1919-1920. In the spring Dodds was offered the editorship of the **National Municipal Review** which moved him to New York. I carried his classes at Reserve during the final month of the school year. Subsequently Dodds became President of Princeton University where he served many years.

[20] The draft of my commentary on these interviews which I prepared for publication is with my papers in the Hoover Institution at Stanford University. I shall tell in a subsequent chapter why it was not published by the Foundation and why I was not able to carry out my intention to publish it on my own account after I left the Foundation. I have written a considerable amount in my life but I have always felt that if anything I ever produced had a claim to fine writing, this report deserved that rating. In reproducing here a summary of what I said in that report, I have had some trouble with the matter of tense, for the original was written in the present but this summary uses past tense. I here register a regret that the time at my disposal does not permit me to publish the report with some additions and corrections now, more than fifty years later.

[21] The unusual length of this chapter and the prosaic nature of its contents warn me that it may seem dull to many readers, for it is not a summary of the findings of the crime survey but an account of how it was conceived and managed. For reasons that I explain later in this chapter, I am omitting all of the findings of the investigation but instead am describing the part that fell under my responsibility. This was to manage the work of the various specialists, to promote community interest in what was going on, and to get the findings well publicized in a way to develop a sound public opinion on what should be expected of the agencies of law enforcement.

This required a high degree of organizing skill which I acquired in my years with the Foundation and later revealed in my work in Missouri, Illinois and elsewhere, and in the 1932 political campaign.

Describing this work makes for dull reading just as is the account of organizing a political campaign. But it is vital and necessary to success in community education just as it is vital in the winning of elections.

[22] An interesting, detailed and accurate monograph on the Survey, and the conditions in the community that led up to it, was written a few years ago by a member of the faculty of Western Reserve, Louis M. Massotti. Dr.

Massotti occupied the position in the Hanna Department of Political Science that I held until 1919. He is now on the faculty of Northwestern University. His monograph has not been published but he generously permitted me to examine it and thus refresh my memory of many of the details described in this chapter.

[23] I have not believed it to be necessary to burden my story with a detailed account of the McGannon case. But since it reveals so much of the atmosphere of those years and it is so interesting a story of official incompetence, and since certain aspects touch so closely my own experience, I shall include some of the details.

I got to know McGannon in 1913 when I was writing my Master's essay on the Cleveland Municipal Court. He had been elected along with Levine to the first group of judges. He was regarded as an efficient and intelligent judge and administrator. In getting material for my essay I sought an interview with him in his chambers.

He was most cooperative, permitting me to sit with him on the bench while he heard cases, mostly from the Conciliation docket. He was crisp and expeditious in disposing of cases, violating, I thought, the principle of conciliation originally proposed by Levine when the court was established. I also heard that in criminal cases he was tough, a "policeman's judge." This was a great advantage to him when he was later tried for murder because the various police officers who appeared in the case all supported the Judge's story. We had a long conversation in his chambers where I was able to appraise him as a judge and as an individual.

He was a big man, tall and very stout. This was especially impressed upon me by a story he told of a car he bought but returned to the factory to have the steering wheel moved back to accommodate his paunch.

The story of the murder and the subsequent court proceedings is narrated at length in my book **Politics and Criminal Prosecution**, published in 1928.

On the evening of the shooting, McGannon and a man named Kagy had driven out to some resort on the eastern lake front. They were in McGannon's car which Kagy had been using while he arranged for some repairs. Presumably after dinner and some drinks (this was in prohibition times) they returned to the city by way of Euclid Avenue which is a major thoroughfare running from the Public Square east to Erie. Fairly well out near the city limits, they stopped at a speakeasy where presumably they had more refreshments. There they met a man named Joyce who was well known to them. He had been the proprietor of a downtown saloon. Joyce was very intoxicated and they invited him to join them in the car for the ride downtown. The car stopped at a corner in the heart of the city but beyond the bright lights. It was testified that there were seen standing near the car some men, including one large man. There seemed to be a quarrel and a shot was heard. Joyce had staggered away from the car, apparently too drunk to know what was going on. Kagy, who had received the bullet, found his way to a doorway and collapsed.

Joyce was indicted but acquitted and then McGannon was indicted. McGannon's defense was an alibi. He said that he had left the car before it reached the place where the shooting occurred and walked through several streets to a streetcar which took him to his home on the east side. There were introduced witnesses, some of them policemen, who testified to seeing McGannon at several points in his alleged walk to the streetcar. A witness said he saw him in the streetcar. Beyond all this, the mystery remains until this day, so far as I know. McGannon, after serving time for perjury, lived in poverty in Chicago where he died of a heart attack.

To my horror during the course of our survey, I discovered that the property where the speakeasy was located, and where they had picked up Joyce, was owned by the Foundation. Someone had included it in his will. I confided my discovery to Garfield and we did all that we could: we got the speakeasy owner evicted and kept the secret to ourselves. This, by the way, is the first time this part of the story has ever been made public. So this is a substantial scoop. I can almost hear the teeth of the departed Cleveland editors grinding in Hades, or wherever they are, for they would have loved to publish this little joke on the Foundation.

[24] In 1917 Frankfurter was counsel to President Wilson's Labor Mediation Board. The I.W.W. had attempted to shut down certain of Arizona's copper production and the authorities had removed some 1,200 disturbers from Bisbee. Frankfurter came out and after a great deal of acrimonious argument, the Sheriff suggested that the mediator leave town.

[25] I freely admit that in taking a stand with Garfield and Thompson I was making a slight compromise with my convictions. For I knew quite well the sins and shortcomings of the press in reporting news about law enforcement. But in this case, as in many other instances where decisions had to be reached, principle had to yield to expediency because a larger objective seemed paramount. It was in the interest of the survey, the Foundation and the Cleveland community that the survey must succeed and it could not succeed without the good will of the newspapers.

Frankfurter did not bear any responsibility except to produce what he conceived to be a fine, rounded study of a social problem. And his temperament did not permit him to share my concern for the local interests I have mentioned. Years later as Research Director of the New York Crime Commission, I was serving a different set of interests. I planned and conducted a critical study of the effect of the press upon the process of law enforcement. When this was published Walter Lippmann wrote a lead editorial in the **World** denouncing the report as a threat to the freedom of the press. This proves once more that in reading written opinions, it is vital to know what interest the writer considers paramount.

[26] My relations with Frankfurter were clouded for years and were not helped by my refusal to sign the Columbia Law School round robin on the Sacco-Vanzetti case. But in 1931, on the eve of Roosevelt's nomination, in which we were both interested, we resumed relations which were as warm and friendly as if we had never quarreled. I regarded Frankfurter, despite his temperament, as useful to our advisory group and he valued a contact with me because it meant a convenient access to FDR.

[27] The unpredictable tide that guides our lives brought Miss Sherwin close to one of my dearest friends in her very old age. After her retirement, with the shadow of the eighties ending her active career, she took a house in Cleveland where she spent the rest of her life. Through some chance she employed as her companion a retired master nurse with whom I was passionately in love when I was in college and she was in nursing school, Irene Kelley. Irene had become a leading figure in her profession and well before she met Miss Sherwin had retired. There was no nursing involved in her association with Miss Sherwin, someone else came in for that. But in the many hours of conversations the two old ladies, according to Irene, mentioned me and my activities in the years since I first knew Belle Sherwin in Cleveland. In my correspondence with Irene since Miss Sherwin's death, she told me of Miss Sherwin's sadness and disappointment because of my later opposition to Roosevelt, for her passionate support of the man never faltered.

[28] I included a study of the grand jury in my book **Politics and Criminal Prosecution**. The article on grand juries in the **Encyclopedia of Social Sciences** I wrote in 1930.

[29] My removal to New York did not completely terminate my ties with the

Foundation. During the winter Malcolm McBride came to New York and asked me to return to the Foundation as acting director during the summer of 1924. Carlton Matson was not to take office until after the summer, and a new survey was to get under way in June. This was a survey of higher education in Cleveland. The main subject to be determined was the creation of a new college, a division of Western Reserve, to be located downtown under the name of Cleveland College. As director of the survey, there had been selected George F. Zook, who ten years later was to become U.S. Commissioner of Education.

I was glad to spend the summer in Cleveland, earning what was a welcome addition to my Columbia salary. My relations with Zook were pleasant and the survey was published in 1925.

[30] I give all this space to this seemingly small episode for several reasons. One is to indicate that the so-called student revolt of the 1960s had certain antecedents in the 1920s and came from so-called educational reformers in Teacher's College. It shows how students can be won over by good and exciting teaching. I have always maintained that much of the later trouble was due to the flight of experienced and mature faculty from undergraduate teaching, leaving green and immature teachers just out of graduate school to hold the attention of large classes. I am almost ready to say that the best and most mature teachers should teach the youngest students. Beard proved that his output of constructive writing never suffered from the fact that he carried undergraduate classes as long as he was on the Columbia faculty. Another reason for including this story is to suggest that teaching women does not differ essentially from teaching men. After I left Reserve, my successor found the large lecture course I had built up falling away in registration. I met him one day and he asked what trick did I use to get women students interested in my courses. I answered, "Try and give an interesting course and forget that they are women." Also, in teaching, as well as in politics, attention to social events as a way of getting acquainted with students is essential.

[31] This doctor was Oswald Jones. From my first contact with him in early 1929 to his death in 1971 — a blessed forty-two years — he kept my fears at bay.

Index

The History of
the United States
1876-1976

1. Robert C. Bannister, Jr. **Ray Stannard Baker: The Mind and Thought of a Progressive.**

2. Irving Bernstein. **Turbulent Years: A History of the American Worker, 1933-1941.**

3. Clarke A. Chambers. **California Farm Organizations: A Historical Study of the Grange, the Farm Bureau, and the Associated Farmers, 1929-1941.**

4. C.H. Cramer. **Newton D. Baker: A Biography.**

5. Jonathan Daniels. **The Time Between the Wars: Armistice to Pearl Harbor.**

6. Robert H. Ferrell and Howard H. Quint, eds. **The Talkative President: The Off-the-Record Press Conferences of Calvin Coolidge.**

7. Waldo H. Heinrichs, Jr. **American Ambassador: Joseph C. Grew and the Development of the United States Diplomatic Tradition.**

8. Herbert Clark Hoover. **American Individualism.**

9. Herbert Clark Hoover. **Memoirs. Volume I. Years of Adventure 1874-1920. Volume II. The Cabinet and the Presidency 1920-1933. Volume III. The Great Depression 1929-1941.**

10. Walter Johnson. **William Allen White's America.**

11. Dwight Macdonald. **Henry Wallace: The Man and the Myth.**

12. M. Nelson McGeary. **Gifford Pinchot: Forester-Politician.**

13. Raymond Moley. **Realities and Illusions, 1886-1931: The Autobiography of Raymond Moley.**

14. William Starr Myers. **The Foreign Policies of Herbert Hoover, 1929-1933.**

15. Anna Kasten Nelson, ed. **The Records of Federal Officials: A Selection of Materials from the National Study Commission on Records and Documents of Federal Officials.**

16. Merlo J. Pusey. **Charles Evans Hughes.**

17. Stephen Roskill. **Naval Policy Between the Wars. The Period of Anglo-American Antagonism, 1919-1929.**

18. Harry Scheiber. **The Wilson Administration and Civil Liberties, 1917-1921.**

19. Homer Edward Socolofsky. **Arthur Capper, Publisher, Politician, and Philanthropist.**

20. Bascomb N. Timmons. **Portrait of an American: Charles G. Dawes.**

21. Ray Lyman Wilbur and Arthur Mastick Hyde. **The Hoover Policies.**